AF471252

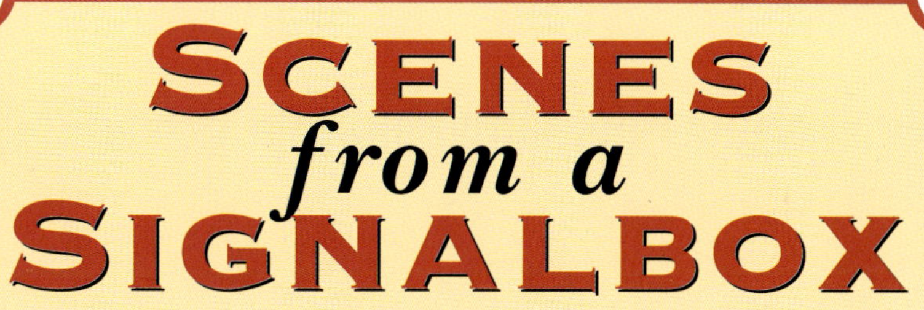
SCENES
from a
SIGNALBOX
A social history of Britain's railways

# SCENES *from a* SIGNALBOX

*A social history of Britain's railways*

David & Charles

A DAVID & CHARLES BOOK

First published in the UK in 2001



A catalogue record for this book is available from the British Library.

ISBN 0 7153 1184 0

Designed, edited and produced by Eaglemoss Publications Ltd, based on the partwork *World of Trains*

Front and back cover photographs: Getty Images/Hulton Collection

Printed in the Slovak Republic for David & Charles, Brunel House, Newton Abbot, Devon

# Contents

# Introduction

'Railroad travelling is a delightful improvement of human life. Everything is near, everything is immediate – time, distance and delay are abolished.' Thus wrote a railway enthusiast in 1842.

The freedom that railway travel brought to people was celebrated in 1850 by *The Times*: 'Thirty years ago not one countryman in one hundred had seen the metropolis. There is now scarcely one in the same number who has not spent the day there.' A year later the newspaper was proved correct: more than six million people visited the Great Exhibition in London's Hyde Park – and most of them had been brought to the metropolis by the great network of railways that was beginning to cover the country.

Today, going on holiday is an accepted part of everyday life. But its roots lie in the advent of the steam train when day excursions, visits to the races, and works and Sunday School outings suddenly became possible. People who had never seen the sea were now breathing in the salty air and feeling better for it. Entrepreneurs like Thomas Cook set up travel companies to introduce people to bigger and better trips at home and abroad. Dreams had suddenly become reality.

Also part of the dream were the railway hotels that were built close to many of the main stations. Today, they are a reminder of the magnificent luxury of a bygone age. The grandest of them all was the Midland Hotel by St Pancras Station, which boasted a lavish dining room, a 'noiseless interior ... shielded (by screens) from the bustle of the adjoining station', and London's first revolving door. Another was Hotel Great Central by Marylebone Station, which after nationalisation became British Rail's headquarters, but today has been restored to its former glory as a lavish and extremely modern hotel.

But the story of steam isn't all about holiday excursions and day trips; there is a darker, grittier side to the account, too. When the steam train first appeared on the scene, the Duke of Wellington was appalled. He saw it as a threat to society, a way by which revolutionaries could spread their message throughout the nation. In fact, when the Chartists rioted in the 1840s, the train became the means by which troops could be quickly dispatched to stop them. A US general in the American Civil War had more foresight. He declared that winning was a question of 'getting there fastest with the mostest' and trains were the way of doing just that.

In fact, trains proved invaluable to Britain's war effort in both World Wars, helping to move troops, ammunition and supplies, and more. In the popular imagination, the railway station will always be the setting for sad farewells between young men going away to fight and their loved ones staying at home. Foremost within living memory is the part played by steam trains during World War II. It was the train that took young city children away from the threat of bombs and into the country; it was there to move the British Expeditionary Force after their evacuation from Dunkirk; and, in the build-up to D-Day, the train took the army and its supplies to strategic assembly points. Finally, at the end of it all, it was the train that brought the war-weary soldiers back home.

Then there were the people who made it happen – the talented, courageous men and women who worked on the railways. The pay was low, the discipline was harsh and the chances of being killed or injured were greater than those normally faced by a soldier in peacetime. And then there were the hours. One Victorian guard was told by his superintendent, 'You've got 24 in the day ... and they are all ours if we want them.' Yet a job on the railway was a coveted prize. Even the lowliest shed sweeper was surrounded by the very latest in technological development, and as for the élite, the locomotive drivers, they were the fastest men in the world – the jet pilots and astronauts of their time.

Today, we can fly to Paris in the time it took Queen Victoria to travel from Paddington to Slough on her first train journey. The steam train has been superseded by the faster, cleaner and far less romantic diesel engine, and the car and aeroplane now share the role of prime mover that the train once held. Nonetheless, thanks to the skill and enthusiasm of a small but dedicated band of volunteers, there is a thriving number of specially maintained steam railways all over Britain. Here we can continue to appreciate the power and beauty of these great engines, ride in carriages pulled by them and travel back in time to the glorious age of steam.

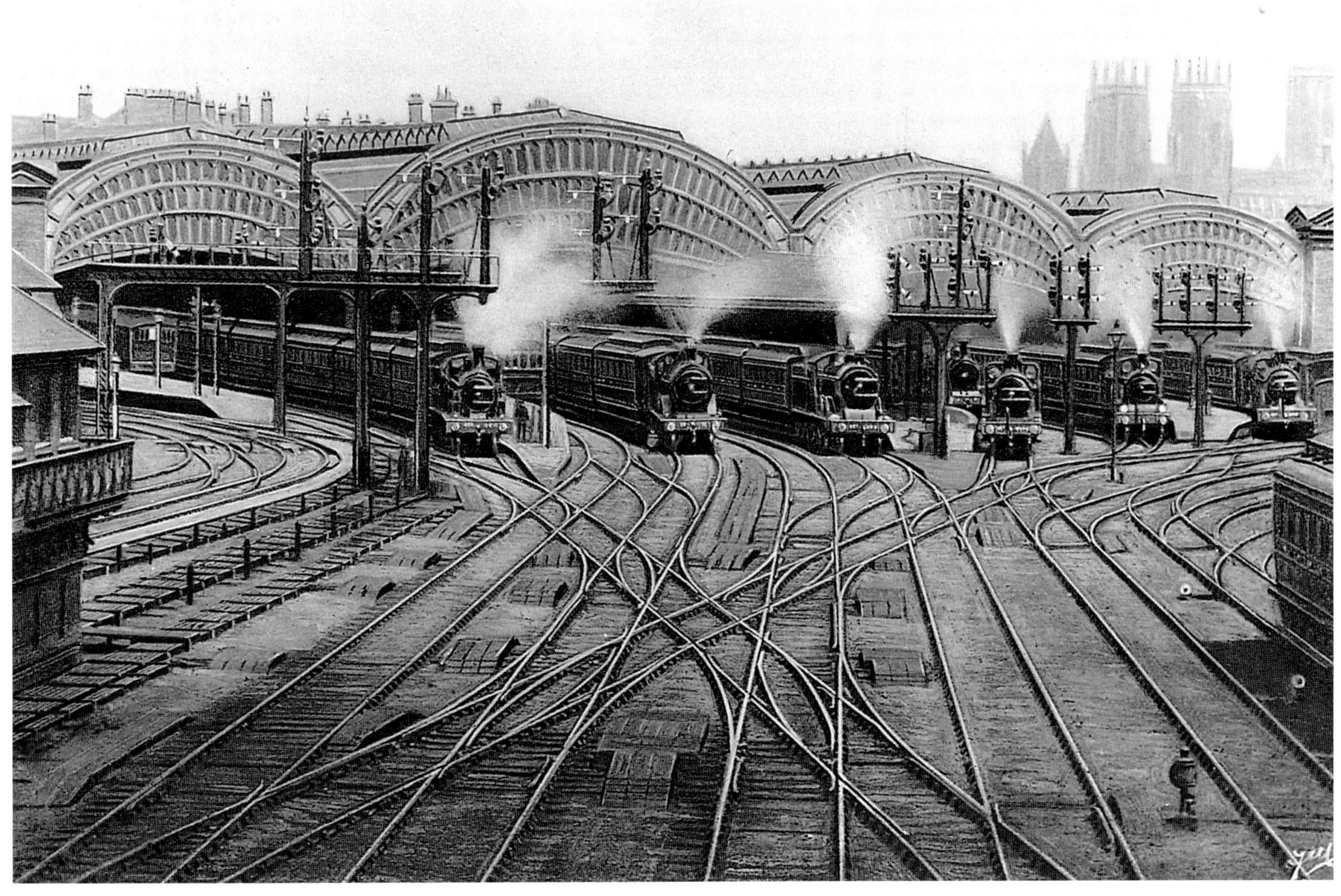

# ALL CHANGE!

*The growth of rail travel and its impact*

# Early reactions to the railways

**From the moment the railway appeared in Britain in the 1820s, it was a source of fierce controversy. Admirers exulted in its speed and novelty, while critics deplored its noise and disruptiveness. But love it or hate it, steam locomotion was here to stay.**

THE RAILWAY—FIRST CLASS.

(Continued from page 325.)

crease, concludes the reader. Alas! for the *hosts* who could testify far otherwise. At the head-quarters of resort in the town of Epsom—where whilom, during the meeting week, you might as well have sought for a bed for yourself or a stall for your horse, as for that *lusus naturæ* that Diogenes looked for with his lantern—only one guest slept the night before the Derby, and three horses constituted the cavalry department. But what of that?

"Tempora mutantur nos et mutamur in illis."

SECOND CLASS.

THIRD CLASS.

'Railways, poisons, enema pumps, cream tarts, royalty and the guillotine.' Thus ran the list compiled in 1836 by the French novelist Gustave Flaubert of civilization's worst inventions. Certainly, he was not alone in his dislike of steam railways. From the moment it appeared in Britain in the 1820s, the country was divided over the value of the 'iron horse'.

Detractors claimed that it was noisy, dirty, obtrusive and dangerous, pointing out that at the inauguration of the country's first all-steam passenger line, the Liverpool & Manchester, in 1830, one of the guests of honour had been run over and killed.

## Benefits of the railway

Supporters of the locomotive argued that it gave fresh impetus to industry, opened up limitless prospects for travel, enabled uninhabited tracts to be made habitable and was in every way beneficial to society.

'Railroad travelling,' declared an enthusiast in 1842, 'is a delightful improvement of human life. Man is become bird; he can fly quicker and longer than a Solan goose...Everything is near, everything is immediate – time, distance and delay are abolished.'

One who remained sceptical was the Duke of Wellington. It was this cantankerous old general who, as Prime Minister, had formally opened the Liverpool & Manchester Railway – and the occasion had done little for his dignity. The 1830s was a time of great political discontent, and a near riot had developed at the Manchester end of the line, forcing the Duke to beat a hasty and unaccustomed retreat.

## Fear of revolution

This humiliation had confirmed the Duke's view that the railway might be used by the 'lower orders' as a means of spreading sedition and revolution through the country. Nor was he alone in his fears.

**◀ First, second and third-class railway passengers embark for the Derby in 1842.**

**Pages 8–9: Engine driver, Bill Perry, waits for the 'all clear' sign from the signalman before he can continue his journey in 1949.**

▲ **As railway travel became increasingly popular, the countryside burgeoned with cuttings, bridges, viaducts and embankments. Here an enthusiastic crowd gathers to watch Prince Albert open the viaduct at Saltash, near Plymouth, in 1859.**

However, with the outbreak of Chartist riots in the 1840s, it was found that the railway could also be a powerful weapon of repression, allowing the swift dispatch of troops to troubled areas. Indeed, the prospect of using it for military purposes excited much support for the 'iron horse', especially on the war-torn Continent.

Another worry shared by some opponents of the railway was that it would bring about an intolerable mingling of the social classes. As one of Benjamin Disraeli's characters says in his novel *Sybil*: 'Equality...is not our métier. If we nobles do not make a stand against the levelling spirit of the age, I am at a loss to know who will fight the battle. You may depend upon it, these railways are very dangerous things.'

## Improper contact

The railway companies' solution was to differentiate carriages by class. Even so, the question of etiquette still proved difficult for some Victorians. The historian Augustus Hare, recalling family journeys of about 1850, wrote that 'for a long time we used to have post-horses to meet us at some station near London: my mother would not be known to enter London in a railway carriage – "it was so excessively improper" (the sitting opposite strangers in the same carriage)'.

Others saw the railway as yet another manifestation of the industrial blight that had settled on Britain. In *Dombey and Son*, published in 1846–7, Charles Dickens gave a depressing picture of rail travel: 'The power that forced itself upon its iron way – its own – defiant of all paths and walls, piercing through the heart of every obstacle, and dragging living creatures of all classes, ages, and degrees behind it, was a type of the triumphant monster, Death.'

Much medical opinion, too, was at first against the locomotive. From Bavaria, in 1835, came a prediction that rail travellers would fall prey to brain damage, or 'delirium furiosum'. Other

**Sunday services**

Nothing piqued pious Victorians more than the thought of trains running on a Sunday. The Sabbatarians, as they were called, attracted a strong following, particularly in Scotland. When, for example, the Tay Bridge collapsed on a Sunday it was considered divine retribution for travelling on the day of rest. And in 1883, inhabitants of Loch Carronside in Wester Ross stormed Strome Ferry station on the Highland Railway to thwart the Sabbath loading of fish. The ten convicted offenders, when released from Calton Jail in Edinburgh, were welcomed by their fellow villagers as heroes.

In 1889, the Anti-Sunday Travel Union had some 8,000 followers and a total of 58 branches nationwide. The demands of running a postal service and the desire to have mail on a Monday breakfast table soon swept away English objections. To this day, however, a Sunday train in some parts of the Scottish Highlands is still a rarity.

▼ **Many critics of the steam locomotive warned that it would ruin the landscape and frighten the animals. One opponent, the writer John Ruskin, declared that railways had 'cut through and spoiled some of the loveliest bits of scenery in our country'.**

**Excursion trains**
One of the major factors in popularizing rail travel was the day excursion, which allowed Victorian workers the once unheard-of luxury of a break away from the city. These trips, usually to the seaside, were organized initially by temperance societies – although Bass brewery would later commandeer hundreds of carriages of the Midland Railway to transport its 10,000 employees and guests to the coast.

But a degree of abandon was sometimes noticeable even on the early trips. In 1838, for example, there were riots when an excursion to Epsom racecourse in Surrey failed to provide enough seats for would-be punters. Before long, excursion trains were being hired for a variety of events. In 1848, special trains were laid on for the thousands of people travelling to watch the public execution of a notorious murderer in Liverpool.

authorities warned of dangers to those with 'exquisite sensibility of the nervous system' or given to 'fullness of blood in the head'.

In 1857, a Frenchman, E.A. Duchesne, identified a 'maladie des mécaniciens' (engineers' disease) caused by constant vibration and appearing as 'generalized, continuous and persistent pains, accompanied by a feeling of weakness and numbness'. A few years later, the authoritative British medical journal, the *Lancet*, drew its readers' attention to 'an often experienced condition of uneasiness, scarcely amounting to actual fear, which pervades the generality of travellers by rail'.

## Brighton blues

The unease in this case was attributed to the possibility of a crash, but as early as 1855 one observer had blamed it on the prospect not of being on a train but of missing one. Whatever its cause, the effect seemed to be cumulative. The *Lancet* article cited a study of business commuters between London and Brighton: 'I have never', wrote the researcher, 'seen any set of men so rapidly aged as these seem to me to have been in the course of those few years.'

Against such gloomy pronouncements was the sheer pleasure to be gained from rail travel. If the trains vibrated, they were nevertheless far smoother than the stage coaches they replaced. The speed was thrilling, the scenery beautiful, the novelty factor undeniable. Even the vast scale of railway construction was to many travellers a source of endless wonder. Following a ride on the Liverpool & Manchester Railway in 1830, the actress Fanny Kemble wrote to a friend:

'You can't imagine how strange it seemed to be journeying on thus, without any visible cause of progress other than the magical machine, with its flying white breath and rhythmical, unvarying pace, between these rocky walls...and when I reflected that these great masses of stone had been cut asunder to allow our passage thus far below the surface of the earth, I felt as if no fairy tale was ever half so wonderful as what I saw.'

The object of Miss Kemble's admiration and delight was Liverpool's 18.25m (60ft) deep Edge Hill cutting, without doubt an outstanding example of railway workmanship. Yet there were many who wished that Edge Hill and its like had never been built, not least the thousands of slum dwellers whose homes were demolished by the gangs of railway navvies relentlessly advancing on the big city termini.

**▶ This cartoon pointing up the risk of travelling by train reflected an attitude deplored by rail chiefs. More people, asserted the chairman of the London & North Western, choked themselves to death than were killed on the railways.**

**▼ Among the earliest opponents of the railway were fox-hunters, who were worried about its effect on their sport. However, as companies began laying on hunting specials for enthusiasts in the cities, it was the foxes who had cause for concern.**

RAILWAY UNDERTAKING.

*Touter.* "GOING BY THIS TRAIN, SIR?" *Passenger.* "'M? EH? YES."
*Touter.* "ALLOW ME, THEN, TO GIVE YOU ONE OF MY CARDS, SIR."

Critics of the railway's impact on the countryside declared that it would destroy crops, disrupt hunting and despoil the landscape. Travelling on most lines, wrote an observer in 1844, meant that 'the face of nature, the beautiful prospects of hill and dale, are lost or distorted to our view. The alternation of high and low ground, the healthful breeze, and all those exhilarating associations connected with "the road", are lost or changed to doleful cuttings, dismal tunnels and the noxious effluvia of the screaming engine.'

## Discomforts and dangers

Even those who welcomed the railway were taken aback by the conditions in which they had to travel. Third-class carriages were likened in 1844 to 'a species of shower bath', and even first and second-class carriages came without corridors, lavatories or heating.

The lack of corridors was the most serious of these omissions, since it encouraged crime. One outraged passenger described how his travelling companion 'bit my thumb off clean to the bone...he held it in his mouth, pushed his head through the glass, spat the thumb into his hand and flung it out the window'.

However, for all its shortcomings, the railway was a breathtaking success. In 1842, 24.5 million train passengers were carried in Britain. By 1850, the figure had risen to 73 million and *The Times* that year could hardly contain its delight:

'There are thousands of our readers, we are sure, who, in the last three years of their lives have travelled more and seen more than in all their previous life taken together. Thirty years ago, not one countryman in one hundred had seen the metropolis. There is now scarcely one in the same number who has not spent the day there.'

By the early years of the twentieth century, the annual passenger head count stood at some 1,100 million – a figure that seemed set only to increase. A hefty portion comprised long-suffering commuters for whom trains were just an unexciting necessity, but for every passenger who took that view there was another who would have echoed Fanny Kemble's words: 'A common sheet of paper is enough for love, but a foolscap extra can alone contain a railroad and my ecstasies.'

**▼ The opening of the Liverpool & Manchester Railway in 1830 (bottom) was an event tinged with tragedy. Politician William Huskisson (below) was knocked down and fatally injured – consequently becoming the first person to be run over by a locomotive.**

# Victoria takes a ride

**Queen Victoria's first journey by rail was an adventure undertaken in secrecy; her last was a state occasion watched by the world. But while the railways grew into a great industry and the Queen enjoyed their convenience, she never entirely trusted them.**

The early years of Queen Victoria's reign were a dangerous time for the young monarch. Twice during the weekend of 28–29 May 1842 would-be assassins tried to shoot her. Her advisers decided, therefore, that she should travel for the first time by train on her return from Windsor Castle to Buckingham Palace two weeks later on Monday, 13 June. They felt that she would be less vulnerable in a railway carriage than in one of her own horse-drawn coaches.

Slough, a station on the Great Western Railway (GWR), was the closest to Windsor, which was still unconnected by rail at this time. However, the company was only notified of the impending trip on the Saturday afternoon and a fevered 36 hours ensued as the GWR did its best to prepare for the unprecedented occasion while maintaining complete secrecy.

The month-old 2-2-2 Firefly Class locomotive *Phlegethon* was chosen to haul the first royal train. The engine left Paddington for Slough a little after 10.15 a.m. on the Monday, pulling the royal saloon together with several carriages and open trucks. The train reached Slough shortly before 11.00 a.m. and waited for the Queen and her entourage to appear.

The party arrived in six horse-drawn carriages an hour later, having driven from Windsor. While the carriages were loaded on to the train's open trucks, the Queen and Prince Albert were shown to a specially prepared waiting room. But the strong-minded young woman declined to wait passively and insisted on being shown her first railway saloon, 'inquiring very minutely', according to a contemporary newspaper report, 'into the whole of the arrangements'.

Meanwhile, as the Queen questioned the GWR officials, the royal coachman demanded to ride the footplate during the journey to London. As the footplate crew consisted of no less than Daniel Gooch, the GWR's superintendent of locomotives, and Isambard Kingdom Brunel, who had engineered the railway, the coachman's presence was hardly necessary. He remained adamant, however, insisting that it was his responsibility to ensure the Queen's safety.

At 12 o'clock precisely, *Phlegethon* set off for London, with Victoria and Albert comfortably ensconced in their flower-decked saloon. Exactly 25 minutes later, the first royal excursion steamed into the original Paddington station, a small, cramped terminus, with only three arrival platforms and two for departures, situated about 180m (200 yards) north-west of its present site.

The following day, Victoria wrote from Buckingham Palace to her uncle Leopold, King of the Belgians, and declared her satisfaction with the journey: 'We arrived here yesterday morning, having come by the railroad, from Windsor, in half an hour, free from dust and crowd and heat, and I am quite charmed with it.'

The royal coachman, however, was less euphoric. Resplendent in his scarlet tunic when he

**▼ The luxurious royal day saloon of the London & North Western Railway was one of a pair of six-wheelers built in 1869 for the Queen's journeys to Scotland. Although the two were connected by a gangway, the Queen refused to pass through it while the train was in motion. In 1895, the coaches were merged into a single unit.**

▲ **Decorated with a crowned headlamp and castings of the royal arms and flying a large royal standard, 4-2-2 No 3041 *The Queen* stands at the head of the GWR royal train, built to celebrate Queen Victoria's Diamond Jubilee in 1897. The train was made up of six carriages in the traditional GWR livery of chocolate and cream.**

▼ **Looking more like a ship's captain than a footplateman, David Hughes served from 1889 to 1901 as the GWR's royal train driver. Hughes was at the regulator when the Queen travelled from Windsor to London for the Diamond Jubilee of 1897, and again in 1901 when her remains were conveyed from London to Windsor.**

climbed aboard the open cab at Slough, he was filthy by the time the train reached Paddington. As one of the Queen's ladies-in-waiting observed, 'Unluckily for him the journey had such an unfortunate effect upon his livery and shining countenance that when he descended he resembled a Christy Minstrel rather than a coachman of the Royal Household.'

The success of this first royal excursion led to other rail journeys and liberated the royal household from its previously rather static lifestyle. It was now possible to convey large numbers of retainers and vast amounts of royal luggage over long distances, free from the difficulties associated with road travel.

## The hazards of rail travel

Many in the royal suite had been apprehensive before the first brief journey because the railways were far from safe in those early days. Only the most primitive traffic control systems existed and mishaps were frequent.

Daniel Gooch, who always insisted on driving the Queen himself when she used the GWR, noted in his diary: 'It was no uncommon thing to take an engine out on the line to look for a late train that was expected, and many times have I seen the train coming and reversed the engine and run back out of its way as quickly as I could.'

To avoid these excitements, strict precautions were taken whenever the Queen was travelling by rail. Points and level crossings were locked in place to avoid accidents. A pilot engine was sent ahead of the royal train and staff were forbidden to alter the setting of any piece of equipment once the pilot had passed.

Even when the block signalling system began to spread during the 1870s, special measures were introduced for the Queen's safety. Normally, a train would travel with one clear section ahead and one behind, but in the case of the royal train this would be increased to two ahead and two behind.

## Close to disaster

With the acquisition in the 1840s of Osborne House on the Isle of Wight and Balmoral House (later enlarged and renamed Balmoral Castle) in the Scottish Highlands, the Queen began to undertake much longer train journeys. The first between Scotland and England was made in September 1848 and almost proved to be the last.

The journey was a hastily improvised affair, planned at the last moment when a heavy fog at sea forced the Queen to abandon plans for a departure south on board one of the royal yachts. In the rush it seems that the normal safety regulations were breached, with the result that the royal train, steaming on the single track between Forfar and Glamis, came within an ace of smashing into a goods wagon that had been inadvertently shunted into its path.

Unaware of how close she had come to disaster, the Queen arrived in Perth, where she spent the night. She rejoined the train at 10.30 the next morning and set off on the four-hour journey to Carlisle. From there she travelled to Crewe,

▶ **Two Caledonian Railway Dunalastair class 4-4-0s steam past Ferryhill Junction, Aberdeen, in November 1900, at the head of the royal train carrying Queen Victoria on what proved to be her last journey from Balmoral to Windsor.**

where she made her second overnight stop. A 7 a.m. start enabled the train to reach Euston about four hours later.

Such long journey times were in part the result of the Queen's insistence that her train should never go faster than 64.25km/h (40mph) during daylight hours or 48.25km/h (30mph) after dark.

She made the whole of her journey from Scotland in an ordinary first-class carriage belonging to the Aberdeen Railway. As time passed, however, the various railway companies competed to provide rolling stock exclusively for the use of the royal family. None of these vehicles ever belonged to the sovereign and journeys were always paid for at the standard first-class rate, plus the appropriate rate per mile for running a special train.

## Royal luxury

The first royal saloon was that used by the GWR on the initial journey to Paddington. The 6m (21ft) four-wheeler had been built at Swindon in 1840 in the hope that the Queen would honour the railway with her patronage because Windsor was only 4km (2½ miles) from the GWR's main line to the west. The vehicle was finished with crimson and white silk panelling and fitted with wooden tyres to deaden noise which might irritate the royal ears.

No less luxurious was the carriage provided by the London & South Western Railway (LSWR), whose station at Farnborough, some 29km (18 miles) from Windsor, served for many years as the starting point for royal excursions to both Scotland and the Isle of Wight.

In 1844, the French King Louis Phillipe made a state visit to England and rode in the royal coach of the LSWR to Farnborough, from where he was driven by road to Windsor. Two years earlier, a terrible rail crash near Versailles – the world's first such disaster – had caused the French government to forbid the King from travelling by train in his own country, and the trip on the LSWR was the first time he had ridden by rail – an experience he seems to have relished.

One effect of the visit by Louis Phillipe was to underline the inconvenience of Windsor's continuing lack of rail connections. Both the GWR and the LSWR had been pressing for years to be allowed to bring the royal town into the railway system. However, opponents of such a scheme, including the Queen, believed that a station would encourage undesirables to come to the area and endanger the morals of pupils at Eton College.

Eventually, in 1849, the railway promoters won their campaign, and two stations opened in Windsor – the GWR, near St George's Chapel, and the LSWR, to the north of the Castle. Many years later, the Queen was transferring from the Great Western station to her coach when a man in the crowd tried to shoot her. As the police hurried the attacker away, they were followed by a mob of muscular Etonians threatening to lynch him.

▲ **As its contribution to the Diamond Jubilee celebrations of 1897, the London & North Western Railway (LNWR) provided two dramatically repainted Webb compound 2-2-2-2 locomotives for the Queen's journeys to Scotland. One of them, No 2054 *Queen Empress*, was turned out in creamy white edged with lavender – including the smokebox and chimney.**

## A new Scottish route

For more than a decade, the royal train to Scotland went via the East Coast route of the Great Northern Railway (GNR). But in 1861 the decision was taken to send it via the West Coast line of the London & North Western Railway (LNWR). To mark this major triumph over the Great Northern, the LNWR built a six-wheeled carriage for the Queen. In 1869, this was replaced by two magnificent six-wheeled royal coaches, one for day use and one for nights, with central gangway connection – the first example in Europe.

Only a short time after the changeover to the West Coast line, the Queen found her life transformed by a far greater event – the death of her beloved husband. The loss of Prince Albert

traumatized Victoria. She surrounded herself with the past and shunned all innovation – including new developments on the railway.

She refused to use the gangway between her two new saloons while the train was travelling, which meant that it had to stop every time she wanted to pass from one to the other. And she maintained her long-standing objection to eating on the move.

Another event of the 1860s affected the Queen's attitude to rail travel – her personal physician, Dr Baly, was killed in an accident at Epsom Junction (later renamed Raynes Park). The doctor was travelling on the LSWR from Waterloo to Portsmouth when the engine was derailed as it crossed a set of points. His carriage overturned and he was thrown through a broken door. The unstable vehicle keeled over and crushed him.

▶ The Queen peers from the window of her train as it traverses the newly erected Tay Bridge at Dundee in July 1879. Six months later, during a violent storm, the bridge collapsed as a passenger train was crossing it, plunging 75 people to their deaths.

Queen Victoria's immediate reaction was to insist that all trains be subjected to the same elaborate safety precautions that applied to her own. She never realized that such orders, if carried out, would have brought the railways to a standstill.

As Victoria grew older, she became increasingly cantankerous. In 1884, the LNWR incurred her displeasure by lighting the royal train with compressed gas. Offended by the unusual glare from the globes – the company had used plain rather than frosted glass – the Queen demanded their instant replacement with her familiar oil lamps.

The nerves of long-suffering railway officials were further strained by the presence on all excursions of the Queen's personal attendant, John Brown. An overbearing and abrasive Highlander, he was the most heartily loathed man in the royal service. Victoria adored him, but his constant interventions on her behalf drove the railway companies to distraction, and G.P. Neele, superintendent of the LNWR, described him as the Queen's 'coarse phonograph'.

The planning of a royal train journey went well beyond considerations of comfort, safety and convenience. The railway companies were also concerned that trains and staff should be appropriately turned out for the occasion. Not only did the royal locomotive have to be spotless and carry a special headboard, the coal on the top of the tender had to be whitewashed. The driver and fireman even had to wear white gloves, although this order could be safely ignored once on the move.

▼ One of the LNWR's Diamond Jubilee locomotives, No 2053 *Greater Britain*, was painted pillar box red for the occasion. With the celebrations over, *Greater Britain* and its sister engine, *Queen Empress*, returned to their normal black livery.

▲ **The locomotive used by the GWR to haul Queen Victoria's funeral train from London to Windsor in 1901, No 3373 *Atbara*, renamed *Royal Sovereign* for the journey, appears with the royal arms draped in purple, its smokebox door surmounted with a wreath of white immortelles.**

The final years of Victoria's reign were marked by the Diamond Jubilee celebrations of 1897. The GWR commemorated the event by building a splendid new royal train of six bogie coaches, with gangway connections throughout – a project that was estimated to have cost £40,000.

The work had not been easy. The Queen, on learning of the company's plans, had made it clear that she was perfectly happy with the existing royal saloon (dating from 1874) and had insisted on the interior remaining unaltered. The GWR, though scrupulously following her wishes, had lengthened the carriage at each end and mounted it on a new frame, with much longer bogies. The new train was provided with electric light, but oil lamps were wisely retained in the main saloon.

Not to be outdone by the GWR, the LNWR marked the Jubilee by painting two of its express passenger engines in fresh liveries. No 2053 *Greater Britain* was painted pillar box red with yellow and black lining, and No 2054 *Queen Empress* was turned out in creamy white, edged with lavender.

Queen Victoria died on 22 January 1901 at Osborne House on the Isle of Wight. Ten days later her remains were carried to the mainland so that they could be conveyed by railway, first to London and then to Windsor, for burial close to where Prince Albert lay at Frogmore.

## The final journey

The journey on 2 February involved three railway companies. The LSWR were to carry the funeral cortege from Clarence Yard, the Queen's private station at Gosport in Hampshire, to Fareham. The London, Brighton & South Coast Railway (LBSCR) would then take over and continue on to their London terminus at Victoria. The GWR would complete the journey to Windsor, departing from Paddington.

But the start of the proceedings was far from auspicious. It had been necessary to reverse the train for its journey to Gosport. This meant that it was the wrong way round according to the plan and pandemonium broke out as distinguished mourners milled around in the rain looking for their allotted places. Moreover, the platform was not long enough to accommodate the whole train, a problem that was hardly helped by the lack of corridors. The result was that the train left eight minutes late.

A further delay occurred at Fareham when the locomotive assigned to pull the train to London, the B4 Class 4-4-0 No 54 *Empress*, developed a braking fault. By now, the party was running ten minutes late and everyone was acutely aware that the new king, Edward VII, who was supposed to meet the train at Victoria, was a stickler for punctuality.

So driver Cooper was asked to try to make up for lost time. In the run that followed, the train touched 128.75km/h (80mph) and arrived two minutes early. For the very first time the Queen had really flown along.

When the train reached London, the Kaiser, who was one of the mourners, sent a message to driver Cooper congratulating him on his efforts. Queen Victoria, on the other hand, would not have been amused.

**Used in emergency**

As Queen Victoria's funeral train steamed into Windsor GWR station in February 1901, royal officials were seized with panic. It was discovered that the hawsers of the gun carriage detailed to bear the Queen's coffin to the burial service had frozen solid in the bitter cold. At the same time, the horses became restive and had to be unharnessed.

The GWR requisitioned communication cords from ordinary passenger coaches and, with these twisted together to make drag ropes, sailors from the Guard of Honour hauled the late Queen on her final journey.

# The development of railway carriages

**For all but a small élite, travelling by train used to be a dreary, daunting and even dangerous experience. But after a slow start, the railway companies began to improve conditions, and by the end of the nineteenth century even third-class passengers were able to ride in reasonable comfort.**

Early rail travel was a bone-shaking experience. The new steam locomotive was able to move people at unprecedented speeds, yet the first railway carriages were hardly different from the horse-drawn mail coaches that had evolved during the previous century. On the Stockton & Darlington Railway, opened in 1825, passengers came second to coal. The passenger trains were formed of road carriages fitted with flanged wheels and were still drawn by horses.

The Liverpool & Manchester Railway of 1830 was planned right from the start as a steam-worked passenger and goods line, but the link with road carriages was still much in evidence. The trains consisted of three mail-coach type compartments mounted on a single four-wheeled underframe. As with the traditional mail coach, the luggage was carried on roof racks and the mail in a boot at one end.

Even the guard was perched high up on a seat so that he could see over the roofs of the other coaches to the engine and respond to any signal from the engine crew to apply or release the handbrake. There was a door to each compartment,

▼ **Fresh flowers, armchair seats, and linen napkins and tablecloths are provided for this third-class dining car used on the Anglo-Scottish expresses of the East Coast Joint Stock around the turn of the nineteenth century. The basket-weave holders below the clerestory roof are intended primarily for top hats.**

with a drop window and, in most cases, a window on either side of the door.

The coach bodies were usually built of timber, with ornate mouldings covering the joints between the panels. Seats were padded, perhaps with arm and head rests, and the inside of the doors and bodywork often had upholstered panels. At night, an oil lamp would be suspended from an opening in the roof.

## A matter of class

These facilities were for the élite only, however, as right from the start, the railways reflected the British class system. Coaches for the middle class were much less ornate than those for the rich, with box-like wooden bodies, possibly glazed windows or even just an open space in the doors, and a semblance of padded seating. These second-class coaches were sometimes divided by partitions into compartments, like their first-class counterparts.

Thus was born the standard British compartment carriage, which survived for over a century and a half and only disappeared as the last of the old Southern Region suburban electric trains were withdrawn from Network SouthEast.

As for the poorest passengers in the early railway days, they often had to ride on slow, lumbering goods wagons, since many railways, fearing that the behaviour of the lower orders would annoy their wealthier patrons, refused to provide third-class carriages. But even where such carriages were provided, they were little more than open boxes, with backless benches and holes in the floor to let out the rainwater.

The Great Western Railway (GWR), with its 7ft (2134mm) broad-gauge, introduced some six-wheel first-class coaches, 7.25m (24ft) long and 3m (9ft 6in) wide, each with four compartments. They were much larger than coaches on standard 4ft 8½in (1435mm) gauge railways, which were often only 1.75m (6ft) and no more than 2m (7ft) wide at that time.

In contrast, the GWR third-class coaches were open wagons with sides just 0.5m (2ft) high, so that there was little to prevent passengers from simply falling off. As a parliamentary inquiry was told in 1839, the GWR provided third-class carriages of 'an inferior description at very low speeds' and, like the London & South Western and London & Birmingham railways, 'combined them with cattle, horses and empty wagons'.

## Disaster heralds new law

On Christmas Eve 1841, a GWR train, including two third-class carriages, ran into an earth slip in Sonning cutting near Reading and inevitably the

**▶ The interior of this third-class compartment of a London Midland & Scottish Railway side corridor mainline coach built in 1946 reflects standards of comfort that would have astonished third-class rail travellers of a century before. Armrests, here folded back, divided the seats into three on each side when pulled down. Decor was in 'Empire timbers' and over-the-shoulder reading lamps were provided.**

**▼ These composite corridor coaches of the early 1900s – one of the Great Eastern Railway (below) and one of the Caledonian Railway (bottom) – included both first and third-class compartments. They also featured two of the most modern amenities – lavatories and electric lighting.**

passengers were tipped out, eight being instantly killed and 17 severely hurt.

In 1844, Parliament passed the Regulation of Railways Act, which required the railways to carry third-class passengers in covered carriages, at an average speed of not less than 19km/h (12mph) and at a fare of not more than one penny a mile. It was the beginning of a new deal.

Carriages themselves also improved, gradually becoming longer and wider. By the 1860s, they were often 9m (30ft) or so in length and – except on the broad-gauge GWR – between 2m (7ft) and 2.5m (8ft) wide. The three-class system still prevailed, however, with well-padded and plush interiors in the first-class, little padding on seats in the second and bare wooden boards in the third.

## Railway revolution

Then in the 1870s came a revolution. The Midland Railway abolished second-class accommodation and improved its third-class carriages, notably by fitting them with upholstered seats and seat backs. It also reduced first-class fares. Other mainline railways gradually followed suit, and third-class passengers, at least on express and long-distance trains, finally began to be treated as people rather than cattle.

It was also in the 1870s that the Midland's general manager, James Allport, made a tour of American railroads and met entrepreneur George Mortimer Pullman. Pullman, disgusted with the poor standards of American railroad cars, had negotiated to run luxury cars of his own design on certain lines, charging the passengers a Pullman supplementary fare.

The upshot was the introduction of Pullman cars on the Midland Railway, including parlour saloons with end balconies, open interiors and armchair seats for day use, and convertible saloons for night services.

For second and third-class passengers, upholstered bench-type seats and backs were installed in the parlour saloons, allowing more people to be seated than in their first-class equivalents. Compared to the conventional British coaches of the time, the Pullman cars were massive, measuring 17.75m (58ft) long and 2.75m (9ft) wide, and running on pivoted four-wheel bogies at each end.

But the British public was not yet ready for such advances and the Pullman trains were not a

**The clerestory roof**

One of the most noticeable features of the early British railway carriage was the clerestory roof, in which the centre was raised above the sides and partially glazed to give extra light. It was first seen on a few early Great Western Railway saloons in 1838, but really came to the fore on the Midland Railway in the 1870s.

By the turn of the century, the design had become common on mainline coaches, with overall heights from the floor to the highest part of the roof of just over 2.5m (8ft). The impression was one of great elegance.

The design did have disadvantages, however. It tended to let in the rain and it made a coach liable to break in two in the event of an accident.

Clerestory roofs began to be phased out after World War I, though they appeared on some coaches produced by the London Midland & Scottish Railway in the 1920s, and were used on new London Underground carriages until the mid-1930s.

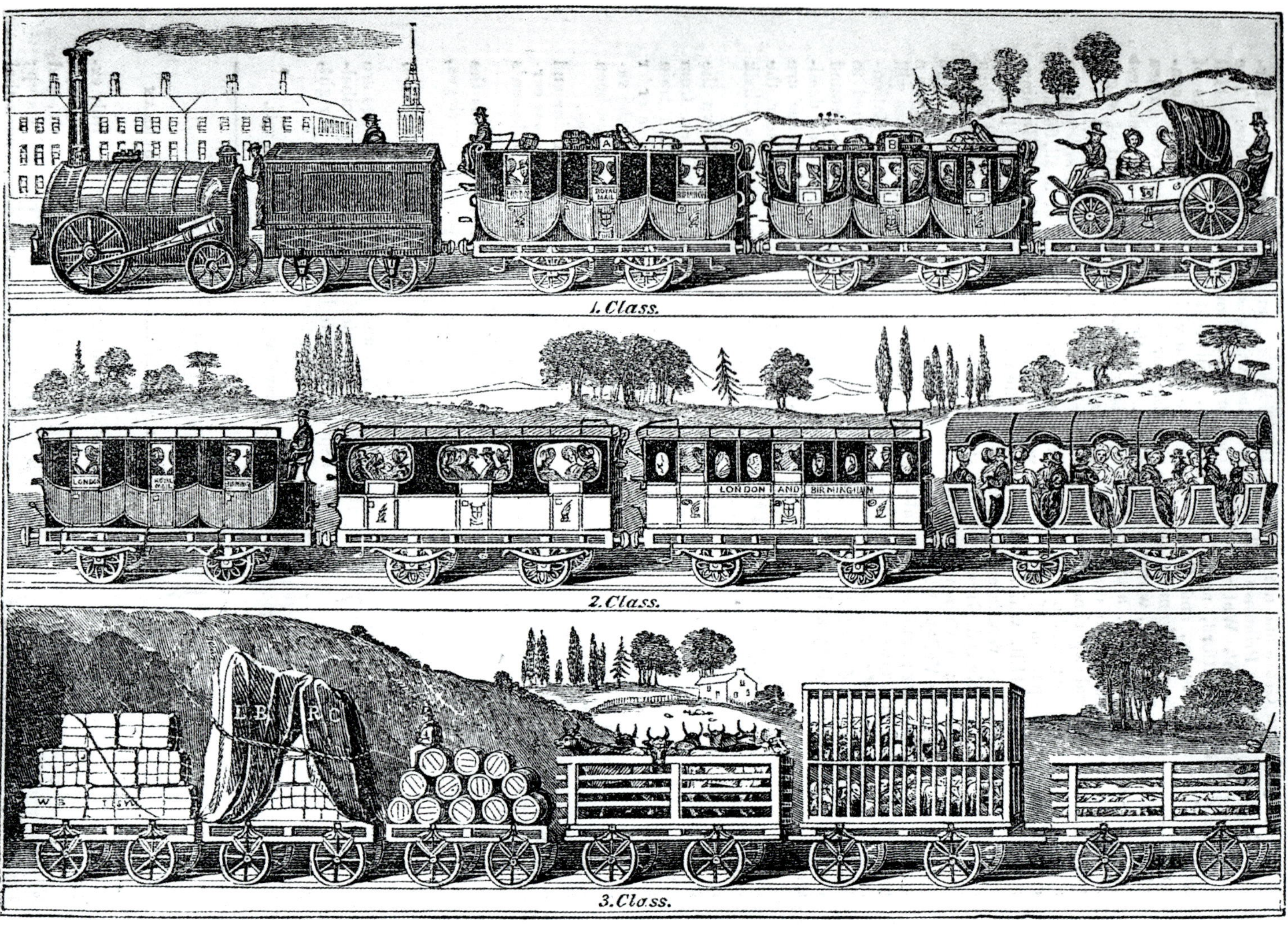


▲ **This print of rolling stock in use on the London & Birmingham Railway in the 1840s highlights the differences between first, second and third-class accommodation. The railways were reluctant to provide proper carriages for third-class passengers, fearing that this would encourage rail travel among the 'lower orders' and thereby offend, or even drive away, higher class patrons.**

success. However, there was a substantial improvement in standards. Again, the Midland led the way, building longer coaches and mounting them on bogies, which gave a much smoother ride than the old rigid four and six-wheelers.

In 1873, the North British Railway introduced the first sleeping cars in Britain. Six years later, the Great Northern Railway introduced the first restaurant car with on-board cooking facilities. However, apart from Pullmans, there was still no means for passengers to move from one coach to another while the train was moving, which meant they had to join or leave the diner at an intermediate station or remain there throughout the journey.

## Improving passenger comfort

It was not until 1892 that the first true corridor train with inter-coach gangways was introduced, on the GWR between Paddington and Birkenhead. Other improvements came with the provision of better heating and lighting. Oil lamps gradually gave way to compressed gas; this was eventually replaced by electric lighting. Radiators fed by steam from the locomotive began to displace rugs and footwarmers, the metal containers filled with hot water and sodium acetate which had been on hire since the earliest days of rail travel.

By 1900, British carriage design had taken on features that are still familiar to us today. Corridor trains with restaurant cars were becoming standard for long-distance services, and non-corridor compartment coaches for short distance and suburban work.

Most new designs were on bogies, and lengths varied from around 15.25m (50ft) to over 21.25m (70ft) on some GWR types where, following the end of the broad-gauge in 1892, larger clearances were available than elsewhere. On the South Eastern Railway, for example, between Charing Cross, Hastings and Dover clearances were tight and remedial work was necessary to run larger coaches with more than 2.5m (8ft) wide bodies. Work was still needed on a number of tight spots to allow free passage of trains to the Channel Tunnel.

## Peak period of design

In the decade between the death of Queen Victoria and the outbreak of World War I, British carriage design reached its zenith. A number of the

### Special trains

Some of the finest coaches available to the general public, as distinct from royalty, have been those in special trains. Probably the best ever were those built in 1907 for the London & North Western Railway's London–Liverpool trans-Atlantic boat-trains. Their large compartments had ornately decorated ceilings and fine timber panelling, and were furnished with sofas and armchairs, in addition to the normal seating.

Thirty years later, both the London Midland & Scottish Railway and its great rival, the London & North Eastern Railway, produced special sets of coaches for certain routes. Most striking were the first-class compartments on the LNER's West Riding and Coronation trains, with their modern interior decor, stainless steel fittings and single armchair seats in alcoves.

▶ **The lavish interior of this first-class dining car on the Manchester, Sheffield & Lincolnshire Railway in the 1890s was typical of the luxury that wealthier rail travellers now regarded as their due. 'They expect not only a seat for themselves,' wrote one contemporary observer, 'but another for their feet.'**

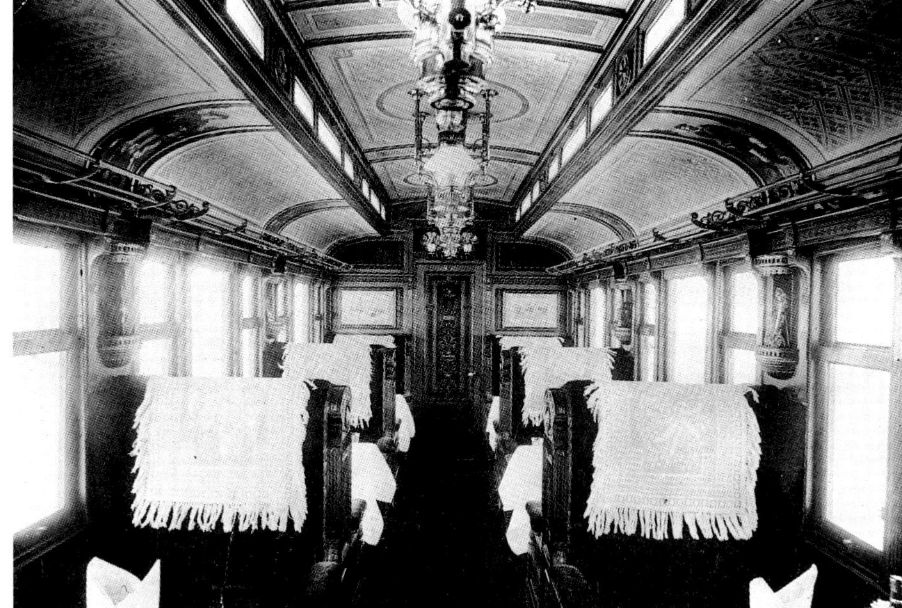

more opulent sleeping and dining coaches were outstanding examples of the coachbuilder's art, featuring finely panelled ceilings and compartment partitions with wood carvings, mouldings and lining. Externally, timber bodies were panelled with raised mouldings picked out in fine lining to emphasize the main background colour.

Colour was what distinguished one railway from the next, whether it was the crimson lake of the Midland, the varnished teak of the Great Northern or the purple-brown and spilt milk of the London & North Western.

However, from around World War I, materials began to change. Steel instead of timber became more common for coach underframes and a number of railway companies started using steel for coach body construction instead of wood. A few even went as far as steel body framing, though this was a development that did not become really noticeable until after the 1923 Grouping.

With the emergence of the Big Four, economy of production became the order of the day. The London Midland & Scottish Railway (LMS), for example, began mass-producing timber coach bodies, with kits for sides, ends and roofs.

Together with the London & North Eastern Railway (LNER), the LMS was also responsible for another far-reaching innovation – the provision of open accommodation for third-class passengers. The open saloon with a row of double seats on either side of a central passageway was more comfortable than the traditional side corridor compartment.

The open saloon style later became standard on British Railways for both mainline and suburban second-class accommodation, and even on some first-class coaches, as well.

World War II brought further design refinements, but little real change, and by 1948, when the Big Four were nationalized, much was as it had been in the 1930s and earlier, although steel body panels had become standard. Further changes would not be made until much later.

▼ **Built in the 1860s, this third-class carriage was open internally above wooden bench seats with low backs. Note the circular door handles and the safety chains in addition to the normal coupling. There were no power brakes in those days, only handbrakes on the tender and on selected carriages.**

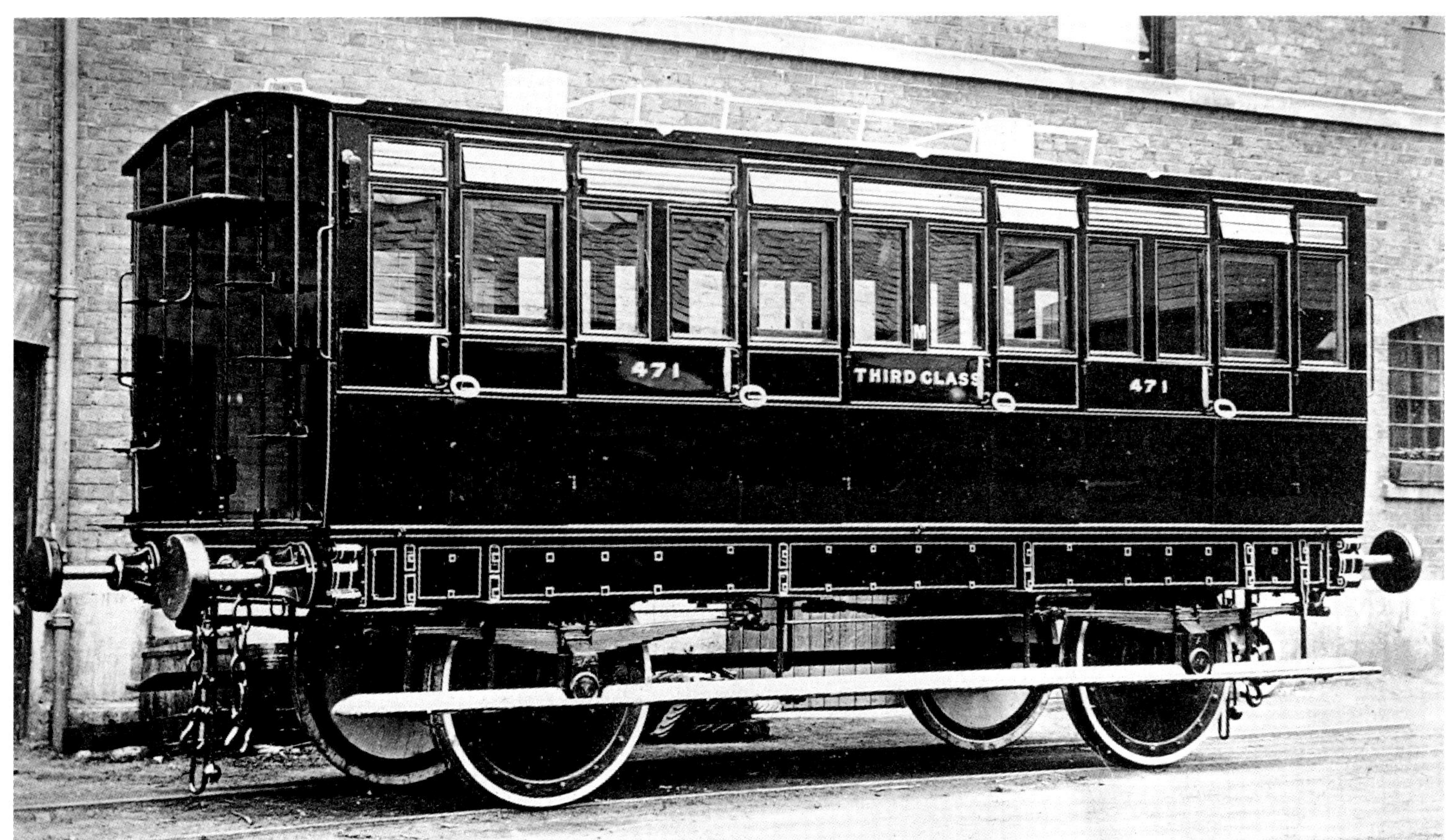

# The Pullman in Britain

**Funeral train**
The turning-point in the fortunes of the young George Mortimer Pullman came in 1865, when his ornate prototype car, *Pioneer*, was used to convey the body of the assassinated President Abraham Lincoln from Chicago to the President's birthplace of Springfield, Illinois. So massive was the vehicle that many bridges, cuttings and platforms along the route had to be altered to accommodate it.

Soon after the funeral, the new President, General Ulysses S. Grant, decided to use *Pioneer* on a journey to his home town of Galena, Michigan, and again many parts of the route had to be altered. But the publicity Pullman derived from the two journeys was enormous. *Pioneer* was not scrapped until 1900, after more than 35 years in service.

**In 1874, the first Pullmans appeared in Britain. The luxury coaches, imported from the United States, were unlike anything ever seen before on British metals, and some cynics doubted that they would ever catch on.**

Pullman is a nostalgic word, evocative of a glamorous past era of rail travel. Its relatively simple and practical origins, however, are less often remembered. In 1858, George Mortimer Pullman (by some accounts a carpenter/coach-builder, by others a building contractor) took his young bride on an overnight honeymoon journey, travelling in a primitive American sleeping car.

So uncomfortable was the experience that he conceived the idea of building a superior type of sleeping car for which a supplement to the normal fare would be charged – the railroad would haul the cars and he would pocket the supplement. He bought a few secondhand cars and refitted them.

At first, the railroads were doubtful, but at length all his Pullman cars – originally, only sleepers, but later parlour and dining vehicles – were adopted on many US lines. In 1872, on a visit to the United States, the progressive General Manager of the Midland Railway (MR), Sir James Allport, invited Pullman to come to England to meet the MR directors. The result was a contract for the import of Pullman parlour and sleeping cars in sectional form, to be assembled at the MR's Derby works and used on its main expresses.

These large, clerestory-roofed bogie vehicles soon attracted attention, because of their extra comfort as well as their American appearance which was so different from that of the ordinary British coach of the period.

**▼ Headed by No 60007 *Sir Nigel Gresley*, the Tees-Tyne Pullman speeds past Hadley Wood in Hertfordshire on the way from King's Cross to Newcastle in July 1952. The service, introduced in 1948, called at Darlington in each direction, with an additional stop at York on the down run.**

▲ **The Midland Railway's first Pullman train ran from London to Liverpool on 1 June 1874. A passenger in the parlour car was particularly impressed by the 'crimson-cushioned easy chairs, in which, by means of a pivot, you might swing yourself round to converse with your neighbour'.**

**The Blue Pullmans**

In 1960, a new series of diesel-electric multiple unit Pullmans went into traffic on BR's Midland and Western regions, operating on routes not previously provided with Pullman services. But these Blue Pullmans, so-called from their striking livery of Nanking blue and white, ran into an immediate problem.

The National Union of Railwaymen objected to the introduction of Pullman services on regions where there were no existing contracts, fearing that this would lead to job losses and a deterioration of working conditions. Eventually, it was agreed that BR staff would be taken on to crew the new trains under their existing contracts.

This proved to be only the first step in the absorption of Pullman into British Transport Hotels – and, in effect, the demise of the true Pullman concept. As for the Blue Pullmans themselves, their working life proved to be short. The Midland service ended in 1966, and the last train on the Western Region was withdrawn in 1973.

'Literally nothing seemed left to desire,' wrote a passenger who travelled in the first train with a Pullman parlour car out of London's St Pancras station in June 1874. 'Entering the train from one end, you were introduced to the parlour car, a luxurious contrivance for short lines and day-travel only. It was a tastefully and richly decorated saloon, over fifty feet [15.25m] long, light, warm, well ventilated, and exquisitely carpeted, upholstered and furnished.'

## Culinary coup

In 1888, the MR's contract with Pullman expired and was not renewed. Instead, some cars were bought by the railway to be operated by its newly formed Midland hotel services. By now, Pullman cars were operating on other lines, including the London, Brighton & South Coast Railway (LBSCR), the London & South Western Railway (LSWR) and the Great Northern Railway (GNR). In 1879, the GNR made history when a Pullman dining car, *Prince of Wales*, went into traffic between King's Cross and Leeds, serving meals actually cooked on the train.

The British Pullman Car company was formed in 1882, with Pullman acting as its chairman until his death in 1897. It was originally a subsidiary of the US company, but in 1907 the financial tycoon Davison Dalziel (later Lord Dalziel) took control. Dalziel later acquired two other famous organizations connected with travel – Thomas Cook & Son and the Compagnie Internationale des Wagons-Lits (the International Sleeping Car Company), often known as the Wagons-Lits Company.

George Pullman had insisted that the comfort of his cars should be matched by a high standard of personal service, and the British company echoed this policy. Following the pattern in America, a conductor was in charge of each Pullman service, and had the responsibility of collecting the supplementary fares and checking the tickets. So far as possible, British Pullman recruited former 'gentlemen's gentlemen' as attendants. (The word 'steward' was thought to convey the wrong image.)

A nice touch was that at station stops, each car's attendant would alight first and wipe the exterior grab handle clean before passengers stepped out – very helpful in steam days.

Not surprisingly, some Pullman staff found the company's standards too exacting, and soon left for easier employment elsewhere. It was said, however, that anyone who remained with the company for two years would never want to leave – they were 'Pullmanized'.

Pullman contracts with the railways were simple. Pullman provided the cars, staffed them, did the catering and charged passengers a Pullman supplement. It furthermore maintained the car bodies and all interior fittings in its own workshops. The railway took the ordinary fares, hauled the cars free of charge and maintained the underframes and running gear.

The extent of Pullman operations varied. 'How far,' wrote the railway historian F.S. Williams in 1883, 'the Pullman car will be generally preferred in England is a matter of some doubt. Americans themselves, when they come to this country, appear well content with the matchless speed of English railway travelling and the comfort of half-filled ordinary first-class carriages.'

Some companies appeared to share Williams's reservations, in particular the Great Western Railway (GWR). It was not until 1929 that the GWR introduced its first Pullman train, on the Paddington–Torquay–Paignton route. However, the constant operating difficulties put in its way by Great Western staff killed it off in less than a year.

The most unlikely provider of Pullman services was the Metropolitan Railway, which was alarmed by the preference that passengers on the Metropolitan & Great Central Joint line showed for the more comfortable stock of the Great Central Railway.

It contracted for two Pullman cars *Mayflower* and *Galatea* (named after two yachts competing in the America's Cup race), which ran from June 1910 until October 1939 in ordinary Metropolitan trains on the Aylesbury line from Moorgate, Liverpool Street and Aldgate. They offered an incongruous sight in the rush hour on the Inner Circle – tea and toast under pink lampshades.

## Tie-up with the Southern

Pullman's most long-standing relationships were with the lines that came together in the Southern Railway after the 1923 Grouping – above all, the line from London to Brighton. The LBSCR began running Pullman cars soon after they appeared on the Midland, establishing a service that was to last for almost a century.

In 1881, the LBSCR inaugurated the four-car Pullman Limited Express, consisting of *Maud*, *Louise*, *Victoria* and *Beatrice*.

'Entering it,' said one passenger, 'you enter a mansion on wheels. You can roam about from parlour to drawing-room, dining-room, and smoking-room. The ladies also have a boudoir. Servants are at your call by electric bell; but you need not call for light or fire.'

'A pleasant and equable temperature is maintained by hot-water pipes, and lighting up is done

### *Working the Highland Railway*

**▲ In 1885, two 11m (36ft) long Pullman sleeping cars were transferred from the Great Northern Railway (GNR) to the Highland Railway (HR) for use on the night trains between Inverness and Glasgow. Named *Balmoral* and *Dunrobin*, they were in use until late 1906–7, when they were replaced by new sleeping coaches built for the HR. The Pullmans were kept as standbys until 1911, when they were returned to the GNR. They ended up as part of a now demolished holiday home in Sussex, close to the Pullman works at Preston Park, in Brighton.**

**▼ This interior of one of the Highland Railway Pullmans, with its handsome woodwork, upholstered seats and elegant fittings, is typical of the cars produced by Pullman in the Victorian and Edwardian eras. Eight compartments, screened by either curtains or doors, were served by two WC compartments and two washbasins in separate recesses. The central gangway with longitudinal sleeping arrangements was a familiar Pullman feature.**

before there is time to demand it. No sooner do you enter a tunnel than the bright but soft and equal light of the Edison electric lamp is shed all over the compartments.'

So popular was the service that in 1908 a seven-car train was introduced to run every day of the year. Called the Southern Belle, it was to become the most celebrated train in Britain.

## Praise for a Belle

'The hand of the decorator,' wrote one rapturous reporter, 'has been laid lightly upon this work, and the beauty of it is a beauty that will endure. There are costly woods, exquisite inlayings, elegant electric fittings, and delicate upholstering; but nowhere is there mere display. It is a Pullman train beautified, and the traveller walking through its whole length of seven cars – it is vestibuled throughout – will find a new delight in every car.'

The Southern Belle continued to run until 1933, when it was replaced by the electric Brighton Belle. The announcement some 40 years later that the Brighton Belle was to be withdrawn led to an angry public protest led by a distinguished Brighton resident and regular user of the train, the actor-manager Lord Olivier. But BR was not to be moved and the Brighton Belle ran for the last time on 30 April 1972.

## Boat-train services

Another constituent of the Southern, the LSWR, also used Pullmans, especially for its Southampton ocean liner trains; a Bournemouth Belle was introduced under Southern auspices in 1931. On the South Eastern side, Pullmans ran on the Dover and Folkestone boat-trains, and in later years the Thanet Belle for the Kent coast resorts.

The Golden Arrow boat-train, with a Pullman counterpart on the French side from Calais to Paris, was perhaps the most glamorous of all Pullman trains. The French Pullmans were owned and operated by Wagons-Lits.

**▲ Pullman car *Coral* awaits the departure of its train at London's Charing Cross station in 1924. At this stage, Pullman cars were still built of wood, and it was to be another four years before the first all-steel Pullman appeared.**

The ties with the Southern were emphasized by the siting of the Pullman head office at Victoria station and of its workshops in the old LBSCR paint shop at Preston Park, just outside Brighton.

During World War II most Pullman cars were stored and mothballed, although *Joan*, one of a batch of all-steel cars built in 1928, was often used by the King and Queen, as well as by the Prime Minister, Winston Churchill. After the war, Pullman services were re-started with considerable enthusiasm on the part of the London & North Eastern and Southern railways.

## British Transport takeover

Nationalization in 1948 had no immediate effect on Pullman. However, in 1954, the British Transport Commission (BTC) bought the equity in the Pullman Car Company, and in 1963, the BTC decided to absorb Pullman into its own restaurant car organization controlled by British Transport Hotels. It was realized that there was real commercial value in the Pullman image and for a time BR restaurant car staff operated a nominal Pullman service on two trains on the Manchester and Liverpool routes.

It would have been uneconomic, however, to go on dedicating BR stock, and what remained of the Pullman tradition was confined to certain limited-stop services simply marked 'P' on the BR timetable. This indicated a superior (and more expensive) menu in the first-class section of the train, with occasional small vases of (plastic) flowers on the tables. George Mortimer Pullman would not have been impressed.

**◀ The Devon Belle – 'Pullman's best to the Glorious West' – approaches Barnstaple in 1952. The service was inaugurated in June 1947 and ran until the end of the summer season in 1954. Three of its cars – No 14, *Lydia* and *Isle of Thanet* – went on to preservation in the United States.**

# Industrial railways

**Established long before the first passenger services, it was Britain's industrial lines that ushered in the railway revolution. Later examples ranged from modest undertakings with a short length of track to vast networks with their own signalling systems and repair shops.**

Although not as glamorous as the mainline railways, industrial railways have a history no less venerable. Indeed, they were operating well before the first major steam passenger service, the Liverpool & Manchester Railway, opened in 1830. The earliest recorded industrial railway in Britain was constructed by Huntingdon Beaumont in 1603–4. It was made with baulks of timber, on which wagons with flanged wheels were drawn by horses from Beaumont's coal pits at Strelley to Wollaton Lane End, near Nottingham. Lines also appeared in Shropshire and Northumberland.

Over the next two centuries, horse-worked tramways became increasingly widespread – first with wooden rails, then with iron plates and finally with iron-edged rails. They were used principally for transporting heavy goods and minerals from the collieries and ironworks to a convenient canal or river. At their greatest extent, they totalled more than 2,400km (over 1,500 route miles).

## Transport revolution

In the early nineteenth century, a development occurred that was to revolutionize the carrying of both goods and people. On 13 February 1804, the first recorded run of a railway locomotive took place. The engine was built by the Cornish experimenter Richard Trevithick, after a business partner, Samuel Homfray, owner of the Penydarren ironworks near Merthyr Tydfil in South Wales, made a 500 guinea bet with a neighbour that it would be able to haul ten tonnes (tons) of iron the 15km (9½ miles) from Penydarren along the old tramway to the canal at

**▼ The network of lines and rows of wagons serving the vast ironworks at Stanton near Ilkeston in Derbyshire illustrate the immense traffic that such a works generated. Both the Great Northern and Midland railways had links with the works, which began substantial production in 1846.**

▲ **Colliery railways were the most common type of industrial line. In 1913, a total of 3,024 mines, almost all being rail connected, raised 287 million tonnes (tons) of coal. Here in 1963, a Peckett 0-4-OST of 1907 shunts at Bagworth colliery, which was served by the former Leicester & Swannington Railway.**

▼ **Ironstone quarries in the East Midlands were served by many railway company and private branches. In 1965, 0-6-OST Stewarts & Lloyd's No 86 takes ore from the Wellingborough Quarries.**

Abercynon – and make the return journey with the empties.

The run was made successfully in just over four hours and Homfray won his bet. A few days later, Trevithick wrote enthusiastically to his patron, Davies Giddy: 'Last Saturday we lighted the fire in the Tram Waggon and work'd it without the wheels to try the engine; on Monday we put it on the Tramroad. It work'd very well and ran up hill and down with great ease, and very manageable. We had plenty of steam and power.'

In fact, Trevithick was to build only one more railway locomotive – *Catch Me Who Can*, demonstrated in 1808 on a piece of waste ground near the site of the future Euston station – and it was left to others to carry on the development of steam traction. Much of the pioneering work over the next two decades was associated with the coal industry, particularly in the North East.

In 1813, William Hedley's celebrated locomotive, *Puffing Billy*, was put to work at Wylam colliery, near Newcastle. A year later, George Stephenson built his first locomotive, *Blucher*, for the nearby Killingworth colliery. (The engine was named after the Prussian general, later noted for his part on the battlefield of Waterloo in 1815.)

Another colliery, at Hetton in County Durham, engaged Stephenson to build a railway to take coal directly to the staithes at Sunderland on the River Wear. Hetton Colliery Railway, opened on 18 November 1822, was the first in the world designed to use locomotives along part of its length, and five of the engines were built under Stephenson's direction.

In 1825 came the opening of the Stockton & Darlington Railway, engineered by Stephenson and linking the Bishop Auckland coalfield in County Durham with the River Tees and the sea, to be followed five years later by the Liverpool & Manchester Railway. The Railway Age had unarguably arrived. But the early railway companies were sometimes unsure about the best method of organizing the traffic.

## Sharing the metals

Some railway companies looked to the experience of the turnpikes and regarded the new railways as 'roads' on which a range of carriers should be allowed to move goods. Several of the Lancashire lines, such as the Liverpool & Manchester, the North Union and the Bolton & Leigh, allowed the colliery owners to work their own traffic over the railway company metals, using tender locomotives of similar design to their own. The system seemed to work to the satisfaction of both sides.

A number of coal and iron works owners bought some of the new locomotives to work the traffic inside their premises. However, the majority continued to rely on horses. Where the terrain was hilly, rope-worked inclines were often to be found. These were well-suited to the slow moving mineral traffic, for which regularity of supply was more important than speed, and a significant number survived on industrial railways well into the twentieth century.

▲ **Where sparks might pose a danger in factories with flammable substances, a fireless locomotive was often used. Such engines had no firebox and were periodically supplied with steam from a central source. This Andrew Barclay 0-4-0 of 1935 worked at the Boots Pure Drug Co in Nottingham.**

**Steam without fire**
An unorthodox type of engine, used almost exclusively on industrial railways, was the fireless steam locomotive. The first to be made in Britain came from the workshop of Andrew Barclay of Kilmarnock in 1912. Designed specially for operation in munition factories, chemical plants, petrol refineries and other places where flying sparks could easily start a major fire, they were also used in locations with a ready supply of surplus steam

Fireless locomotives resembled ordinary engines, but without a chimney. Instead of a boiler, they were fitted with a steam container, surmounted by a dome and safety valve. The container, having first been three-quarters filled with water at a high temperature, was then charged with superheated steam from a central stationary boiler – with the result that it was able to keep the cylinders working continuously for several hours.

## Early tank locomotives

In 1851, thousands flocked to the Great Exhibition held at London's Crystal Palace. Two small locomotives on view here came in for much attention. The engines, both well tanks, were a 2-2-2 from George England of the Hatcham Ironworks at New Cross, London, and a 2-4-0 from E.B. Wilson of Leeds. They were among the earliest tank locomotives built and the type was to prove ideally suited to the industrial railway, with its tight curves and short sidings.

From the 1860s, there was a tremendous expansion in the number of industrial railways worked by steam engines. This was matched by a rise in the number of locomotive manufacturers, many of which would go on to become household names. Although E.B. Wilson's business at Leeds had collapsed in 1858–9, Manning Wardle & Company had already been set up on the adjoining land, and it perpetuated some of the tank locomotive designs. Nearby, Hudswell Clarke & Company was founded in 1860 and the Hunslet Engine Company was set up in 1864.

The demand was such, both at home and abroad, that many already established firms also began to build industrial locomotives – Fox Walker in Bristol, Andrew Barclay in Kilmarnock, W.A. Bagnall in Stafford, Hawthorn Leslie in Newcastle and the Yorkshire Engine Company in Sheffield, to name but a few. They were complemented by many smaller Victorian companies serving local markets, some of whose locomotives possessed an individual, not to say idiosyncratic, character.

## Increasing diversity

The range of industrial railways was now immense, serving not only ironstone quarries and coal mines, but a multitude of other undertakings besides, including farms, factories, dockyards and the armed forces. They even helped with the construction of canals, roads and housing estates. For example, a fleet of some 200 locomotives was assembled for the construction of the Manchester Ship Canal.

The shunting locomotive was an ever-present feature of many industrial towns. Nowhere was this better exemplified than in Burton-on-Trent in Staffordshire, where several of the brewery companies used their own locomotives to move ingredients – barley, malt and hops – as well as beer and coal over both their own lines and those of the four railway companies serving the town. As a result, there seemed to be a level crossing every few yards, with a red, green or blue locomotive puffing across. This might seem far fetched, but Burton-on-Trent did have a total of 32 such crossings. Anyone taking a tram journey along its two main streets would encounter five level crossings in less than 1.5km (one mile), each adjacent signalbox carrying the warning: 'Caution – these gates will be opened when the bell rings!'

One of the most notable industrial railways in Britain was owned by the Gas, Light & Coke Company. Within the boundaries of its gasworks at Beckton in Essex were more than 112.75km (70 miles) of railway track, which were connected to the London & North Eastern Railway. The system was so extensive that it once had as many as 20 trains working simultaneously and featured 14 signalboxes ranging from simple ground frames to a complex 70-lever box.

## Scottish pioneer

There were, of course, many more modest industrial railways, with a short length of track serving just a couple of loading banks and a connection with a waterway or mainline railway. An unusual member of this minor league was the 1.5km (one mile) railway operated by the British Aluminium Company at Kinlochleven in Argyllshire. Used for transhipment between the harbour and the works, the 3ft (915mm) gauge line was electrified in 1906, becoming the first electric railway in Scotland.

It was in the years following World War I that industrial railways began gradually to decline. There were several reasons for this: improved operating techniques, such as conveyor belts at quarries; the shift of general goods traffic from the railways to the roads; and the closure of many mines and factories in the Great Depression of the 1930s. The situation was exacerbated in the 1960s and 1970s by the effects of the Beeching cuts.

The coal industry, with a cheap source of fuel immediately available, was one of the last users of steam locomotives in Britain. It was still possible in the 1970s, several years after its disappearance on BR, to visit collieries where steam was hard at work. At Wheldale colliery in Yorkshire, a steam service was operating in the 1980s.

In November 1981, Hunslet maker's No 3168 was moved here for three weeks' trial so that the manufacturer could test a new variant of its mechanical stoker equipment. The National Coal Board continued to use the engine periodically on the run to Fryston until September 1982. The following month, it left by road for the preserved Embsay Steam Railway at Skipton.

▲ **The 29km (18 mile) sugar beet railway that left the Great Eastern Railway Stoke Ferry branch at Abbey was typically neglected. Hudswell Clarke 0-6-OST *Wissington* of 1938 was named after the British Sugar Corporation beet refinery that the line fed.**

It is possible that the last regular steam-worked industrial system was at Glaxochem's plant at Ulverston in Cumberland, which used a fireless locomotive until 1989, when it acquired a secondhand BR Class 08 diesel shunter.

Locomotives continue to play an important role in transporting goods around industrial sites in Britain but, as with their mainline brethren, the past seems to exert more fascination for the railway enthusiast than the present.

▼**Crane tanks were used in engineering works where relatively modest weights had to be moved around the factory on an internal railway. Shipbuilders were typical users, and one is seen here at William Doxford & Sons' yard at Sunderland.**

**Private prefererences**

The majority of industrial locomotives fell into three categories: the outside-cylindered four-coupled tank, and the outside or inside-cylindered six-coupled tank.

Saddle tank locomotives predominated, followed by side tanks. A number of companies used well tank locomotives, but the industrial tender engine was quite rare, a reflection of the fact that most operators wanted simple, reliable machines with a short wheelbase and good visibility for shunting.

Many industrial operators undertook their own engine repairs and overhauls, calling in outside specialists, such as wheel turners and boilersmiths, as and when they were needed. In some cases, operators with large locomotive fleets set up substantial repair facilities. One of these was the Gas, Light & Coke Company, whose enormous railway system at Beckton in Essex was served by 34 saddle tank locomotives and more than 1,000 wagons.

# Working on the railway

**The pay was low, the discipline was harsh and the chances of being killed or injured were greater than those normally faced by a soldier. Yet a job on the railway was considered a coveted prize.**

Karl Marx was able to influence millions and to set continents ablaze, but he failed to impress the Great Western Railway. When he applied for a job, he was turned down on the grounds of poor handwriting. It was a bitter disappointment. But then, as he later expounded in *The Communist Manifesto*, life could not be expected to give people what they wanted.

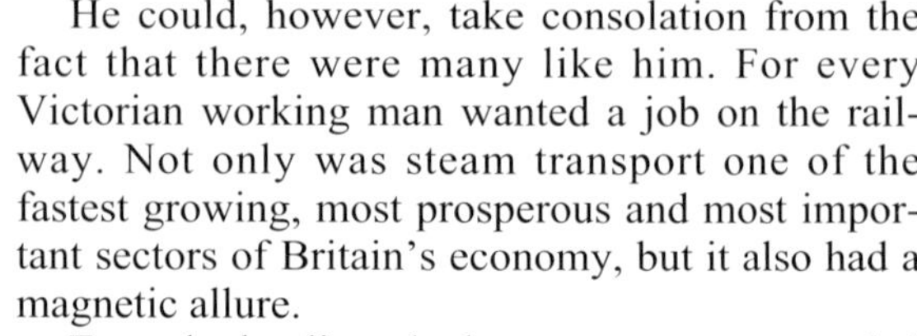

He could, however, take consolation from the fact that there were many like him. For every Victorian working man wanted a job on the railway. Not only was steam transport one of the fastest growing, most prosperous and most important sectors of Britain's economy, but it also had a magnetic allure.

Even the lowliest shed sweeper was surrounded by the very latest in technological development, and as for the élite, the locomotive drivers, they were the fastest men in the world – the jet pilots and astronauts of their time.

A high regard for safety and good time-keeping was, of course, paramount for anyone working on the railway. But many other qualities were also demanded, and staff selection methods were remorselessly stringent. An employee was expected to be healthy, literate, courteous, well-dressed, physically strong, sober, vigilant, quick-witted and of impeccable character.

A railwayman safeguarded the national interest as much as a soldier, and initially the two callings had a lot in common. They were both subject to extreme discipline, they both wore uniforms that reflected their sharply differentiated ranks and they were both expected to obey, without question, the precise orders of their superiors. Indeed, many railway managers were men who had served long years as army or naval officers.

## Breaking the rules

Infringement of company regulations brought stern retribution. Offences for which employees were dismissed ranged from exercising a dog while on sick leave, to betting on a horse. One man who quit without giving proper notice was prosecuted and sentenced to three weeks of hard labour.

The prevailing attitude was vigorously expressed by E.B. Ivatts, an official of Ireland's Midland Great Western. In his *Railway Management at Stations*, published in 1885, Ivatts wrote that 'Obedience is gained by fear and respect, and lost by a deficiency of firmness and moral courage...Submission to a leader is given tacitly upon the belief that the leader is able

**◀With his carefully waxed moustache and neat collar and tie, this Southern Railway driver is the epitome of the old-time engineman. Note the medal ribbon, no doubt a legacy of World War I, worn prominently on his waistcoat. The picture, taken at Clapham Junction in 1944, also shows No 788 *Sir Urre of the Mount*, which was to haul American soldiers to Southampton.**

to lead, and on that account is a superior kind of man.'

And then there were the hours. One Victorian guard was told by his superintendent, 'You've got 24 in the day like every other man and they are all ours if we want them.' Often that was an understatement. In 1871, the Board of Trade received a report detailing instances of men working for 37 hours continuously. Days of 16 hours and upwards were commonplace.

## Huge casualty rate

On top of – and often because of – the hours, there were accidents. Men were crushed between buffers; collisions lit up rural horizons like a harvest sunset; and spilled embers from racing locomotives were constantly starting fires.

Even the simple act of reducing speed could maim – the transmitted jolt of braking a long goods train could toss the guard from one end of his van to the other. As late as the first decade of the twentieth century, some 5,000 railwaymen were killed and almost 240,000 injured.

Even so, the railwaymen stuck by the railways. The pay was as good as in any other industry, on top of which there was cheap accommodation, free fuel, free uniforms and later free rail travel. Tips for station staff were forbidden at first, but in 1857 the London & North Western Railway permitted them and other companies fell into line. More important than all this, however, was the knowledge that, whatever happened, the 'guv'nors' would look after you.

From early Victorian times, railway companies operated schools, orphanages, banks and friendly societies on behalf of their employees. When the railwaymen became unable to fulfil their duties because of old age, ill-health or injury, posts were often found for them elsewhere in the company.

## The all-powerful presence

An observer who visited the new railway town of Wolverton in Buckinghamshire was struck by the 'considerable number of men who have lost a finger, hand, arm or leg. All, however, whether whole or mutilated, look for support to "the Company", and not only their services and their thoughts, but their parts of speech are more or less devoted to it: for instance, the pronoun "she" almost invariably alludes to some locomotive engine; "he" to "the chairman", "it" to the London Board.'

### Decorating zeal

Pride in their work was the hallmark of the true railwayman. Drivers were particularly devoted and often spent hours of unpaid overtime lovingly grooming their locomotives.

On top of this, they would add their own decorative touches. Some painted the chimney or smokebox, others inscribed their names in gilt script or advertised the insignia of their Masonic lodge.

During the 1870s, a visitor to Carlisle noted of one bright green engine that 'Her driver has further embellished her with a pair of polished-brass antlered stags in her uncompromising stove-pipe chimney and there is a gaudy transfer picture of the Royal Family on her sandbox...'

Occasionally, the zeal for decoration could become excessive, as in the case of the North British Railway whose royal engine was so covered in tapestry, shrubbery, flowers and painted carpentry, that it was virtually impossible to make out its livery.

**▲ The yard inspector looks out from the signalbox at London's Victoria station in 1939. The senior ranks of the railway hierarchy had to be particularly mobile, often uprooting family and home every few years in order to climb further up the promotion ladder.**

**▼Dining car attendants line up at Euston station, the London terminus of the London & North Western Railway (LNWR), in 1906. According to one LNWR manager, the railway service demanded 'a high degree of smartness, alacrity, energy and zeal on the part of every individual engaged in it'.**

The price for the security offered by the railway companies was loyalty, and most employees were happy to pay it. During the nineteenth century, few strikes by railway workers occurred – only ten are recorded in the 40 years from 1830 to 1870 – and men willingly followed their fathers, uncles and brothers into the paternalistic embrace of the companies.

## Community of the railway

The railwaymen and their families comprised a separate, close-knit community, with their own rules, their own traditions and their own strict hierarchy. In his book *Men and Rails*, published in 1913, Rowland Kenney, who had himself worked in a goods yard in the north of England, wrote that: 'The man in one of the higher grades was regarded as socially superior to the lower grade man. The goods porter was looked upon as an inferior animal by the shunter. The shunter was tolerated as a necessary evil by the goods guard, who had wild hopes that some day he might be able to look a passenger guard squarely in the eyes as a man and brother of equal rank.'

**▼ Silhouetted against a curtain of steam, a guard carries rear warning lamps along one of the platforms at Liverpool's Lime Street station in 1954. 'It is very doubtful,' wrote one observer of the inter-war rail scene, 'if even in the most unfavourable circumstances anyone has ever seen a guard "rattled" or in any danger of losing his dignity.'**

Another striking aspect of railway life was its distinctive vocabulary, some of which passed into common usage. 'Light at the end of the tunnel' and 'full steam ahead' were obvious examples of footplate patois. Other phrases, however, remained obscure. Outsiders might possibly have guessed that 'Australian days' and 'birth-control hours' referred to night work. Only initiates could have recognized 'the razor gang' as company auditors, or know that a 'set of Huns' was nothing more alarming than enginemen from another depot.

## Company name-calling

There was, in fact, a good deal of rivalry between the different companies, with employees scoffing at competitors' uniforms, facilities, liveries and rolling stock. Derogatory nicknames emerged for different lines. So the Lancashire & Yorkshire became the 'Languish and Yawn', the Somerset & Dorset the 'Slow and Dirty', the London, Chatham & Dover the 'London and Cheetham', and the London, Midland & Scottish the 'Elleva Mess'.

In cities such as Carlisle, which boasted sheds belonging to five different companies, crews would cross the street to avoid each other, and intermarriage between the children of opposing liveries was regarded as outright betrayal.

However, the early 1900s saw a gradual fall in company loyalty. The railwaymen, increasingly restive over their low pay, long hours and poor

▲ **An 0-6-0 tank engine holds centre stage at the opening of the Midland Railway's Barnoldswick line in Yorkshire in the early 1900s. The stationmaster and footplate crew, the latter in their Sunday best, pose on the locomotive itself, while the lowlier staff merely stand in its shadow. The man in mufti with the brass armband is probably a shunter. He is flanked on one side by a porter, and on the other by someone whose appearance suggests that he is the local postman.**

working conditions, turned in growing numbers to the rail unions.

The reaction of the employers was summed up in the comment of the London & North Western's Sir George Findlay, 'that you might as well have trades unions in Her Majesty's Army as have it in the railway service.'

Discontent came to a head in 1911 with the first ever national rail strike. Two further all-out stoppages followed in 1919 and 1926 – the latter as part of the General Strike called by the TUC.

A further blow to the traditional style of master-servant relationship was the Grouping of 1923, which combined some 120 privately owned railway companies into just four. Yet loyalties still remained strong in the regions.

At their peak, after World War I, the railways employed more than three-quarters of a million workers. After World War II the payroll still numbered an impressive 635,000. But the decline already apparent in the inter-war period became even more marked after 1945. Morale slumped disastrously and the long-awaited nationalization of 1948, rather than improving the situation, removed much of the partisan pride that had infused the old regional lines. A few years later, the British Railways chairman, Richard Beeching, removed many of the lines themselves.

Steam trains were soon superseded by diesels and electrics, which were themselves outstripped by jet aircraft. Computerization and technological advance shrank the workforce still further. Nevertheless, despite all the upheavals the railway workers have faced over the past years, it would be hard to dispute Rowland Kenney's verdict of 1913: 'I do not suggest that railwaymen are better or worse, or more or less necessary than any other section of the national labour forces, they are different, that is all.'

▼ **A GWR guard, beard groomed and boots shining, awaits the 'right away' with the 9.15 a.m. local service from Solihull to Birmingham Snow Hill in 1899. The early railway managers, many of whom were ex-army men, insisted on station staff presenting a parade ground appearance.**

# The Railway Inspectorate

**Set up in 1840 to promote the safety of passengers, the Railway Inspectorate at first had few powers save those of persuasion. And with many of the railway companies implacably opposed to reform, the Inspectorate's officers faced a tough battle.**

There could have hardly be a more typically British institution than Her Majesty's Inspecting Officers of Railways – known simply as the Railway Inspectorate. Its Britishness came from a compromise, long maintained during the nineteenth century, between leaving business to regulate itself and enforcing regulation in the public interest. The Inspectorate was expected to rely upon the enlightened self-interest of the railway companies to improve standards of rail safety – though, in the end, it had to be given long overdue powers of enforcement.

The Inspectorate was born in 1840 through the Regulation of Railways Act. This followed the Report of a Select Committee of the House of Commons which concluded that, while it was desirable for some control to be exercised over railway safety, it should, in the true spirit of Victorian *laissez-faire*, be kept to a minimum.

The Act required the railway companies to notify the Inspectorate of their intention to open new lines and to inform it of all accidents involving death or injury. Just reporting, however, meant little; so in 1842, the Inspectorate was given the power to prevent the opening of any line it considered unsafe.

The Inspectorate, responsible at this time to the Board of Trade, consisted of a handful of retired officers from the Royal Engineers. However, it would be wrong to imagine that they had any

**Hair-raising methods**

The early railways indulged in some hair-raising operating methods. The Taff Vale, for example, often ran goods trains without a brake van, merely hanging a tail lamp on the coupling hook of the last wagon. The Rhymney, always short of engines, used to make up immensely long trains of 130 or more wagons for the downhill run to the docks, which could temporarily become runaways.

Recalling pioneering days on the Great Western Railway, Daniel Gooch, the company's one-time Chairman, wrote in his diary: 'When I look back upon this time, it is a marvel to me that we escaped serious accidents. It was no uncommon thing to take an engine out on the line to look for a late train that was expected, and many times have I seen the train coming and reversed the engine and run back out of its way as quickly as I could. What would be said about such a mode of proceeding now?'

**◀ Unaware of Stephenson's locomotive, *Rocket*, approaching with a train on the track behind him, the President of the Board of Trade, William Huskisson, was struck down and fatally injured at the opening of the Liverpool & Manchester Railway in 1830.**

kinship with Colonel Blimp; they were able, even distinguished, professional engineers who were trying to protect public safety with virtually no powers of enforcement.

Resemblances to Colonel Blimp can more easily be found in the resistance, often expressed in choleric language, of some railway chairmen to the sensible proposals of the Inspecting Officers. It was typical of the Victorian age that, while the Inspecting Officers had a duty to investigate the causes of accidents reported to them (and their reports were soon recognized as models of clarity), the railway companies were not obliged to act upon their comments or recommendations.

Even so, individual Inspecting Officers could be pretty forthright, as one would expect of former military men. The redoubtable Colonel W. Yolland was once asked to approve a locking frame in which a signalman at Kentish Town Junction on the North London Railway had to depress a stirrup with his foot to clear a signal. The Colonel managed to put both his feet simultaneously into two stirrups, which nullified the locking; he refused to approve the installation.

It was also he who commented acidly about an accident at Sittingbourne on the London, Chatham & Dover Railway in 1862 that, 'it is apparent that nearly every servant of the company that had a responsible duty to perform, neglected it'.

◄ ▼ **The early part of the twentieth century saw a number of railways adopting Automatic Train Control (ATC). Although systems varied, the principle was the same.**

**A shoe under the locomotive controlled a battery-generated current that held a valve in the vacuum braking system closed. When the locomotive ran over a special ramp fixed in the track before a distant signal, the shoe was lifted, automatically breaking the circuit from the locomotive battery. If the signal was at clear, the ramp was energized by a battery in the signalbox, so that current picked up by the shoe continued to hold the brake valve closed. It also sounded a bell in the engine cab.**

**But if the signal was at caution, the ramp remained 'dead'. With the circuit from the locomotive battery broken, air rushed into the vacuum pipe, sounding a siren and applying the brakes.**

## Aiming for the best

One function of the Inspectorate – to ensure that new railways were built with proper regard to safety – grew steadily. A later Chief Inspecting Officer wrote about his predecessors that, 'Their method seems to have been to study the practice adopted by the many Companies who were building railways throughout the country and to try to ensure that all were as good as the best'.

Codes of practice were built up until, by 1858, the Board of Trade was able to issue guidance booklets of 'Requirements' for passenger lines and 'Recommendations' for goods lines. These were progressively expanded into substantial manuals of good engineering practice.

Operating methods were a more difficult area than engineering; they only came under review following an accident. This was not felt to be satisfactory even by so sturdy an individualist as George Stephenson. From his retirement home in 1841, 'Old George' wrote to the President of the Board of Trade suggesting that speeds should be limited to 65km/h (40mph) 'on the most favourable lines, excepting on special occasions' and that 'no train should be allowed to travel which has not two brakesmen, and four coaches in each train should be provided with brakes'.

Time after time, the Inspecting Officers' accident reports drew attention to unsatisfactory operating methods, such as time-interval working and inadequate brake-power. As the mileage of railways increased, and trains became faster and more frequent, the Inspectorate began to press for improved safety measures in four principal fields.

These were: full interlocking of points and signals, with standardization of signal design; absolute block signalling procedure in place of both time-interval and permissive block on passenger lines; provision of a reliable continuous braking system in all passenger coaches; and effective means of passenger-guard communication in an emergency.

A case study of the frustrations experienced by the Inspectorate can be found in the long-drawn-out search for passenger-guard communication. In the early days, guards rode outside their vans on a raised seat like those of a stage-coach, from which they were supposed to look out for 'passengers exhibiting signs of alarm'.

## Nail in an iron coffin

The Great Western Railway (GWR) put a 'travelling porter' in a cubicle at the end of an express locomotive's tender, facing backwards, known as the iron coffin. The problem had to be solved otherwise, and in 1868 Parliament passed a new Regulation of Railways Act requiring the provision, 'as the Board of Trade may approve', of efficient means of communication between passengers and 'the servants of the company in charge of the train' wherever trains travelled more than 32km (20 miles) without stopping. A deadline of 12 months was set.

The companies long experimented with unsatisfactory outside cords ringing bells in the guard's van and/or operating the engine whistle. These were Heath Robinson expedients, however, and it was not until 1899 that the simple and effective communication cord applying the brake – vacuum or Westinghouse – and thereby attracting the attention of the train crew was standardized. Not one year but 30 were required to meet the Board of Trade requirement.

**Cup final trio**

In 1899, the Railway Inspectorate included three men – Sir Francis Marindin, P.G. von Donop and G.W. Addison – who had all been members of the Royal Engineers team that reached the FA Cup final of 1874. The captain had been Marindin, who served from 1895–9 as Chief Inspecting Officer. He was later President of the FA. Von Donop had gone on to play in the Royal Engineers team that won the FA Cup in 1875.

**◀ A driver of the 1950s at the controls of a locomotive fitted with BR's Automatic Warning System (AWS). On approaching a signal, a magnetic impulse was sent to a receiver in the cab. Where the signal was at clear, the receiver's dial was unaffected, but where it was at caution, the dial split into segments like those on a dartboard, as here. If not promply overridden, the system applied the brakes.**

Progress with interlocking and absolute block working was hardly more rapid. A crude form of interlocking had been provided by the South Eastern Railway in 1843, yet as late as 1870 there was a serious accident on the North Eastern Railway line between Sunderland and Gateshead, where there was no interlocking whatsoever.

Block telegraph working, to ensure that only one train could be in a section at a time, was first used on the North Midland Railway at Clay Cross in 1841. As late as 1873, however, the GWR had less than half of its lines worked on the absolute block, still elsewhere clinging to time-interval and permissive block.

The attitude of some railway directors to the question of new safety devices was summed up by Lord Houghton of the Lancashire & Yorkshire Railway, who asserted that the public 'were well satisfied to run a small risk of accident for the great convenience of frequency and celerity'.

So far as continuous brakes were concerned, there was initially genuine doubt about which of the several competing systems available was the most reliable. However, even when the superiority of two of them – the automatic vacuum and the Westinghouse air brake – had been clearly demonstrated, the companies continued to drag their feet. A long list of fatal accidents underlined the cost of their vacillation.

In 1880, following the derailment of an express train at Wennington in Lancashire, Colonel Yolland, his zeal undiminished, took the railway companies to task. The Board of Trade, he declared, had been asserting the need for better brakes for 20 years, and 'it may be truly stated that the principal railway companies throughout the kingdom have resisted the efforts of the Board of Trade to cause them to do what was right, which the latter has no power to enforce...'

It was to take the horrific accident at Armagh in June 1889 to spur Parliament into action. The result of the runaway of part of a Sunday School excursion colliding with a following train, it was Ireland's worst railway disaster. Some 80 passengers, including 22 children, were killed or died later, and 260 seriously injured. Before the year

**Hard Struggles**

The nineteenth century railway companies were not alone in their dislike of the Railway Inspectorate. Many rank and file railwaymen also had reservations. One such was a disgruntled ex-Great Western Railway Stationmaster, Hubert Simmons, who produced an angry memoir under the pseudonym Ernest Struggles.

'What a satisfaction it must be to the public, when an accident has happened,' he commented sourly, 'to know that a "real gentleman", appointed by the Government, goes down to the spot, taking luncheon in a saloon carriage on his way thither, accompanied by the officials of the line on which the accident has happened, and whose very frown or hint beforehand, accompanied by their presence, will undoubtedly have the effect of "the whole truth and nothing but the truth" being laid before the enquiring Colonel or Captain Inspector.'

▶ BR workers search through wreckage at Scotland's Paisley Gilmour Street station in 1979 following a head-on collision that claimed seven lives, including those of both drivers. Assessing the evidence gathered in the aftermath of such disasters was a crucial part of the Railway Inspectorate's task.

**Risk to railwaymen**

Although the Railway Inspectorate was set up primarily to promote the safety of passengers, injuries and loss of life among railway workers was a much greater, if less publicized, problem. According to a survey carried out in 1865, the risk of accidents was 50 times greater among railway servants than railway travellers. In 1874, a year when the system had attained about the same size as British Rail in its later years, there were 788 men killed – an average of two a day – on the railway.

A century later, in 1974, the number of men killed was down to 39. The Railway Employment Act of 1900 established a team of Railway Employment Inspectors to enforce safety precautions, and this, helped no doubt by improved technical practices, led to the steady fall in fatalities.

◀ In their eagerness to travel by the new steam railway, passengers tended to ignore its potential dangers. They often opened the doors while still travelling at speed and some even leapt out to retrieve hats lost in the breeze. In an attempt to reduce accidents, many of the early companies resorted to locking in their passengers – a practice which posed its own risk in the event of a fire.

was out, Parliament passed another Regulation of Railways Act making both continuous automatic brakes and the absolute block system compulsory on all British railways.

Interlocking had already been made a statutory requirement, despite opposition from reactionaries like the Chairman of the London & North Western Railway, Sir Richard Moon, whose more progressive Superintendent, G.P. Neele, recorded that 'we never failed to hear from the Chairman that these mechanical appliances were all inducements to inattention on the part of signalmen and drivers.'

With the main battles over, relations between the railway companies and the Inspectorate became more cordial in the twentieth century, although need remained for improvement in a number of areas, including the substitution of electric for gas lighting in carriages, track circuiting, Automatic Train Control and the replacement of semaphores by colour-light signals.

In addition to its responsibilities for safety, the Inspectorate had another duty – that of giving technical advice on railway matters to its political masters. This was important particularly in the 1950s, when heavy investment was proposed under the Railway Modernization Plan. The Inspectorate was required to give an impartial view, based on familiarity with modern railway practice in other countries.

The improvement in relations between the railways and the Inspectorate was clearly seen in 1935 when, following a signalman's error, a north-bound express ran into the back of another at Welwyn Garden City on the main line out of King's Cross. The railway companies welcomed the Inspecting Officer's recommendation for a link between track circuits and block instruments, and the system, which eventually became known as the Welwyn control, was widely adopted.

Accidents, alas, continued to provide plenty of work for the Inspectorate, but at least it no longer had to carry on a war of attrition against the railway companies. The new relationship was perhaps illustrated by the career of Brigadier C.A. Langley, CBE, MC, who was Chief Inspecting Officer from 1956–63, but who had personal ties with a number of senior railway managers who had served with or under him during World War II.

Ardagh Langley, as he was known, was an expert on railway electrification; he had been seconded to the Great Indian Peninsula Railway in 1927–33 to assist in the electrification of the main Bombay–Poona line; and when he retired from the Inspectorate he was appointed a consultant to the British Railways Board. To railwaymen he was very much 'one of us', liked and respected by management and trades unions equally.

## End of a tradition

Ardagh Langley was also the embodiment of a tradition which seemed set to continue indefinitely. However, in December 1990, the Inspectorate was transferred from the Department of Transport to the Health and Safety Executive under the Department of Employment. At the same time, after 150 years, an end was made to the exclusive recruitment of Inspecting Officers from the Corps of Royal Engineers, though some former military men remained. Perhaps as a sop to compensate for any regrets about the change, the Inspectorate was re-christened Her Majesty's Railway Inspectorate. That, at least, would have had the full-hearted approval of Colonel Yolland and his colleagues.

# The Railway Clearing House

**Set up in 1842, the Railway Clearing House ironed out the worst of the problems arising from a rail system owned by a multitude of different companies. It was here that company representatives regularly convened to discuss important railway issues.**

For over a century, one of the most important organizations in the railway world functioned, almost entirely unknown to the public, in a long, gloomy building beside London's Euston station. Even to many railwaymen it was nothing more than an address to which documents had to be sent and to which an office chief might routinely disappear for a meeting. But the work of the Railway Clearing House affected almost every aspect of the railways' activities.

Its origins were straightforward. Almost as soon as the Liverpool & Manchester Railway had opened for traffic in 1830, various other companies started the construction of connecting railway lines. By 1841, a traveller from London could reach Birmingham, Manchester, Liverpool, Nottingham, York, Leeds and a host of other places, but only by using the rails of different companies. Constant changing of trains and, even worse, the transhipment of goods between wagons, were intolerable handicaps. (It remained inescapable between the broad-gauge Great Western trains and those of the rest of the network.)

## Double expense

Not untypical was a letter to *The Times* from an indignant horse owner, complaining that the 'unaccommodating spirit' of the railway companies had obliged him to send a servant all the way

**Letting off steam**

One of the worst problems faced by the toiling clerks of the RCH was monotony. In March 1849, a Mr Tysen tried to dispel this in a way which provoked the displeasure of the controlling committee. Its minutes record that he 'was called in to answer a complaint against him for having thrown an apple against a fellow clerk'. He was not allowed to take a holiday that year and the details of the case were made known to his colleagues as a warning.

This, however, did not deter a Mr Glover, a part-time soldier in the Third City of London Rifle Corps, who in 1851 brought his firearm into the office and performed some 'platoon drill', the high point of which was the shooting of the office clock. Mr Glover and a colleague, a Mr Metcalf, who had joined in the high jinks, were each fined 50*s*. for their misdemeanour and ordered to pay for the repair of the unfortunate clock.

**◀It was this anonymous looking building, to the east of London's Euston station, that served for more than a century as the nerve centre of the British railway system. The Railway Clearing House had its headquarters here from 1849 until its disbandment in 1963. Much of the building was later demolished as part of the scheme to rebuild Euston station.**

from London to Derby simply to lead his horse from one train to another on its journey to Barnsley. As a result, the expense of sending the horse was 'nearly doubled'.

An irate traveller from Preston wrote that he had travelled to London in January and had been 'very desirous' of remaining in one carriage. 'I found there was no chance of it, and that I could only book to Parkside [near Manchester], then from Parkside I had to book again to Birmingham, and the inconvenience was so great at Birmingham that I had no time to get refreshment properly, having to look after my luggage.'

## Time for change

The travelling public demanded both through booking and the through running of passenger trains, while traders agitated for a system of through invoicing and through running for goods traffic. The railway companies' response was to set up the Railway Clearing House (RCH), which would record all the debits and credits arising from through transits and make a periodic settlement of the final balances due.

Robert Stephenson, son of George Stephenson, Kenneth Morison, auditor of the London & Birmingham Railway (LBR), and George Carr Glyn (later Lord Wolverton), a banker and a director of the LBR, are generally regarded as the founding fathers of the RCH. It opened in 1842 with the participation of nine companies. Just six clerks formed the nucleus of the new organization, which was situated in a house in Drummond Street, almost opposite the main entrance to Euston station. Kenneth Morison was appointed the first Secretary.

The railway network was expanding at an astonishing rate and the volume of work flooding into the RCH increased accordingly. Within three years, the railways included in the RCH system had grown to 16, with more than 965.5km (600 route miles) of track. In 1849, the RCH leased from the London & North Western Railway a new three-storey office which it had built on the east side of Euston station, in Seymour Street (later renamed Eversholt Street).

▲ **Hundreds of documents stored at the RCH in the early 1930s reflect the huge workload handled by the organization. In 1850, the companies included in the RCH system controlled 55.8 per cent of the country's total route mileage. Half a century later, this had increased to 94.5 per cent.**

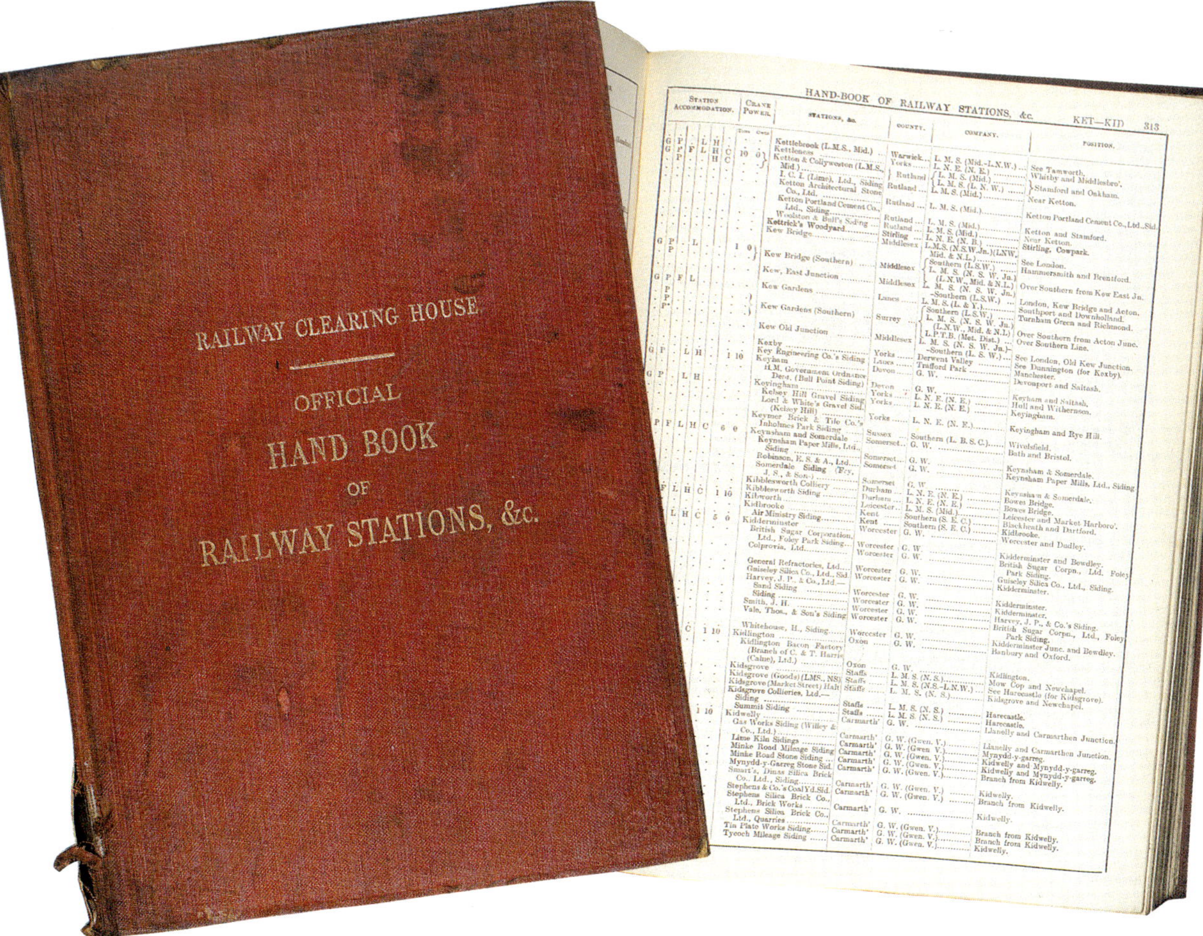


◀ **Arguably, the most useful publication of the RCH was the *Official Hand Book of Railway Stations, &c*, including junctions, sidings, collieries and works, which listed the station accommodation, crane power, county, company and position. The 1938 edition, seen here, ran to 654 pages and cost 10*s*. 6*d*. carriage paid. The key to the letters describing station accommodation was: G – Goods Station; G* – Coal Class, Mineral and Station to Station Traffic in Truck Loads; P – Passenger and Parcel Station; P* – Passenger, but not Parcel or Miscellaneous Traffic; F – Furniture Vans, Carriages, Motor Cars, Portable Engines, and Machines on Wheels; L – Live Stock; H – Horse Boxes and Prize Cattle Vans; C – Carriages and Motor Cars by Passenger Train. (The Crane Power referred to the lifting capability of a fixed crane, but most companies had portable cranes of five tonne (ton) capacity that could be moved from station to station as required.)**

▲ **The board room of the Railway Clearing House was the venue for meetings of the organization's controlling committee. This comprised four representatives from the board of each of the participating companies. Numbering nine at the RCH's founding in 1841, these had increased to 43 by the spring of 1848.**

On the ground floor was the famous Long Office, the epitome of Dickensian gloom, with its vast rows of desks and its gas lighting. On the floors above were meeting rooms of varying size and dignity, including the Board Room, where the general managers of the participating railway companies met to decide grand policy.

There were also catering facilities renowned in the rest of the railway world. *Haute cuisine* and cigars were produced for the general managers, and roast beef and Yorkshire pudding, with bottled beer, for the humbler officials.

## System of working

The routine work of the Clearing House was divided between the clerks, who toiled at their desks sorting out the traffic returns and apportioning the receipts, and the number takers at junctions and interchange points who had to record the details of every van, wagon and carriage which passed from one company into the hands of another.

'The number takers,' observed *The Times* in 1892, 'must be capable of exposure to all kinds of hard weather, and possess the requisite amount of smartness and intelligence to enable them to perform their different duties with the utmost accuracy and dispatch. It is to them in great measure that the efficiency of the Clearing House is due.'

A Mileage Department checked journey distances and ensured that all rolling stock was returned to its parent railway company or private owner. (By 1911, there were 4,000 private owners, with a total of 650,000 wagons.)

The day to day control of the Clearing House rested with the Secretarial Department. In addition to dealing with administration and personnel, it provided a forum in which the managements could meet to hammer out policies and make progress in commercial, operating and technical procedures.

There was a great pyramid of conferences and committees, with the General Managers' Conference at the top dealing with major issues affecting all railways (other than political issues, which were reserved for the chairmen). Lower down the pyramid there were conferences of the other echelons – goods managers, superintendents, passenger managers, accountants, engineers (civil and mechanical), even solicitors and chemists. In fact, just about every kind of railway official had his appointed conference or committee.

An organization chart of the RCH issued in 1947 showed a total of 132 conferences, committees and sub-committees. The RCH provided meeting rooms, agenda papers and secretaries for this mass of business; in 1946, just before nationalization occurred, there were 2,859 meetings in 12 months.

## Setting new standards

It can be argued that the RCH, though it had to work through consensus, made more progress possible in, for instance, railway safety than even the Railway Inspectorate. Rules and regulations were standardized, and a uniform signalling system was gradually introduced.

The dangers of the old system were underlined by a director of the Brighton and Greenwich railways. Giving evidence to a parliamentary committee in 1841, he pointed out that the signals of some railways 'were almost the converse of those on others', and that the signal for 'safety on one line was that for danger' on another.

Other important decisions by the RCH concerned the positioning of head and tail lamps,

▶ **A Class G2 0-8-0 heads north on the West Coast main line with a train of empty coal wagons in the mid-1930s. Details of all wagons passing from one railway system to another were recorded at exchange junctions and forwarded to the RCH.**

▶ **Although taken when most of the clerks were conveniently absent, this photograph still captures the barracks-like atmosphere of one of the RCH's offices. Note the chief clerk in his special cubicle. Until 1912, the RCH was an entirely male establishment, but in that year 27 women were employed.**

### Railway lobbying

In 1858, railway company chairmen and directors, meeting at the premises of the RCH, launched a new body – the United Railway Companies Committee. It was later renamed the Railway Companies' Association (RCA) and moved to Westminster.

Unlike the RCH, the RCA was directly concerned with political matters, its main tasks being to monitor all proceedings in Parliament which might affect the railways and to lobby for legislation of benefit to the railway companies.

Towards the end of World War II, the RCA produced a detailed plan for the future of the railways. But this was ignored by the newly elected Labour Government whose own plan was nationalization. Following the winding up of the railway companies, the RCA was also dissolved.

the height and size of buffers, and the standard of brakes and couplings.

On the commercial side, the RCH laid down rules on a host of subjects, ranging from the movement of dangerous goods to the conveyance of monkeys 'in charge of organ grinders etc', which were to be charged 'as for one dog'.

Publication of books and maps was an important RCH activity. The huge *General Railway Classification*, which listed everything that could conceivably be carried by train, and the standard of charging to be applied, was the bible of goods managers and the bane of the trading community. There was a massive *Official Hand Book of Railway Stations, &c*, showing all facilities for the receipt and despatch of freight. Junction Diagrams were issued, showing the distances between stations and interchange points on each company's line. And splendid Railway Maps of England and Wales, Scotland and Ireland were produced, many of them now collectors' items.

The RCH had the difficult task of persuading the Great Western Railway (GWR) to agree to anything which was acceptable to the other companies. There was a story, probably apocryphal, that the GWR chairman of a committee once instructed the secretary to draw minutes recording that a decision had been taken, 'the LMS, LNER and Southern Companies dissenting'.

By the time of the 1923 Grouping, a record number of 3,400 staff was employed by the RCH. However, the effects of amalgamation, the introduction of pooling schemes and the onset of trade recession reduced this number to less than 2,000 over the next ten years.

During World War II, the RCH was moved to Amersham in Buckinghamshire, but its committee structure formed a basis for the detailed operations of the Railway Executive Committee through which the government exercised its emergency control.

The nationalization of the railways in 1948 was expected to spell the end for the RCH, and therefore, a number of 'farewell' lunches and dinners was held. In fact, the Clearing House proved remarkably resilient. Its property, powers and liabilities were not transferred to the British Transport Commission until 1954, and even then it was to linger on for almost another decade.

## Secret of survival

What explains the survival? Although the role of the RCH steadily dwindled away after nationalization, it suited several interests to use the facilities and the remaining staff at Eversholt Street. The Ministry of Transport found the organization useful in furnishing statistics, maps and secretarial services at meetings with railway officers.

It was also well known, if not officially accepted, that the regions of British Railways maintained a communications network of their own, and their representatives often preferred to meet on the neutral territory of Eversholt Street rather than at BR's own premises in Marylebone Road, with a headquarters officer almost inevitably in the chair.

However, the appointment of Dr Richard Beeching as Chairman of the new Railways Board in the early 1960s was to mark the end. He and his henchmen saw the Clearing House as a symbol of a bygone age, and it was finally closed on 31 March 1963. Not long afterwards, part of its premises in Eversholt Street, including the Long Office, was demolished in connection with the reconstruction of Euston station. So ended 120 years of useful service to the railways of Britain.

*A Day in the Life of...*

# A Shedmaster

**The 1950s Shedmaster reigned supreme in his dirt-caked domain. Enginemen, fitters, cleaners, coalmen – all looked to him as the ultimate Boss. And when an emergency arose, it was usually his good sense and sound judgement that saved the day.**

It is exactly 8.15 a.m. as the Shedmaster parks his bicycle and makes for his office. His domain is a typical Midland roundhouse, with a turntable in the centre and 24 stabling roads radiating from it, of which four have high-pressure mains for washing out boilers. A fifth is reserved for major inspections and has a sheerlegs for lifting.

The small adjoining workshop contains benches but little in the way of machine tools; anything beyond the scope of a pillar drill and a tool grinder has to go to the District main depot for machining.

The engines, all 49 of them, are a pretty workaday lot, used mostly for hauling freight. There are five 8F 2-8-0s for working coal trains, mainly to Finedon Road (Wellingborough), and six 2-6-0 Crabs, which do the fitted freight and 'Maltese Cross' (vacuum-fitted head) trains to London, Carlisle, Edge Hill and Bristol.

The 17 4F and ten 3F Midland 0-6-0s perform a variety of tasks, working coal and empty wagon trips to and from the numerous collieries, including one or two block trains to the nearby power station.

On the passenger side, the stopping trains are in the hands of four elderly Midland 2P 4-4-0s, while the branch provides work for an Ivatt 2-6-2 tank

▼ **A cleaner trundles his wheelbarrow through the steam, shadow and glancing sunlight of a Midland roundhouse in the early 1950s, while a colleague tackles the tubes of a Jubilee Class locomotive, No 45660 *Rooke*. Tube cleaning, like most other jobs connected with the day-to-day maintenance of steam engines, relies more on sweat and muscle than machinery.**

on a push-pull. The extensive hump freight yard has two shunting tanks working round the clock; there is no mechanization, just shunters braking the wagons as they roll down.

## Shortage of engines

The sound of an ex-LMS Class 4F 0-6-0 moving out of the roundhouse, cylinder cocks open, penetrates the cramped office, and the Shedmaster glances out of the window. But his attention is on what the two men facing him across his desk are saying.

They are Wilf Collins, the shift Running Foreman, in blue slop coat and trilby, and Jim Bridges, the Leading Fitter, wearing a greasy flat cap and boiler suit. Collins is short of locomotives for later in the day.

'I've got two trip cancellations advised by Control, but all *that* gives us is a couple of Class 3Fs, so it doesn't help. I can't see a Crab for our Carlisle fitted tonight. The one on last night's Edge Hill ran a hot box and whatever they send in its place won't be here in time to dispose and reprepare. I've asked Control to find us something, but no promises yet.'

The Boss suggests having a 4F standing by, just in case.

**▲ Hunched between the engine and the ashpit, a fireman uses a long rake to clean out the ashpan. This lung-choking procedure has to be carried out once, and sometimes twice, a day on every locomotive.**

**▼ Under the watchful eye of the fitter a young apprentice uses callipers to measure the gap between the guides of a tender axlebox. Overheated axleboxes are a regular problem for repair crews, demanding hours of tedious labour.**

'How are you for power for this Women's Institute excursion to Bourneville tomorrow?'

'Well, the best I can see at the moment is another 4F, unless District can find a Compound or something.'

The Shedmaster promises to speak to District about the problem, then turns to the question of coal stocks. Collins is none too happy about the situation.

'We'll get by the next couple of days, but we'll be scratching around for Grade 2A if we don't get any more by then.'

'Right, keep me posted. Oh, and Wilf, there's a lot of coal spillage in front of the stage. Get the coalmen picking it all up, will you? It'll fill a bunker for you.'

## Stopped engines

Jim Bridges, meanwhile, has put his list of stopped engines on the Shedmaster's desk. This details all locomotives undergoing repairs or inspections, awaiting spare parts or having their boilers washed out. The Boss examines it.

'What's this 8F, waiting brake valve? Surely we keep one in stock?'

'Yes, we do, but District were stuck for one last week and I let them have it. Now *we're* stuck for one and the stores van doesn't come till tomorrow.'

'Okay, I'll press District for it. What about this 4F with the hot box?'

'We've cleaned up the journal and it should be all right. The box is coming from District on the 2.35 this afternoon, so we should have her finished tomorrow night with a bit of luck.'

### Washday blues

One of the least enviable jobs in a steam depot is washing out – the removal of scale and sludge from the boilers. Clad in oilskins and clogs, the boilerwashers use high pressure hoses to dislodge the deposits, which are then raked out at the base of the firebox.

However, so great is the amount of waste swilled out that the pit drains often become clogged. Washing out is done at intervals of one to four weeks, depending on the type of engine and usually takes about 30 minutes.

▲ **A Jubilee Class 6P 4-6-0, No 45562 *Alberta*, has been shunted into position over the inspection pit. Like other passenger engines, *Alberta* is checked over daily by an examining fitter. If a defect develops while an engine is in service, it will be reported by the incoming driver.**

'Right. Wilf, we'll need to start getting that coal off the ...'

The Shedmaster's words are cut short by the jangling of the telephone. It's the Assistant District Motive Power Superintendent (ADMPS) wanting up-to-date information for the 9.00 a.m. telephone conference with Division. After giving him details of stopped engines and coal stocks, and discussing the requisition for the brake valve, the Shedmaster raises his two most pressing concerns – that night's Carlisle engine and the WI special the following day. The ADMPS promises to ring back after the conference.

Various administrative chores keep the Boss busy for the next hour. Then Control telephones with information about the Carlisle. They've got a Kingmoor Class 5 unbalanced at Nottingham after working a troop train. Can he send a set of men to collect it? He certainly can, even if he has to cover on overtime. The shift Running Foreman is delighted.

Emerging from his grimy sanctuary, the Shedmaster notes how the four washout engines are progressing, then strolls over to the sheerlegs to have a look at the 4F's journal. Satisfied with it, he inspects the two ashpits.

Clearing a firebox of hot ash and clinker is one of the most unpleasant tasks on the railway, but it is a vital one and if neglected, it will cause trouble on the train's next trip. In some sheds, the job is handled by so-called fire-droppers, but here, as in the majority of sheds, it is done by firemen, who are either drawn from incoming crews or are on full-time standby.

Beyond the pits stands the elevated coal stage, with its steeply ramped approach track up which coal wagons are propelled twice a day. Two coalmen on each shift shovel from wagons into

▶ **A BR Standard ex-Crosti boilered 2-10-0, No 92026, awaits for its next duty. Carried out by a steam-raiser, the firing process usually begins several hours before a locomotive is due to leave the shed and can consume a tonne (ton) of coal.**

half-tonne (ton) wheeled skips, which are pushed across the stage and tipped into tenders below. This is another dirty and tiring job, and the Boss gives his coalmen some words of encouragement.

A shout brings him striding towards the Foreman's office. Three wagons have overshot the buffer stops at the far end of the marshalling yard and are hanging dangerously over the embankment, threatening the road below. The Yardmaster has alerted the police.

'I'll go and recce the situation. Get an engine and men on the tool vans, but don't send them until I give the word. It sounds like a crane job, so alert District.'

Off he goes at a fast trot the length of the yard. On the way, a down express behind a Jubilee comes by, braking instead of going through at 60 plus with steam on. Since all signals are off, he wonders why.

## Rough shunt

At the scene, it has obviously been a rough shunt that the brakie failed to catch. The stops are demolished and two empty 21-tonne (ton) minerals are hanging down the bank, wheels buried to the axles, and threatening to fall on to the road. A third wagon, a 16-tonner, is still on a fairly even keel, sitting on the sleepers. Police have closed the road and the traffic is in chaos.

The Shedmaster weighs up the situation and decides that it *is* a crane job, but he must anchor the wagons until the crane arrives. He phones his instructions to the Leading Fitter and makes his way back to the shed, lunch forgotten.

By this time, the down express is sitting engineless in the platform, while in the shed yard a column of smoke tells of furious efforts to prepare a locomotive in a hurry. The Jubilee is on an ashpit, looking forlorn.

The Foreman explains the problem: 'Failure on the express – both injectors. The only thing I can give them quickly is the 2P for the 1.50. The driver's not exactly thrilled with a 2P for nine bogies, but I've sweetened him and he'll be off shed soon. I'll put a 3F for the 1.50 and the other spare is on your tool vans.'

The Shedmaster considers for a minute. 'You know, Wilf, that Jubilee might just be our salvation for the Bourneville tomorrow, if the fitters can get the injectors right in time. I'll have a word.'

By the time the tool vans are ready to leave, the Shedmaster has spoken to the Mechanical Foreman at District about arrangements for the breakdown crane and established that the specialist fitter will work overtime on the Jubilee. Muck from the tender is probably blocking the injector cones, in which case the tank will need emptying to examine the sieves – a time-consuming process.

Back to the marshalling yard. Within an hour the gang has stabilized the two wagons down the bank, using the Kelbus pulling tackle to hitch them to three loaded 16-tonne (ton) minerals, with brakes pinned hard down as an anchor. They return to the shed as the breakdown crane appears.

By now, the power position has eased a little. The Black 5 from Kingmoor has arrived for the Carlisle. Like most Kingmoor engines it looks unkempt and is down on its boxes, but it will no doubt do the job. The Jubilee is in the shed, water draining from the tender into the pit, and the fitter has started work on the exhaust injector. The Shedmaster can only leave him to it.

Back in the office, there are letters to sign, as well as a couple of Shopping Proposals for tired engines which Jim Bridges has prepared. At 5 p.m. the Boss tells the Back Shift Foreman where he can be contacted later – he is on call every night except for holidays – and heads for home. With luck, he and his wife will be able to enjoy an undisturbed evening at the cinema.

### A fireman's lament

A locomotive produces up to half a tonne (ton) of ash and clinker on a single journey – and its disposal is one of the first tasks to be carried out after arrival at the shed yard. Armed with a long rake, the fireman bends double to clear out the grate, dodging the inevitable specks of hot ash.

But this is not the end of his ordeal. From the ashpit he has to clamber on to the buffer beam, there to perch precariously while clearing the smokebox of char – fine pieces of partly burned coal.

This clearing of the hot ash and clinker from the firebox is sometimes done by a fire-dropper.

# British railway electrification

**In 1847, George Stephenson is said to have predicted 'that electricity will one day power the railways of the world'. In Britain, this was to prove a slow and sporadic process, marked by a last-minute change of heart.**

**▶ A pioneer of electric locomotive traction was the North Eastern Railway (NER), which introduced the system on its heavy mineral line between Shildon and Newport, Co Durham, in 1915. The line's 1100hp Bo-Bo locomotives are seen here in their Shildon depot in 1927.**

An old poster in London's Science Museum announces, 'Mr Robert Davidson's Exhibition of Electro-Magnetism as a Moving Power', and promises rides behind a 'Locomotive Engine carrying passengers on a circular track'. The poster, undated, shows a four-wheeled vehicle, presumably the 'locomotive engine' because it carries a massive battery box, coupled to an elegant passenger car with curtained windows.

It is known that Davidson demonstrated a battery-powered locomotive, the *Galvani*, on the Edinburgh & Glasgow Railway in 1842, and the picture probably shows what it looked like. Little is known of the trials or final fate of the locomotive, but the story goes that it was broken up by angry workmen who saw it as a threat to their employment on steam railways.

In fact, batteries in the 1840s were an inconvenient and cumbersome source of power. They produced current for only a short time and they could not be recharged. The real breakthrough came in the 1870s, following the invention of the dynamo, which was driven by steam or water, and generated a continuous current that could be carried through a third rail between the tracks.

The first railway to take electric power from a steam-driven dynamo was demonstrated by Dr Werner von Siemens at the Berlin Trades Exhibition in 1879. His 3hp engine hauled three open passenger cars on an oval track 300m (985ft) long, making the circuit in two minutes. The current, running along a centre rail from the dynamo, was fed into the locomotive's electric motor and then returned to the dynamo along the outer rails.

**▼ A coal train headed by a BR Class 76 goods locomotive, No 76056, pulls into Dinting station in Derbyshire in 1974. Although more than 90 years had elapsed since the opening of Britain's first electric railway, electrification schemes covered less than 20 per cent of BR routes.**

**Classroom to cab**

Before electric traction began between Manchester and Sheffield in 1954, a training school was opened for drivers who had been working on steam locomotives. Here they learned basic electrical theory and became familiar with the intricacies of circuit diagrams.

There were problems of language, however. When an instructor talked of opening a circuit he meant stopping the current. To a driver, opening the regulator meant letting steam flow into the cylinders. A similar confusion arose over closing a circuit and closing a valve.

Two weeks in the classroom were followed by a technical exam. Practical training began with handling a locomotive in the sidings. More tests followed, and trainees who passed them then spent at least 30 hours on the main line with an instructor before receiving their appointment as electric locomotive drivers.

The new phenomenon appeared in Britain in August 1883, when the first half-kilometre (¼ mile) section of an electric railway was constructed along the sea front at Brighton. Its designer, Magnus Volk, was the son of a German watchmaker, but he had been born and bred in Brighton and was electrical engineer to the town's corporation.

His line was extended the following year to Black Rock, giving it an overall length of about 2.5km (1½ miles). From here, Volk built his celebrated but short-lived Brighton & Rottingdean Seashore Railway. The track was laid on concrete blocks on the shore and at high tide was covered by 4.5m (15ft) of water. The passenger car was perched on four long steel legs, however, which kept it clear of the water, the electric current being collected by metal arms from wires on the shore.

## Driven by water power

Five weeks after Volk's original line opened, the first electric railway in the world to take current from a dynamo driven by water power was opened from Portrush to Bushmills in the north of Ireland. Another innovation was a side contact third rail, which ran alongside the track like a fence, and transmitted current via a metal arm attached to the cars.

According to the line's founder, W.A. Traill, he and a colleague, Edward Hopkinson, convinced the Board of Trade Inspectors of the side rail's safety by taking down their trousers and sitting on it. 'But did it not hurt, Papa?' Traill's daughter asked some years later. 'It hurt like blazes,' Traill replied, 'but we weren't going to tell them that.'

In 1890, the City & South London Railway between King William Street and Stockwell was opened and scored two notable firsts. It was the first of London's deep-level tubes; and it was the first line in the country to use electric locomotives, though these soon gave way to motorcoaches – vehicles with their own driver's cab, power equipment and passenger seating.

**▼ Opened on 4 February 1893, the electric Liverpool Overhead Railway (LOR) was the first such line in the world. Its ten kilometres (6¼ miles) of double track ran the length of the Liverpool Docks on a viaduct, later known as the 'dockers' umbrella'. The LOR continued to carry passengers until 30 December 1956.**

**Unlucky 13**
In 1922, the North Eastern Railway (NER) built a prototype electric passenger locomotive, No 13, to run on its main line between York and Newcastle. Designed by the NER's Chief Mechanical Engineer, Vincent Raven, and outshopped at Darlington, it had a 4-6-4 wheel arrangement and six 300hp traction motors.

Its promise was unfulfilled, however. With the absorption of the NER into the London & North Eastern Railway in 1923, the electrification of the York–Newcastle line was abandoned, and No 13 went into store. It was later renumbered No 26600 by British Railways, but was scrapped in 1950 without having turned a wheel in revenue-earning service.

Trains were formed of units of one or two motorcoaches and several trailers. Units could be coupled into longer trains with all motors controlled from the leading cab. Such was the electric multiple unit (EMU) system, which was to dominate electric railway traction in Britain for the next half century.

In 1893, the electric Liverpool Overhead Railway was opened, affording passengers a panoramic view of the docks. This was the first electrically operated elevated railway in the world and the only line of its kind in the British Isles. It survived until the end of 1956.

Electrification of steam-worked lines began with the Mersey Railway in 1903, followed in 1904 by the North Tyneside line of the North Eastern Railway (NER) and the Liverpool–Southport line of the Lancashire & Yorkshire Railway. Liverpool–Southport was claimed to be the first mainline electrification in Britain, since it connected two separate centres of population.

The trains on these lines ran on third-rail direct current (DC) supply at between 600 and 750 volts (V). However, in 1908 the Midland Railway electrified its lines between Lancaster, Morecambe and Heysham using alternating current (AC) at 6,600V. The supply came from the local generating authority at the normal commercial frequency of 50 Hertz (Hz). It was then converted at a trackside feeder-station to 25Hz and fed into a wire above the line at 6,600V. Transformers on the trains reduced this to a suitable voltage for the motors.

**▼ The first electric train service in Britain, Volk's Electric Railway, was opened along the Brighton seafront in 1883. The public was enthusiastic about the new line, and the local press declared that it was a 'real means of locomotion and not a mere amusement'.**

**▲ To mark the electrification of the Southern Railway's Brighton main line in 1933, the Pullman Car Company built three five-car electric multiple units for the new Brighton Belle service. One is seen here south of Quarry Tunnel near Redhill. The line was electrified using the DC third-rail system.**

## The Overhead Electric

The London, Brighton & South Coast Railway (LBSCR) began electrifying with low frequency alternating current at 6,600V in 1909, and by 1929 the system had been extended as far as Coulsdon on the main line to Brighton, and Sutton on the line to Dorking and Horsham.

The new services, advertised as the 'Overhead Electric,' were much faster, and passengers responded accordingly. In 1909, the LBSCR carried under four million on its electric sections.

▼ **An electric train waits to pull away from Surbiton in Surrey in 1953. More than 20 years earlier, a Royal Commission on Transport had stated that it would 'tend to the great convenience of the public, if all suburban lines were electrified...where there is intense passenger traffic'.**

A year later, the figure had grown to more than 7.5 million, and by 1920 it stood at approximately 37 million.

Under the 1923 Grouping, the LBSCR became part of the new Southern Railway, whose General Manager, Sir Henry Walker, was an enthusiastic proponent of electrification. In 1928–9, however, he scrapped the AC overhead system on the old LBSCR network to conform with the DC third-rail system adopted by the SR's other constituents.

## A question of voltage

Although there was much discussion about railway electrification, this centred not on the choice between AC and DC, but on which DC voltage to adopt. In the case of a heavy goods train drawn by a locomotive, this needed to be higher than the voltage obtainable from a third-rail system.

The trailblazer was the North Eastern Railway (NER), which in 1915 installed a 1,500V DC overhead system on its heavy mineral line between Shildon and Newport, County Durham. Designed to transport coal to the Erimus marshalling yard at Newport, it was the first major example of electric locomotive traction in Britain. One of the locomotives on trial hauled a 1,400 tonne (ton) train on the level at 40km/h (25mph) and averaged 37km/h (23mph) up a 1 in 230 gradient with 800 tonnes (tons).

Encouraged by the Durham project's success, the NER's Chief Mechanical Engineer, Vincent (later Sir Vincent) Raven, proposed introducing a 1,500V DC overhead system on the main line between York and Newcastle for passenger services. However, when the NER became part of the London & North Eastern Railway (LNER) in 1923, the mainline project was shelved.

The first 1,500V DC railway to carry passengers in Britain was the Manchester, South Junction & Altrincham joint line in 1931. Shortly before World War II, a government-aided programme of new works authorized 1,500V electrification of the LNER from Liverpool Street to Shenfield and from Manchester to Sheffield (together with the branch from Penistone to Wath marshalling yard).

The Manchester–Sheffield line was the first in Britain on which all traffic – passenger and goods – was hauled by electric locomotives. The electrification, suspended during the war, proceeded in stages, the final link being forged in September 1954. With the scheme completed, the first of seven 2,490hp express passenger locomotives (BR Class 77) went into traffic. These joined 58 1,870hp goods locomotives (BR Class 76) already in service on the line.

## Following the French example

When the plan for the modernization of British Railways was published in 1955, it was assumed that DC electrification would continue. By now, however, developments on the Continent were calling for a rethink. In France, great strides were being made with an AC system, which enabled current to be taken direct from the National Grid without conversion to the lower frequency required for the traction motors.

After long deliberation, the British Transport Commission felt obliged to depart from its earlier decision. In November 1955, it announced that a 25,000V AC overhead system would be used for future electrifications outside the Southern Region and that the lines out of Liverpool Street, already working at 1,500V DC, would be converted. But it was not only the traditional DC system that was under threat. In little more than a decade, steam would disappear from Britain's railways.

# Railway works towns

**One consequence of the Victorian railway boom was the growth of a new kind of town, where life revolved around the manufacture of railway equipment and the word of the railway company was law. Here are four examples of towns, each with its own unique identity.**

The growth of the railway system in the nineteenth century produced a need to house the increasing army of railway workers close to their place of employment. Sometimes the demand could be met by private developers, but often, because accommodation was needed quickly, the railways built their own houses and let them to their employees. As a result, enclaves of railway housing developed in towns and villages where there were major railway installations such as junctions, locomotive depots, marshalling yards and locomotive works.

If there was no existing settlement, a railway would create its own. The pattern was not new; factory towns had existed since the early days of the Industrial Revolution. The railways simply created their settlements on a larger scale. This applied particularly to communities involved with building locomotives and rolling stock.

Because the railways' rapid expansion in the 1840s and 1950s quickly outgrew the capacity of outside manufacturers, the industry was forced to build its own, and factories were erected either near an existing town or on a green field site, including houses for workers. Frequently, the railway company came to dominate the locality – at some places well into the twentieth century.

## Convenient junction

In 1841, the Great Western Railway (GWR) bought land near the small Wiltshire town of Swindon for a locomotive works. At the junction with the line to Gloucester, it was a convenient point at which to change engines for the steeper gradients westwards. There was also a canal close by, for bringing in building materials.

To accommodate the workers, the company's chief engineer, I.K. Brunel, designed the layout

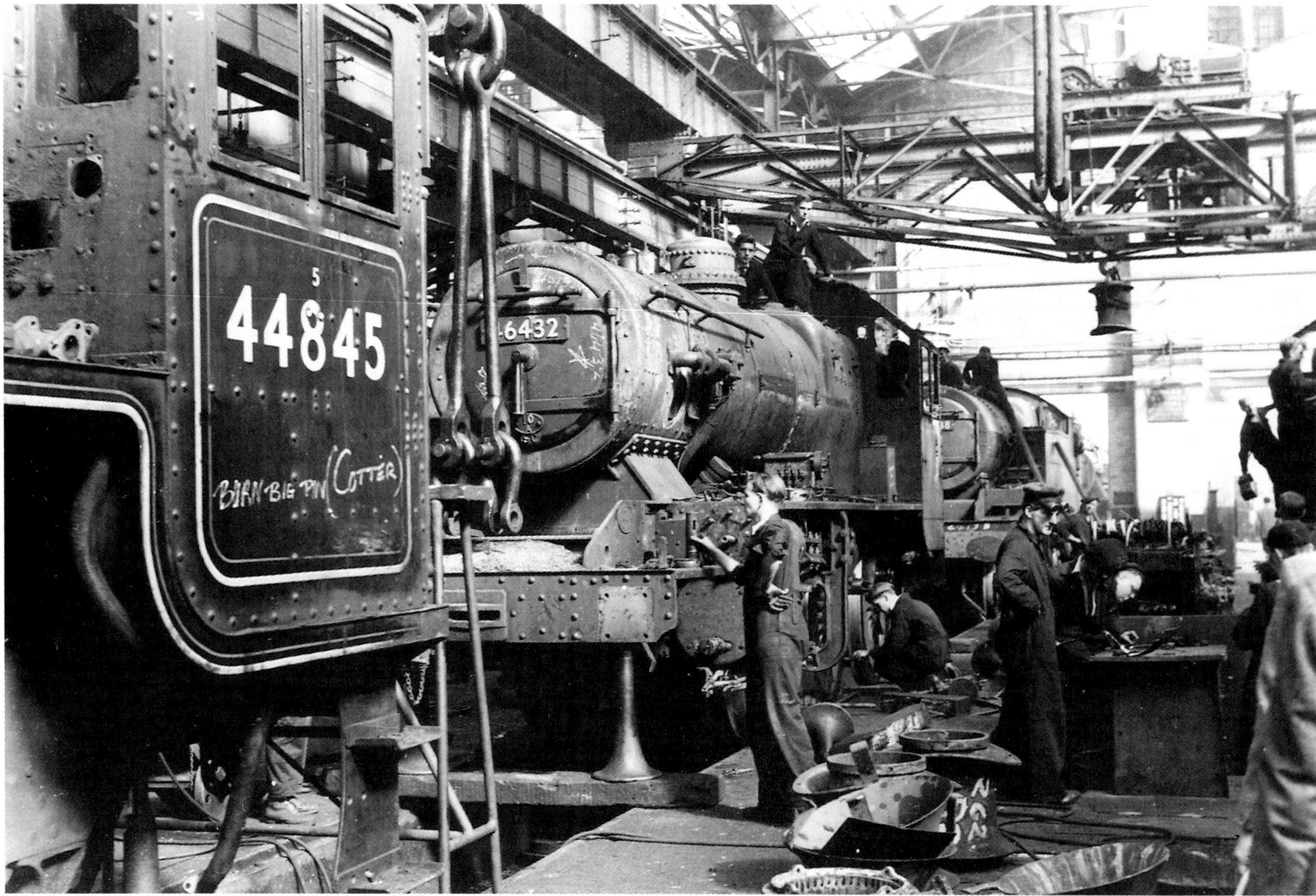


**▼ Locomotives undergo repair at Crewe works in 1953. In earlier years, under the London & North Western Railway (LNWR), the works turned out a large range of products, including steel rails, bricks, leather and soap. The LNWR even printed its own tickets at Crewe.**

▲ **Like most of the big railway companies, the London & North Western was keen to encourage self-improvement among its employees. The cultural and recreational facilities at Crewe included an art room, seen here in 1907.**

for a new town which was constructed by one of the railway's contractors, for whom the GWR collected the rents. The houses were built in neat terraces, using stone excavated from Box Tunnel, and for their day they reached a high structural standard for workmen's dwellings.

But other conditions were poor. For some years there was an inadequate water supply and no mains drainage, and in 1853 a typhus epidemic put a stop to building, which was not resumed. The result was endemic overcrowding, which went on until the early 1920s.

The problem was caused by the need for engines, which was so great that the works was opened before the houses and services were ready. A young engineer, named Edward Snell, wrote that, eight weeks after production started, he 'took a walk through the mud up to Swindon'. He hated it and thought it made him ill:

'A precious place it is at present, not a knocker or scraper in the whole place. Most of the houses very damp and containing only two rooms. Not a cupboard or a shelf... and the unfortunate inhabitants obliged to keep the grub in the bedrooms. Not a drop of water to be had but what comes from the [engine] tenders or out of ditches and what little we do get is as thick as mud – not fit for a jackass to drink. The Company make the men pay extortionate rents... 3*s*. 6*d*. for a single and 7*s*. for a double cottage and won't allow any of the men in their employ to sell anything whatever. We have a couple of Doctors' Shops which are pretty frequently visited, a Great Western Sick Club, a school... and a chapel.'

By the end of 1843, the population of New Swindon was approximately 550, and already overcrowding and lack of amenities were producing drunkenness and crime. Daniel Gooch, the Locomotive Superintendent who rose to become Chairman of the GWR, recorded in his diary that local gentry and villagers complained that Swindon works was a curse.

Gooch tried to alleviate conditions by establishing a workmen's institute and reading room, and by organizing dances and concerts in one of the workshops. However, although anxious to keep his men from 'sipping and sopping in a public house hour after hour', he was not opposed to the occasional drink, recognizing that 'a glass of good beer is good for a working man'.

Later, the company provided piped water, a sewerage system, a library, a market house and a large mechanics' institute. It also contributed to the building of a church and paid the vicar's stipend. A park was laid out, and in 1892, the GWR opened swimming baths, for which water came from the company's supply, being heated at the railway works before being piped to the baths.

For many years New Swindon was separate from the old town, becoming an Urban District in its own right, but in 1890 the two towns became physically joined and ten years later were incorporated as a single borough, by which time the population was approaching 50,000.

By 1931, it had reached 62,700, and by the mid-1970s the figure was 90,000. By then railway employment was declining and new high-tech industries were well established. Now, Swindon forms the core of the district of Thamesdown, while the railway works has closed and been sold, and a considerable part demolished. However, the original houses of the New Town have been saved and restored by the local authority as part of a conservation area.

## Moving to Crewe

Roughly contemporary with Swindon, Crewe developed in much better fashion, to become Britain's best known railway town. The Grand Junction Railway (GJR) had a small works at Edge Hill, Liverpool. This rapidly became inadequate, so the company laid out new workshops and housing on virgin land close to the junction of the Liverpool, Manchester and Chester lines at Crewe in Cheshire. There was little else here but a station and a few cottages that took their name from Crewe Hall nearby.

**▲ The Lancashire & Yorkshire Railway cricket pitch at Horwich was part of 11 acres (4.5 hectares) of land which the company placed at the disposal of its employees. The land was also laid out with tennis courts, a bandstand and a bowling green.**

**▼ The dinner hour dash begins at the Swindon works of the Great Western Railway in 1904. 'It is a mystery where they all come,' wrote one employee of the daily comings and goings. 'They are like an army pressing forward to battle.'**

The transfer was made in March 1843, when the new town was populated by 800 inhabitants almost overnight. Because, unlike the GWR at Swindon, the GJR pursued a more vigorous and sustained housing policy, nearly everything was ready for them, and by the end of the year the town had schools, an assembly room, a magistrates' court and a temporary church.

Expansion continued rapidly, so that by 1848 the London & North Western Railway (LNWR), of which the GJR was now part, had built 520 houses. Another 300 were privately owned. The population was already nearly 4,500; by 1911 it was ten times that figure, the large majority in railway families. Eventually, the LNWR was to own more than 900 houses in Crewe.

## A variety of housing

A commentator in 1846 remarked: 'The dwelling houses arrange themselves into four classes: first, the villa-style lodges of the superior officers, next a kind of ornamental Gothic constitutes the houses of the next in authority; the engineers [mechanics] domiciled in detached mansions which accommodate four families, with gardens and separate entrances [they were really two-storey maisonettes] and last, the labourer delights in neat cottages of four apartments, the entrances within ancient porches. Each house is supplied with gas; the water is at present in the street, but is to be immediately introduced into the houses.'

Four years later, it was noted that 'The streets are wide and well paved... The accommodation is good and it would be difficult to find such houses at such low rents.' For their time they were, indeed, well designed and constructed, and Crewe was considered to be a model town. Once the initial layout was completed, development was

▲ **Railway employees often formed their own militia units. Here the Diamond Jubilee Detachment of the Crewe Engineer Volunteers stands on parade at Crewe on 19 June 1897, in preparation for Queen Victoria's Diamond Jubilee.**

**Crewe paternalism**
The influence of the London & North Western Railway (LNWR) affected every aspect of public life in Crewe, including politics and religion. Through its autocratic works manager, F.W. Webb, the company opposed the incorporation of the town, which would have weakened its influence, and when it ultimately had to give way, it ensured that senior LNWR officials were elected to the council. In 1887, Webb became mayor.

He wielded enormous power in both the town and the company, even securing the appointment of his brother as vicar of St Paul's, a living in the gift of the LNWR. He is also said to have set up a committee of foreman to dragoon men into attending the church on Sundays. Even so, he was motivated by a strong desire to further the town's well-being. For example, he secured company support for a hospital, which bore his name, and bequeathed a personal legacy of £10,000.

less orderly as the LNWR took little interest in formal planning, although it provided four churches, a hospital, eight schools, a market house, and various other facilities.

The company also equipped the whole town with water and gas, and a police force. The first permanent church, Christchurch, was begun in 1843 and consecrated in 1845, with a tall tower that is still a landmark today, even though the rest of the building was demolished in 1977 and replaced by a smaller modern structure.

The market square was roofed over by the LNWR in 1854 to make a covered market. This was followed by a cheese market which, although provided at the expense of a contractor, was constructed according to a plan and under regulations approved by the directors of the LNWR. The company built a siding from the main line, so that Cheshire cheese could be shipped out in covered vans with minimum handling

In this and many other ways the works, as at Swindon, dominated the life of the town. Crewe works eventually became the largest establishment of its kind in the country, at which the LNWR pursued its policy of manufacturing itself as many of its requirements as possible. These included steel rails, bricks, leather and soap; the company even printed its own tickets at Crewe. The joinery shops produced ready-made woodwork for buildings of all kinds, which were built with Crewe bricks and Crewe ironwork.

Although some smaller industries were established, Crewe remained predominantly a railway town until Rolls-Royce opened a factory in 1938, followed by other firms. By the 1970s, when the population was 50,500, the railway works had diminished. In 1988, it was privatized and undertook locomotive work.

## Seizing the chance

Horwich was a small, insignificant Lancashire textile town on a short branch line when it became the home of the Lancashire & Yorkshire Railway (LYR) locomotive works in 1884–6. The previous site at Miles Platting, Manchester, was cramped and incapable of expansion, so when a trade slump led to a fall in land prices, the LYR seized the opportunity to move.

Nineteen streets, named after famous engineers, were laid out for employees' houses. But rather than put up the dwellings itself, the company sold off plots to private builders, bringing in a handsome profit that enabled it not only to cover the cost of the 300 acres (121.5 hectares) it had acquired, but to pay for the erection of some of the workshops as well.

The LYR provided a large mechanics' institute and a technical school, which was opened in 1888, while the directors combined to pay for a sports ground, bandstand and cottage hospital. In five years, the population of Horwich trebled and the works came to employ 4,000 men.

Other industries gradually followed, so although the railway's presence and power were significant, it never dominated to the same extent as at Swindon and Crewe. From 1983, the works was progressively sold, by which time the railway passenger service had long gone.

## Under the influence

In 1882, the small Norfolk parish of Melton Constable, where there was little more than the seat of Lord Hastings at Melton Hall, was shaken by the opening of workshops by the Lynn & Fakenham Railway (LFR). Under Lord Hastings's influence – he owned most of the land – Melton became the junction of four railways.

The LFR became part of the Eastern & Midlands Railway (EMR). After bankruptcy, the EMR was acquired in 1893 by the Midland and Great Northern companies, which operated it as the Midland & Great Northern Joint Railway (MGNJR). The works expanded and Melton considered itself to be a railway town, although it was still really no more than a village.

At first, there was just one row of terraced houses, Melton Street, but after the MGNJR took over, the population gradually increased, rising to 1,157 by 1911. Railway workers arriving in Melton Constable during the early years described the place as 'a godforsaken spot', without shops, school or pub.

Two further rows of railway houses were erected, one of them, Astley Terrace, constructed by a local builder after the MGNJR's Engineer and Locomotive Superintendent, William Marriott, guaranteed the rent of 1*s.* 6*d.* per week for each house. Staff who rented these houses had to take up to four lodgers nominated by the company – a practice that led to frequent overcrowding.

Marriott, who ruled over Melton Constable for more than 40 years, was a stern enforcer of the professional pecking order. Walking into the drawing office on one occasion, he found a junior clerk making up the fire. He ordered the hapless youth to make himself scarce, pointing out that fires should be left to the head messenger.

After some time, the local amenities improved. The company provided gas, water and a sewerage system, opened a railway institute and built a school. A pub was also opened and a bowling green was laid out at the end of Melton Street. This was overlooked by one of the engine bays, and it is said that, if the MGNJR team was losing, their opponents would be showered with cinders.

In its small way, Melton Constable was to the MGNJR as Crewe was to the LNWR, although its nickname, the Crewe of North Norfolk, reflected a large degree of poetic licence. In 1936, locomotive work ceased, and the railway closed entirely in 1964, when the population sank to 650. The works site is now an industrial estate, but the terraces of Victorian houses remain, looking oddly incongruous in the rural landscape.

**Concrete achievements**

William Marriott, the Midland & Great Northern Joint Railway's Engineer and Locomotive Superintendent at Melton Constable works from 1883 to 1924, was a pioneer in the use of concrete on railways. He introduced concrete fencing posts in 1909 and took out no less than 135 patents for concrete components such as signal and telegraph posts, girders, level crossing gate posts, platform walls, sleepers, building blocks and station nameboards.

During World War 1, they became a valuable substitute for brick, timber and steel, then in short supply, and some items were sold to other railways. Marriott Way, leading to the works site at Melton commemorates his name, as does the long-distance footpath on part of the old railway trackbed north-west of Norwich.

**▼ The fire brigade train at Horwich works turns out for a realistic rehearsal in December 1915. The train was kept on permanent standby and volunteer staff were required to practice regularly in case of emergency.**

*A Day in the Life of...*

# A signalman

**The railway of the 1950s was a world apart, and no inhabitant of that world was more independent than the signalman. Ensconced in his glass-ribbed domain, which not even the stationmaster would enter without permission, he was charged with a burden few would have wished to share.**

It is 5.45 on a weekday morning in March 1953, and the daylight is breaking through the mist and low cloud over the Wiltshire countryside as Jack free-wheels his bicycle down the hill along Marlborough Road from the town centre towards Wootton Bassett station. He left home on the other side of town about ten minutes ago on a journey he has done now for more than a decade.

A local man, he started on the Great Western Railway (GWR) at the age of 15, working as a booking boy in the signalboxes at Swindon. Passing out as a signalman, he worked his way through the grades until now, in his mid-40s, he is a Class 1 signalman, one of three working at Wootton Bassett East signalbox.

A short but athletic looking man, with powerful shoulders and forearms gained through years of pulling the signal and point levers, he passes the Beaufort Inn on his right, enters the station yard and pushes his bicycle across the tracks on the public footpath close to East signalbox. Although it is still early in the year, the weather over the past few weeks has been remarkably warm and today promises to be no different.

Propping his bicycle under the signalbox steps, Jack climbs up to the cabin door, which bears an uncompromising black cast-iron sign with the word 'Private' spelled out in white letters. Stepping inside, he is greeted by Fred, the night man. 'The milk empties are just off Swindon,' Fred explains, 'and I'm waiting the out for the Tavistock Junction goods, which was a few minutes early.'

Jack signs the train register to show he is on duty a minute or two before 6.00 a.m. and Fred signs off duty at the same time. Although Fred lives at Swindon, it is not easy getting to work at Wootton Bassett by train because the few stopping passenger services do not always accord with the booked shift changes. And it is no good hoping to hitch a lift on a goods train, since it may be cancelled or running late. So Fred travels to and fro on his motorbike, which he parks out of the way on the up platform.

Jack, on his own now, glances at the block indicators to see if there is anything Fred has forgotten to tell him. But all is in order. There are two indicators to Studley, the next signalbox up

**▼ No 5096 *Bridgwater Castle* approaches Wootton Bassett station with a Bristol to Paddington express in 1952. The East signalbox can be seen beyond the bracket signal. The left-hand arm controls entrance to the down goods avoiding line which passes to the rear of the signalbox. Beyond the signalbox is the splitting signal for lines to Bristol and South Wales, with home and distant arms. The GWR prided itself on its signalling and was the first to equip its main lines with automatic train control.**

the line – the repeater instrument for up trains and the accepting instrument for down trains.

However, to Wootton Bassett West signalbox there are six indicators: the repeater instruments for the down main to Bristol, the down to South Wales and the down goods avoiding line; and the accepting instruments for the up main from Bristol, the up South Wales and the up goods avoiding line. The block instruments are of the typical GWR Spagnoletti type, with a swinging disc which shows half and half for 'line blocked'. It swings one way for 'line clear' and the other for 'train on line'. There is quite a knack in pegging the instruments to one or other of these positions, pressing down the appropriate key and pushing the brass retaining rod across the key to hold it in place – using just one hand.

## A promise fulfilled

Glancing at the small stove, which not only heats the signalbox but is the permanent resting place for the kettle and the teapot, Jack sees there is enough coal on the fire for the time being. In fact, the promise of another warm day is being realized and, with the temperature inside the cabin gradually rising, Jack throws open some of the windows.

Two-pause-one rings out on the bell from Studley and the block indicator disc swings to mid position to tell him that the Tavistock Junction goods has cleared the section and is heading towards Swindon. This is followed by two rings from Studley to say that the milk empties have entered the down line section.

Jack replies with two beats and pegs the down line instrument at 'train on line'. Dealing with the milk empties means some shunting to get the tank wagons into the United Dairies sidings, which are off the up main line at the Swindon end of the station and are controlled from a ground frame released by East signalbox. By the time the York to Swindon and Bristol overnight passenger and mail train passes ten minutes later, the empties have all been moved off the main line.

A steady stream of trains builds up as the daytime passenger services get under way, interspersed with the odd goods working. All have to be offered and accepted on the block instruments; points levers have to be operated to change points; signal levers have to be pulled to clear; and the times of all block bell signals have to be recorded in the train register.

Jack checks each train as it goes past, making sure that there are no passengers in obvious distress, that there is nothing wrong with the train itself and, above all, that the tail lamp is on the rear to show that the train is complete. Only then does he pass it out of section.

The shunter at the United Dairies ground frame rings to say that the milk engine is ready to come back through the station *en route* to the down sidings where it will pick up the coaches for the train carrying staff to the Swindon workshops, due to be away at 7.10 a.m.

An hour or so later, the pace quickens. At 8.10 a.m., West signalbox rings three-pause-one for the

**▲ In this GWR signalbox, BR standard block instruments have replaced the GWR Spagnoletti type, but still retained are its rare dial route indicators, only required where there were numerous options. At Wootton Bassett East trains for the South Wales line were billed as 'branch' trains as a route code.**

**▼ King Class 4-6-0 No 6004 *King George III* roars through Wootton Bassett with the eastbound Red Dragon from South Wales in December 1961. It was less than a year before the Kings were withdrawn, and No 6004 is showing signs of poor maintenance, leaking steam from around the piston glands.**

### Express derailment

In the early hours of 27 June 1946, the 11.50 p.m. express goods from Paddington to Carmarthen was wrecked at Wootton Bassett. Somehow the signalman had managed to get the lever of the facing lock bolt into the locked position, allowing the signals to be cleared. However, the diamond crossing switches were not fully home and locked, with the result that the train was derailed on the switch diamond crossing at the intersection of the down South Wales and up Bristol lines. No lives were lost.

6.40 a.m. Bristol–Swindon stopping train. As this goes past East signalbox at 8.21 a.m., Jack realizes he has not had a Stoke Gifford–Hanwell goods off the South Wales line offered up the goods line to make way for a couple of faster trains. 'Just off Brinkworth now,' comes the response from a call to West box. 'That's cutting it fine,' says Jack.

The 7.18 a.m. stopper from Bristol via Badminton to Swindon is only a section behind the goods. Booked 12 minutes behind the 7.18 towards Swindon is the 7.00 a.m. from Weston-super-Mare, the first morning express from the Bristol line to Paddington. This is one train a signalman delays at his peril.

No use holding up the local to let the 7.00 a.m. run ahead because the 3.55 a.m. Fishguard boat-train is also coming up the South Wales line, booked only five minutes behind the 7.00 a.m. But it all just about works. Out of section for the 7.18 from Studley, offer four bells for the 7.00 a.m., accepted, pull off, check the repeater for the up distant arms to ensure they have come off.

A few minutes later, the 7.00 a.m. speeds through, a Castle Class 4-6-0 at its head, whistle shrieking two long blasts and a crow (cock-a-doodle-do) to confirm that it is alright for water and does not need to stop at Swindon. Jack checks its special red and white tail lamp on the rear of the last coach, to be slipped at Didcot, then telephones Swindon West to tell them, '7 o'clock Weston TL (through line)'.

In a quiet moment, Jack fills a bucket from the cold-water tap at the small sink and starts mopping the lino floor. The signalbox chores are divided between the three regular men. The middle turn man, who takes over from Jack, will clean the windows, and the late turn man will polish the brass of the instruments.

All goes well until about 10.15, when the code ring for East signalbox sounds on the omnibus telephone circuit. It is Shrivenham advising that the 8.55 express from Paddington to Pembroke is eight minutes late and could clash through the junction. Jack rings Chippenham. 'How's the 7.50 Taunton? – right time OK.' That means both trains coming together. Better to let the up train run, as it is still on the slight climb to Swindon.

Two 'Is line clear?' bells sound almost simultaneously – one from Studley for the 8.55 and one from West box for the 7.50. Jack offers both trains on, changing the one-three code for the 8.55 train to four beats to West box. Nothing for it but to pull off on the up for the 7.50. This train is going well as Jack dashes backwards and forwards along the frame pulling and resetting levers. The frame is not entirely in sequence, with the mainline switch diamond lever separated from its locking levers. As usual, Jack does the work armed with a

**▼ GWR 2-6-2T No 5547 pauses during shunting of the up sidings, as seen from the window of Wootton Bassett East signalbox on a gloomy afternoon in the 1950s. The same locomotive was also used to shunt the United Dairies sidings and prepare the early afternoon milk train to London.**

**East and West**
Wootton Bassett had a remarkably complex layout controlled from two signalboxes, East and West. East box was the larger and more important of the two since it controlled the points of the route split between the South Wales and Bristol lines. West box also controlled both routes, but was concerned mainly with the exit from the down goods loop and down sidings on the Bristol line and the entrance to the up goods loop from the South Wales line.

West box was sometimes switched out, but East box was open continuously. It was worked in three eight-hour shifts during the week and two 12-hour shifts on Sunday. The late turn man one week did the early turn the following week, and the night shift the week after that.

cloth, which prevents the levers from being corroded by sweat from his palms.

The 8.55 a.m. missed the distant, but Jack has the home and starting signals clear, and West box distants are clear as the train coasts through the station. With the 80km/h (50mph) restriction through the junction towards the South Wales line, it has not lost much more time.

Footsteps outside the signalbox herald the daily visit of the stationmaster, or SM. In spite of his rank, he gives a nominal tap on the door before entering. 'Hello Jack.'

'Morning Guv'nor, it's a warm one today.'

'The sunshine's fine,' says the SM, 'but a month without rain has dried my garden up. A bit different to a few weeks ago with all those floods in the east. Now, let's have a look at the book. Bristol wants to know why somebody stopped the Dragon last week.'

The SM had just received a memo from the District Operating Superintendent's office in Bristol inquiring about an incident involving the Red Dragon express from Carmarthen.

Someone let a goods out too close in front of the Dragon and it was checked approaching Swindon. The signalman may not have been at fault. The engine of the goods might have been steaming badly. Either way, the register will show the times of the block bell signals.

'And what about the hot box you had last week?' asks the SM. 'Why wasn't it taken off here?'

'Well Guv'nor, I had all boards off, and I didn't see the wisp of smoke on a wagon near the middle until after it had gone by the box. But it would have been pushing it to have stopped an unbraked goods in time, so I sent 'Stop and examine' to Studley. It may not have been smoking when it went by Brinkworth. That's the trouble with the old grease box wagons.'

'Well, we stopped the job for over an hour,' says the SM.

Jack is philosophical: 'We can never win with Bristol.'

A ring on the block bell from West signalbox heralds the four-beat 'Is line clear?' bell signal for the 11.45 a.m. Bristol–Paddington off the South Wales line. Soon after, the 9.00 a.m. all stations stopping train from Weston-super-Mare to Swindon is offered on the main line, reminding the SM that he has to attend the local train. 'I'm off. Don't worry, I'll square that hot box.'

Between trains, Jack finds time to eat his sandwiches and make tea. He empties about two days' worth of tea-leaves out of the pot, but makes no attempt to wash it. That would spoil the taste of traditional signalbox tea, which is produced simply by adding hot water and tea to what is already there. He has brought a container of milk with his lunch box and, after pouring some of this into a clean mug, he tops up with a torrent of dark brown liquid from the pot.

## Weighing the balance

The signalbox clock shows 2.00 p.m. and Les, the late turn man, arrives. In the eight hours since he came on duty, Jack has handled about 50 trains, sent a few thousand passengers safely on their way, made sure that London received its milk and passed or shunted thousands of tonnes (tons) of goods. He earns a basic wage of £8 a week, plus overtime if he works a rest day, a Sunday or a night shift. But it is a secure job and, although his wife is not too happy about shift work, the railway is his way of life. He could earn half as much again working in a factory, but money isn't everything.

**▼ GWR 2-8-0 No 3846 hauls an up goods past the East signalbox in September 1955. It was vital for signalmen to keep a careful eye on such trains: an undetected wagon hot box could lead to fire or even derailment and cause chronic delays to following trains. A tell-tale wisp of smoke was the first sign that the axlebox was beginning to overheat.**

# The General Strike

**In May 1926, Britain's railways were caught in the grip of the General Strike. The railway companies responded with a call for volunteer train crews and signalmen, and for nine days, rail enthusiasts had the chance to fulfil their fondest childhood dream.**

On Tuesday 4 May 1926, Britain was paralysed by the first – and so far, the only – General Strike in its history. Called by the Trades Union Congress (TUC), its aim was to force the government to intervene on behalf of the miners, who were locked in bitter dispute with the coal owners. The government and most members of the public who were not trade unionists saw it as the nearest approach to a revolution that the nation had experienced since the Chartist riots of a century before.

The three railway unions – the National Union of Railwaymen (NUR), the Associated Society of Locomotive Engineers & Firemen (ASLEF) and the Railway Clerks Association (RCA) – were not involved in any dispute with their own managements. There had been a national rail strike in 1919, which had won them important concessions.

But in the present conflict, which was to last for nine days, they had nothing to gain and everything to lose by responding to the TUC's call. Yet even more railwaymen came out in 1926 on behalf of the miners than had come out in 1919 in support of their own claim.

Although about a third of the RCA's members stayed on duty, the walk-out by the two blue-collar unions was almost complete. On the nation's largest system, the LMS, only 62 out of 14,000 firemen and 207 out of 15,000 drivers reported for work on the first morning of the strike.

On the employers' side, policy was directed by the general managers of the Big Four railway companies – the LMS, GWR, LNER and SR – plus the Metropolitan. Their aim was to run as many trains as possible. The staff available for this purpose, however, were a very mixed lot.

Apart from the few non-striking staff, there were a handful of men – the exact number is unknown – who sought to escape the censure of their comrades by working for railways other than their own. There were also some retired railwaymen

**▼ Mainline stations such as London's Waterloo were almost deserted during the strike. But travellers who did arrive were sometimes pleasantly surprised. One girl wrote to her mother in the country of the 'awfully nice' Oxford students she had encountered acting as guards and ticket collectors. 'It's all very jolly, and such an improvement on the ordinary humdrum state of things.'**

▶ **On 10 May, the public was outraged by a serious act of sabotage – the derailment of the Flying Scotsman near Cramlington in Northumberland. The culprits were striking miners who had loosened one of the rails. Fortunately, the volunteer driver had been warned of possible trouble on the line and was running under caution. Even so, he was unable to prevent No 2565 *Merry Hampton* and five of its 12 coaches toppling off the rails, with minor injuries to the fireman and two passengers. The eight offenders were quickly arrested and received sentences of between four and eight years.**

who disapproved of the strike and were willing to come back for a short time. Further help was provided by managerial and clerical staffs who undertook operational and manual work.

Finally – and in the folklore of the strike, most conspicuously – there were the members of the public who responded to the general managers' call for volunteers. The abiding image is of young bloods in Fair Isle sweaters and plus-fours, looking on the whole thing as a lark.

One such was the writer Spike Hughes, then an undergraduate at Cambridge. 'The truth is', he wrote later, 'that I and some 2,000 other young men at Cambridge went to work in the General Strike with no thought of strike-breaking, of being "patriotic", saving the country from Bolshevism or anything like it. We saw in the whole business nothing more or less than a heaven-sent opportunity to run a railway.'

## Lords on the railway

Although students made up the largest contingent, volunteers came from a wide range of backgrounds – a few even from the House of Lords. Lord Monkswell, a prolific writer on railways, acted as a signalman at Marylebone station, and Spike Hughes found himself sharing a signalbox outside Cambridge with a viscount.

So many volunteers applied for work at Paddington station that the recruitment office had to be closed by the second day of the strike. Indeed, the problem was not numbers but suitability. It is not too difficult to drive a steam locomotive, but driving a train requires skill and experience. The railway companies were therefore cautious about accepting volunteer steam drivers.

But there were some amateur drivers and, naturally, a number of hair-raising mishaps. On Hughes' first day as a volunteer guard on the Ely to Cambridge milk train, the fireman, a fellow student, unwisely stood up on the tender as the train went under a bridge – and was lucky to escape with no more than a sore head.

On another occasion, the driver, also a Cambridge student, overshot a station by 45.75m (50 yards) and was only saved from worse disaster by a small boy who had had the foresight quickly to open the level-crossing gates that lay ahead of the train.

Driving a Southern electric, Metropolitan or Underground train was a less difficult task than handling a steam train, so that volunteer labour was more acceptable in replacing motormen. On both the Underground and the Metropolitan, over a third of the normal service was in operation by the end of the strike.

In an effort to boost public morale, the Chancellor of the Exchequer, Winston Churchill, decided to travel on the Underground. This was only his second ride on the Underground, however, and according to his wife Clementine, 'he went round and round' on the Inner Circle 'not knowing where to get out and had to be rescued eventually'.

▼ **Clad in Fair Isle sweaters and plus-fours, two undergraduates operate the signalbox at Bletchley station in Buckinghamshire. Despite the inexperience of the volunteers, there were few serious accidents during the strike – a state of affairs that was probably due to the low speeds and small amount of traffic.**

▲**The Hon. R.F. Anson watches for the guard's signal to move off. Other upper-class volunteers included the Hon. Lionel Guest who, according to the LNER, brought 50 friends to work at Liverpool Street station before using 'his expert knowledge and experience' to drive a train from London to Yarmouth.**

The railways produced a short manual which emphasized basic safety rules for volunteer drivers. But it was shortage of signalmen that caused the greatest problem. Many signalboxes, of course, could be switched out by putting the signals at clear and connecting the block instruments between the adjacent boxes. Telephone contacts between key boxes and control offices were also invaluable.

Where serious gaps occurred in block signalling, trains could be sent forward on the primitive time interval system, with drivers instructed to run at caution to the next block post. It was decided to avoid running trains during the hours of darkness when safety would be harder to maintain.

## Rear-end collisions

The sparseness of the traffic and the low speeds probably accounted for the small number of serious accidents which the rudimentary signalling methods might otherwise have caused. The worst incident happened at St Margaret's, Edinburgh – a rear-end collision which killed three passengers. Another rear-end collision at Bishop's Stortford led to one fatality; a third, at Brixton, produced minor injuries.

Strikers were very amused at the shortcomings of the volunteer railwaymen. 'We understand that luncheon cars are to be put on trains running between Westminster and Blackfriars,' declared the *Westminster Worker*. The bulletin of the St Pancras Strike Committee reported that notices posted on the walls of Highgate Cemetery called for volunteers and suggested that it should be 'picketed by Underground men'.

The bulletin of the Bristol Central Strike Committee, in a verse entitled *To Heaven by LMS*, mocked the middle-class airs of many of the volunteers:

*Early in the morning, per broadcast from*
*London,*
*See the little puff-puffs all in a row.*
*D'Arcy on the engine, pulled a little lever,*
*Expansion of the boiler – UP WE GO!*

## Eruptions of violence

But the strike was not all schoolboy jokes and *bonhomie*. Contrary to popular belief, a good deal of violence occurred during the nine days, not least on the railways. In many places, strikers gathered to throw stones at any trains that passed. So serious was the missile throwing in Glasgow on 9 May that the LNER felt obliged to inform the District Civil Commissioner, Sir Arthur Rose, that volunteer train crews were unable to work many of the goods depots in the city 'owing to injuries already received and the menacing attitude of the mobs at different points'.

Nor was stone throwing the only problem. At Middlesbrough, a mob of 4,000 wrecked the goods and passenger stations and chained lorries to the tracks. At Nine Elms depot in London, there was a clash in which a police sergeant was struck on the head with a hammer and a special constable stabbed in the back. And at Anstruther in east Fife, police made baton charges to clear the railway line.

How many trains were actually run, day by day, was not easy to establish. A government newspaper, the *British Gazette*, the editorship of which Winston Churchill combined with his ministerial duties, tried to paint an encouraging picture. But figures that were later issued by the railway companies themselves show that even after nine days the strike was still remarkably solid.

On the SR and GWR, passenger services were just over 19 per cent of normal, while on the LMS

### A grave issue

The railwaymen were virtually solid in support of the strike, and they were quick to make clear their hostility towards the handful who refused to join in. Few, however, went as far as the railway workers of Swindon, the great GWR centre in Wiltshire.

Here they decided to treat the nine non-strikers as if they were dead. Led by a railwayman wearing a top hat and tails, nine coffins were paraded through the town to the municipal rubbish dump.

One of the striking engine drivers, draped in a white tablecloth to represent a surplice, said a burial service over the coffins. Having been dowsed in paraffin, they were then set alight by the bogus vicar, whose final words were 'May the wind blow their remains to the four corners of the earth, and to hell with them all.'

▶ Not everyone who volunteered to work on the railways could be an engine driver, and many of the volunteers had to take on rather less glamorous jobs such as the manning of level-crossings.

▼ A volunteer locomotive crew, in trilby and boiler suit, poses proudly on the footplate. The efforts of these crews provoked much sarcasm from the strikers. 'The strike is over,' declared one of the London strike bulletins in a mock announcement on 7 May. 'Only 400,000 NUR men are now on strike, plus one million miners and two million others. But three trains are running in Manchester and there is a five minute service every two hours on the tubes. A bag of coal has been brought from Newcastle today.'

and LNER they were just over 12 per cent. The comparable figures for freight were even lower. At the end of the strike, the GWR goods service was 8.4 per cent of normal, the SR 4.5 per cent, the LMS three per cent and the LNER 2.2 per cent.

In fact, there had been little attempt to run freight trains apart from mails, perishables and foodstuffs, especially milk. Private road hauliers, largely with non-union labour, had jumped into the breach.

On Wednesday 12 May, having despaired of changing the mind of the government and fearful of losing control to the local strike committees, the TUC unconditionally called a halt to the strike. The railway companies were in a pugnacious mood and their terms of settlement were humiliating to the unions. There was a flat refusal to give a 'no victimization' undertaking. Every man's staff history recorded his 'loyalty' or 'disloyalty' to his company during the strike.

## Terms of surrender

Men would be reinstated only 'as traffic offers and work can be found for them'. The unions had to 'admit that in calling a strike they committed a wrongful act'; to give an undertaking that they would never again call a strike without negotiations; and to promise to discourage unofficial strikes and strikes by supervisors. The companies reserved the right to transfer men to other work at their existing rates of pay.

As it turned out, there was delay in finding employment for everyone, and five months after the end of the strike the NUR leader, Jimmy Thomas, claimed that 200,000 railwaymen were working three days a week and 45,000 were still without jobs.

This was due partly to victimization, partly to diminished traffic and partly to the continuation of the miners' strike, which created shortages of locomotive fuel, as well lost coal freight. The miners went back to work in October, having been forced to accept longer hours and lower pay.

If the rail unions had foreseen the damage the strike would do to the long-term employment prospects of their members, they might have held back. Much traffic that had moved independently of the railways during the strike never returned. This was the price paid by the railwaymen for their solidarity with the miners.

For many of the volunteers, too, the end of the strike was more a cause for gloom than celebration. As Spike Hughes said: 'I have been told by strikers who were "out" during the General Strike that they felt they had lost something when it was all over. They were not the only ones; those few days in May 1926 were, for thousands of us, pure, ecstatic wish fulfilment'.

*A Day in the Life of...*

# A steam engine driver

**The 1950s were the last of the great years for the long distance engine driver. His recognition was earned on a daily schedule that often took him away from home on overnight trips in all weathers.**

On a cold, frosty winter's afternoon, a driver in his late 50s, small and dapper, carrying a cheap attache case, is walking down the slope from Dean Lane, Manchester, into Newton Heath engine shed. His boots glow with a shine that relieves some of the gloom from the pall of smoke that hangs in the air. His shiny greasetop cap sits firm and straight on his grey hair.

Seeing him walk into the shed lobby, the foreman's assistant riffles through the plastic-covered work dockets and hands the driver his itinerary: the 4.12 p.m. from Manchester Exchange station to Glasgow, followed by the 10.50 a.m. return the next day. It's 2.15 now and the engine is due off shed at 3.30.

The driver is a member of a group known as the Glasgow link, which covers the run from Manchester to Glasgow and other work. Promotion to this link of eight driver-fireman teams is a normal step for senior drivers attached to Newton Heath shed, although they can opt to avoid it. The fireman volunteered to work in this link for two years because the high mileage bonuses are attractive, although the work is difficult and can sometimes involve overnight stops.

## Final checks

Today's journey to Glasgow has two temporary speed restrictions: one caused by mining subsidence south of Wigan, and a 32.25km/h (20mph) slowing just before the train reaches Penrith. But even that is not the final word, and the 'Late Notice Case' in the lobby is checked for last minute alterations.

Collecting a greasy overall coat from his locker, the driver sees the fireman at the stores counter drawing his firing shovel, bucket full of spanners and a gauge lamp and brush. The two men carry the equipment to the waiting locomotive, then the driver runs a practised eye over the engine. Although not immaculate – she has run 64,373.5km (40,000 miles) since her last works overhaul – her lined green paint is clean and the 18,184 litre (4,000 gallon) tender is piled high with good Yorkshire coal.

**◀ At the start of another long haul the driver waits, ready for the off. Over 40 years of life on the railway have placed him at the top of his profession – his present status is a far cry from his first days as a cleaner at the age of 14. In charge of an express passenger locomotive, a driver in the mid-1950s could expect to earn about £10 12*s*. a week, supplemented by an average of £4 mileage allowance.**

## Making ready

The crew have an hour to prepare the locomotive. The fireman replenishes the sandboxes and builds up the fire while the driver concentrates on dealing with the brakes and lubrication. The more inaccessible parts are usually covered in oil and dirt, which is why the driver has taken the precaution of wearing the overall coat.

Once both men are satisfied, the fireman hoses down the cab floor while the driver eases the engine down the shed yard and signals to the outside foreman's cabin. The driver then pulls to a halt at the shed outlet so that the fireman can ring off to Thorpes Bridge signalbox. So far they are on time.

At Red Bank sidings they pick up four carriages and drift slowly down to Exchange station. A second section of seven coaches from Liverpool, including the dining car, will be attached at Preston, making up the full permitted load of 365 tonnes (tons) for their engine.

Over each buffer are the two express headlamps which glint in the gathering, late afternoon gloom. The train leaves Manchester and heads for the junction with the West Coast mainline at Springs Branch. It's an easy task with their light load of four coaches and they are able to draw down to the north end of platform three in Preston on time.

The Liverpool section arrives soon after and stops well back on platform two. As the second engine is uncoupled and moved off, the Manchester driver draws his coaches out of the station and reverses back into platform two to couple the sections together. Preston is not well laid out for this manoeuvre and the darkness does not help.

Leaning from his cab window with one hand on the brake, the driver looks down the train. The shunter hangs from the last coach waving his handlamp which forms a pinpoint of light to guide the driver. One bad judgement and the train will buffer up too hard, jolting passengers and spilling the aperitifs being enjoyed in the diner.

After a quick brake test and a glance round the cab to make sure everything is in order, the driver looks back down the platform for the right away signal. Four minutes late, the guard waves his green lamp and the driver feeds high pressure steam to the cylinders – the pistons begin to move and the train inches forward. Next stop Carlisle.

There is plenty of hard work ahead – 101 minutes are allowed for the 90 mile (145km) journey, which includes the climb from close to sea level at Carnforth to Shap Summit at 915ft (279km).

## A testing time

As he approaches the Lancaster curves, the driver shuts off steam and lets the train coast through the 97km/h (60mph) restriction. With no speedometer in the cab, he must judge how fast he is going from the motion of the engine and the passing landscape.

Now drizzle starts to fall, blown in from Morecambe Bay. The cab windows blur and the reflected glare from the firehole only adds to his difficulties in sighting signal lights. A good knowledge of the route is the key to spotting them.

The driver is constantly wiping the small glass windshield with his sponge cloth. Now and then he glances round to check how his mate is doing and to keep an eye on pressure and water gauges. Hardly a word passes between the two men.

The drizzle adds to the driver's problems by bringing the risk of wheel slip. With hard climbing ahead, he decides to rush the gradients to keep up

**▼ The Manchester–Glasgow express speeds through the countryside – during the five to six hour journey the Jubilee Class 4-6-0 engine works hard, consuming six tonnes (tons) of coal and thousands of litres (gallons) of water.**

**A banking engine may be needed to push the train up the steep inclines of Shap and Beattock. But it isn't only the engine that feels the strain. By the time the train reaches its destination the driver and fireman will have had a hard day.**

◀ Even an engine driver has to do paperwork. At the beginning of his shift the driver signs on and picks up all the notices for the journey. Later he may have to make out a repair card listing faults with the engine needing attention.

▼ Before they leave the depot the driver and fireman have to satisfy themselves that the engine is fit for the road. An engine such as this one with two outside cylinders was easy to prepare – but in order to oil the inside valve gear of a Jubilee it was necessary to climb up between the frames from the pit.

▲ After signing on, the driver examines the Engine Arrangements Board to see which engine is allocated for his trip. No 45642 *Boscawen,* stabled on road 14, is scheduled for the Glasgow journey. Apart from engine provisions for this and the following day, the board lists engines under repair and those needing maintenance.

speed and gives his engine more steam to do so. His hand is poised to release sand on to the track to remedy any wheel slip but he is lucky.

## Over the top

The rain is falling harder; the climb to Shap Summit becomes a battle against gravity. The engine is pounding away but only doing 40.25km/h (25mph). Once it is over the top, the run into Carlisle is mainly downhill and steam can be shut off.

As the train reaches platform three, the driver carefully brakes so that the engine halts with the rear of the tender opposite the water column. While the tender is replenished, he checks all the bearings to ensure that none is running hot.

Despite the mountain of mail at Carlisle, they get away on time and head for the Scottish border. The climb to Beattock is particularly hard with two crests before Lockerbie. But the final ascent for 16km (ten miles) to the summit up a 1 in 75 gradient is the toughest test on the line.

Wet lineside trees increase the likelihood of slipping and the driver errs on the side of

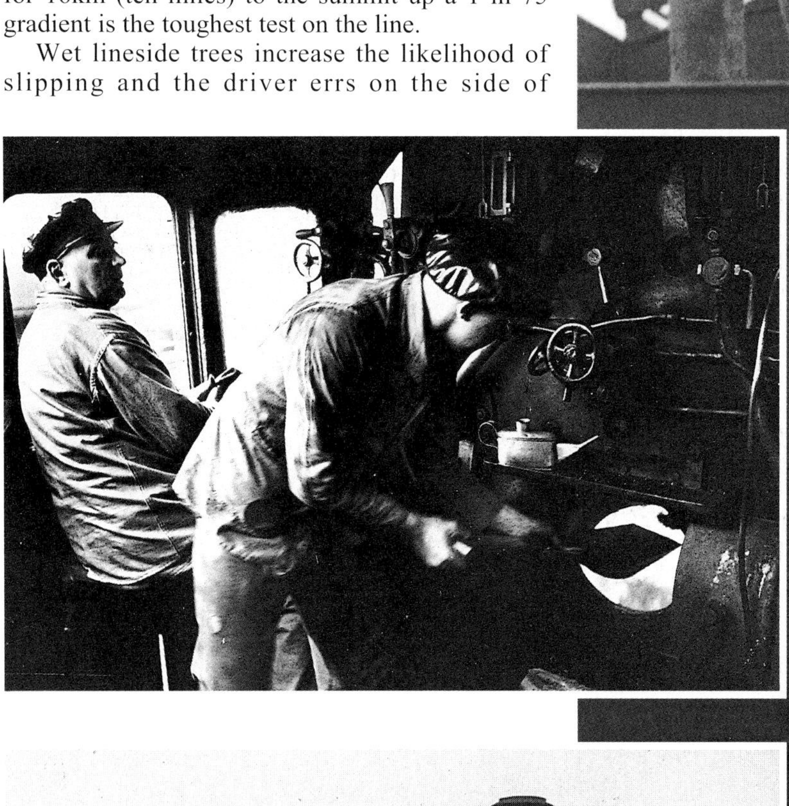

**▲ Before leaving the yard the engine has to take on water. The fireman puts the leather bag into the filler hole while his driver turns the water on at the valve. Alongside stands a fire cresset on a stove – a simple but effective way of preventing the water freezing in winter.**

**The tender holds up to 18,184 litres (4,000 gallons) – it needs 36,368 litres (8,000 gallons) to complete the journey. There are four water troughs on this route which allow the supply to be replenished on the move.**

**◄ The journey begins, with the enginemen at work in their traditional greasetop caps and bib-and-brace jackets. Having built up a good fire, the fireman maintains the boiler close to maximum pressure, without wasting fuel and water by blowing off at the safety valves.**

**◄ The correct ordering of engines to take up their duties off shed needs great organizational skills from the running shed foreman. At many depots turntables are used – some are vacuum operated, using the engine as power, others are pushed round by hand.**

caution. He crows on the whistle as he passes Ecclefechan signalbox so that the signalman can warn Beattock that they will have 20 minutes to provide a banking engine to push them up the hill.

The train seems hardly at a stand before the banking engine buffers up at the rear. The banker crows on the whistle to indicate that it is ready to push. The train driver replies in kind and the two engines start their 20 minute battle to the summit.

Once they are over the top, the banking engine drops off. The express rolls down Upper Clydesdale to Carstairs, where the section for Edinburgh is uncoupled from the rear. The final stage is a gentle roll downhill into Scotland's industrial belt with a brief stop at Motherwell. The last short sprint brings them into platform two at Glasgow Central just five minutes late. They have used over 36,368 litres (8,000 gallons) of water and six tonnes (tons) of coal since they left Manchester.

### A well-earned rest

Local men take charge of the engine and deliver it to Polmadie shed while the tired crew take their ease with a beer apiece in the dining car.

From Larkfield carriage sidings they have a short walk to the railway hostel where they will spend the night. They have earned almost 14 hours' pay on their eight-hour shift, thanks to a bonus scheme in which every 24.5km (15 miles) over 225 (140) count as an extra hour of pay. Consoled by that and drained by their mental and physical effort, they sleep soundly in their cubicles.

The following day is a mirror image of their journey north. Another crew relieves them on arrival at Newton Heath shed so that the driver can make out a card for any repairs that might be necessary, check his schedule for tomorrow and head home for tea. With a few home comforts on his mind, he is glad to leave the noise and the smoke behind him for another day.

**▲ Contact with Control was a regular feature of a driver's day. The graffiti on the wall, with the message 'Control can hear', sums up the rivalry that often existed between footplate staff and those they referred to as 'bank clerks and bureaucrats'. But, while drivers may have resented Control's supervision of operating matters, they were always glad when Control found relief crew at short notice.**

### *Learning the road*

When he joined the link, the driver had to learn the route. Until that point he knew the line only as far as Carlisle. Now he had to learn all the signals, gradients and speed restrictions on the 164.25km (102 miles) from Carlisle to Glasgow. These varied from the formidable climb to Beattock Summit to the complexities of the track on the approach to Glasgow.

To pick up these points, he rode with old hands and worked under their guidance. Then he learned the *Sectional Appendix*, a book which lists local details such as the location of passing loops of track and their holding capacity and special local whistle codes. It was three weeks before he 'signed the road', certifying that he could handle any type of train on the route, night or day in complete safety. This signed card is kept by the train crew foreman for reference should he need to replace a driver at short notice.

# The Railway Modernization Plan

**In 1955, the British Transport Commission published its Railway Modernization Plan. At last, Britain was to have a train service as good as any in the world, and the Press, the public and the government were all duly impressed. What no one had foreseen were the problems that lay ahead.**

▼ For devotees of steam, 11 August 1968 was a day of sadness as 143 years of public steam operation came to an end on the national railway network in Britain. The swansong was provided by a series of specials in the north-west of England, the final one being a 15 guinea per seat train that is seen here at Ais Gill in Cumberland with two Class 5 4-6-0s, Nos 44871 and 44781.

When the railways were nationalized in 1948, the Labour Chancellor of the Exchequer, Dr Hugh Dalton, said that the state was acquiring 'a poor bag of assets'. Although this was unfair, the railways were certainly in poor condition, having suffered the effects of heavy wartime traffic and bomb damage. Furthermore, there were many ageing locomotives and rolling stock in urgent need of repair.

Across the Channel, the war-devastated railways, especially West Germany, Belgium and Holland were embarking upon huge programmes of renewal that included mainline electrification. The state-owned British Railways (BR) had to make do and mend.

The government, which did not benefit from the vast amounts of American aid poured into Europe, maintained a regime of post-war austerity in which export industries had absolute priority. Not only food, but coal, steel and timber were strictly rationed or controlled.

BR, through its new overlord, the British Transport Commission (BTC), pleaded annually for more investment, but was told by the government that it would have to 'live off its fat' for a bit longer. Only the fat had already been eaten.

**Death bed proposals**
Almost the last act of the Railway Executive, set up by the Labour government in 1945 and abolished by the Conservatives in 1953, was the production of a Development Programme, which contemplated an outlay of £500 million on many of the items that were to be contained in the 1955 Modernization Plan. The Development Programme, which was never put to the Cabinet, had two striking features. It proposed to spend £160 million on electrification, but absolutely nothing on diesel locomotives.

Its other curious feature was a provision of £40 million for 'helicopter terminals and services'; it expected that frequent intercity helicopter services would soon appear and urged that the roofs of major passenger stations should be adapted as helicopter terminals.

▲ **Driver Charles Carter turns his head away as No 70013 *Oliver Cromwell* leaves the BR workshops at Crewe in Cheshire in 1967. Driven by the Mayor of Crewe, himself a railwayman, *Oliver Cromwell* was the last steam locomotive to be given a complete overhaul in a BR works.**

Hopes began to rise in 1951, with the election of a Conservative government pledged to 'make a bonfire of controls'. One of its first acts was to abolish the Railway Executive, the body charged with the day to day management of the railways, which were placed, instead, under the direct control of the BTC.

The Commission had for a long time thought that the Executive was too traditional in its outlook and now wanted to see new ideas brought into effect, especially regarding traction.

## Attachment to steam

All over the world, steam seemed to be losing its place to electric or diesel traction. However, the Railway Executive, though sponsoring some suburban electrification schemes and introducing diesel multiple units on a limited scale for branch lines, had proposed no plans for mainline electrification or diesel mainline locomotives. Instead, it had concentrated upon designing new types of 'standard' steam locomotive, which the Commission thought misguided.

The first task of the BTC, itself reorganized in 1953 under a new Chairman, the formidable and beetle-browed General Sir Brian (later Lord) Robertson, was to set up a Modernization Committee. This was divided into sub-committees which covered subjects such as way and works, signalling and telecommunications, and forms of traction.

The sub-committees had no difficulty in showing that serious deficiencies existed in virtually every aspect of railway operation. Their proposals were contained in the document *Modernization and Re-equipment of British Railways* – usually referred to simply as the Modernization Plan – published by the BTC in 1955.

The Plan covered a 15-year period, and during this time there was to be improvement of track and signalling; modernization of passenger rolling stock and station facilities; and the recasting of goods services, especially through the fitting of continuous brakes on all wagons.

However, the crucial element in the Plan was the changeover from steam to diesel and electric traction. This proposal had only been put to the Commission and approved after long and sometimes bitter debate, with the supporters of steam fighting a strong rearguard action.

One of these supporters was Roland Bond, recently appointed BR's Chief Mechanical Engineer. A dedicated ex-London Midland & Scottish Railway (LMS) locomotive man, he had helped to mastermind the introduction of the BR Standard steam engine, of which a total of 999 was to be built between 1951 and 1960.

Bond loyally supported the argument brought forward by his former chief at the LMS, Robin Riddles, that steam still had some way to go in technical development. In the end, however, the voting went against him. There was so much in favour of the alternatives – cleanliness, greater availability, reduced labour requirements and almost unlimited power potential. Unfortunately, the teething troubles were not foreseen, nor was the trauma of the changeover.

**▲ The old and the new at Carlisle Kingmoor in October 1967 – a Class 5 4-6-0 stands at the end of a pair of Type 1 Clayton Class 17s. On the adjoining track is a Class 46 1-Co-Co-1, D192. The rapid rate of dieselization meant that many steam engines less than ten years old were scrapped.**

So the fateful words were included in the Modernization Plan: 'The Commission accordingly propose to...terminate the building of all new steam locomotives within a few years.' The emphasis was to be on electrification, though the Commission was forced to recognize that 'there is a limit to the amount of mainline electrification that it appears practicable to complete within the period covered by the Plan...as regards the remainder of the principal mainline services, it is intended to introduce diesel traction as quickly as possible'.

The total cost of the Plan was put at £1,240 million, spread over 15 years. Although this sum was enormous, the government welcomed the BTC's proposals as 'imaginative'. There was also general approval by the public and the Press. 'All that we have read about or seen of the modernized railway systems of the United States and the Continent', enthused the Manchester Guardian, 'is to be transferred to England's green and pleasant land. The prospect is exciting.'

But designing the Plan was a good deal easier than carrying it out. To begin with, there had to be a drive to recruit more technical staff. This took

**One of the least successful products of the Modernization Plan was the Metropolitan-Vickers Class 28. It had a unique Co-Bo axle arrangement, but its two-stroke engines were most unreliable. D5702 is seen at Carlisle Upperby in October 1967.**

time. Then there was the agonizing question of which system to adopt for major mainline electrification – 25kV AC overhead or 1,500V DC overhead. (The Southern Region would continue to expand its 750V DC third-rail network.)

The 1,500V DC system had already proved its worth on the Liverpool Street–Shenfield and the Manchester–Sheffield–Wath lines of the Eastern Region; the AC system was still experimental, but offered greater possibilities for the future. The BTC, pressed by its Chief Electrical Engineer, Stanley Warder, chose the long-term solution.

## Choice of region

But was it really practicable to electrify, as the Plan proposed, both the London Midland and Eastern Region main lines simultaneously? Stanley Warder believed that it was. However, as further studies progressed, it became clear that a choice had to be made – and it was the London Midland Region that was selected.

Further difficulties arose over dieselization. BR had failed to obtain any substantial experience of diesel mainline locomotives, completely ignoring what had been happening in, for example, the United States and West Germany. Indeed, when the Modernization Plan was published there were only seven diesel mainline locomotives in the whole of the United Kingdom.

It was decided to order a few widely different designs for exhaustive testing before placing bulk orders on the basis of standardization. However, the inconvenience of the changeover period became so great that much larger orders were placed – some almost directly off the drawing board – resulting in a mixed bag of successful and reliable machines alongside many which had to be withdrawn after a short time.

More controversy flared in the wake of the BTC's decision to equip all freight wagons with continuous brakes. Here, political forces, which had demanded more power for the Regions, exercised an unfortunate influence.

The choice lay between the vacuum brake and the Westinghouse air brake. The headquarters technical officers had no doubt that the air brake

### Dutch resistance

One of the foreign experts brought in by the British Transport Commission to help implement the Modernization Plan was Dr F.Q. den Hollander, retiring President of the Netherlands Railways (then completing its own huge modernization programme).

Dr den Hollander had been a leader of the Dutch Resistance during World War II and did not conceal his distaste for everything German. The German Railways were using diesel locomotives with hydraulic transmission, apparently successfully, whereas diesel-electric was the norm elsewhere. Under the Modernization Plan, the Western Region insisted upon diesel-hydraulic locomotives, which provoked the fiercest opposition from Dr den Hollander.

In the debate over electrification, he strongly supported the 1,500V DC party against the proponents of 25kV AC. This may have been because the Netherlands Railways was using the former – or possibly because the French had pioneered the extensive use of the latter.

**◀ This was a common scene on the West Coast main line between the start of electrification work in the late 1950s and 1974, when electrics took over the final section to be completed, between Carlisle and Glasgow. An electrification team is seen at work at Edgeley Junction, Stockport, near Manchester, in the mid-1960s. Electrified services between Euston and Manchester/Liverpool began on 18 April 1966.**

▲ **A Swindon-built Class 124 six-car unit, or so-called Trans-Pennine, leaves Leeds on its way to Manchester in 1963. It was the use of these DMUs on the Trans-Pennine route that gave them their unofficial designation. The proliferation of types of DMU produced under the Modernization Plan was to create problems for both engineers and operators.**

was superior to its rival, and they recommended its adoption accordingly.

However, what headquarters called the 'Regional Mafia' (a strictly private meeting of Regional General Managers away from headquarters) decided to support the vacuum brake because its installation would involve fewer immediate complications and problems of compatibility – in other words, short-term convenience was considered more important than long-term advantages. The BTC reluctantly accepted the Regional view – an expensive mistake which ten years later had to be rectified.

Was the Modernization Plan a success? It is undeniable that the railway would have been in a far worse state if the Plan had not existed. It has been calculated that at least half the expenditure under the Plan was for undertaking essential work deferred since the war years. Mistakes were certainly made in the traffic estimates, because the huge increase in private motoring, the motorway building programme and the container revolution were not foreseen.

In consequence, money was wasted on freight facilities, such as new marshalling yards and the great concrete flyover at Bletchley in Buckinghamshire. On the credit side stands a great deal of electrification and a phenomenally rapid introduction of diesel traction, the gradual replacement of mechanical by colour light signalling from a small number of power boxes, the upgrading of track for higher speeds and some handsome new stations.

Of course, an easy criticism of the Plan was to say that it should have come *after* the 'reshaping' carried out in the 1960s by the new BR Chairman, Dr Richard Beeching, since money was spent on parts of the system that he decided to axe. However, in 1955 no-one could reasonably have foreseen how changed the world of transport would become in later years.

▶ **A Class 40 (then Type 4) diesel locomotive works a down express up Stoke Bank near Little Bytham on the East Coast main line in May 1971. Built by English Electric and introduced between 1958 and 1962, Type 4 was one of the more successful classes; the last Class 40 locomotive was not withdrawn until 1988. By 1971, continuous welded rail had been introduced on the East Coast main line, but the telephone pole route had yet to be replaced by modern telecommunications.**

*A Day in the Life of...*

# A country stationmaster

**The country stationmaster of the 1930s was a jack of all trades, as likely to be selling the tickets as working out the accounts. He was also the eyes and ears of the local community, with an unrivalled knowledge of its failures and successes.**

It is 6.30 on a Monday morning in September, the beginning of the autumn school term. The Stationmaster closes the door of his house and strides along the footpath across the fields, his domain spread like a model railway layout in the valley below.

He counts the wagons in the goods yard and the quarry siding; he knows they total 23, the same as when he left work on Saturday night, since when not a wheel has turned. But during the ten years he has been in charge here, counting the rolling stock has become compulsive.

Tall, with a reddish face and a second chin that looks as though it has been chiselled, he is regarded by his staff and customers as a retiring man with few obvious pleasures. Now in his early 50s, he is a confirmed bachelor, and lives, as well as works, for the Great Western Railway (GWR). He is proud to have come up through the ranks – he joined the GWR as a cleaner at the age of 14 – and is happy with his posting to a branch line station and seeks no further promotion.

He thinks of his station as the most important business centre for miles around, with himself at its heart. He knows how the farmers and market gardeners are doing, which shops are thriving or declining, who can afford a holiday or even a trip to the funeral of a distant relative, and, above all, how the quarry is faring.

It is now the mid-1930s, but the train service has not changed since before World War I and there is nothing to suggest that it ever will. On weekdays, six passengers and two freights stop at the station, all but one bound for either the terminal or the main town with its junction and connection to London. There is one exception, a short working, which runs between here and the town.

**▼ A shunter prepares to uncouple coal wagons at a branch station goods yard in the Midlands in the 1920s. To save time, the uncoupling of goods trucks is often done while the vehicles are on the move – a dangerous job which can result in injury or even death.**

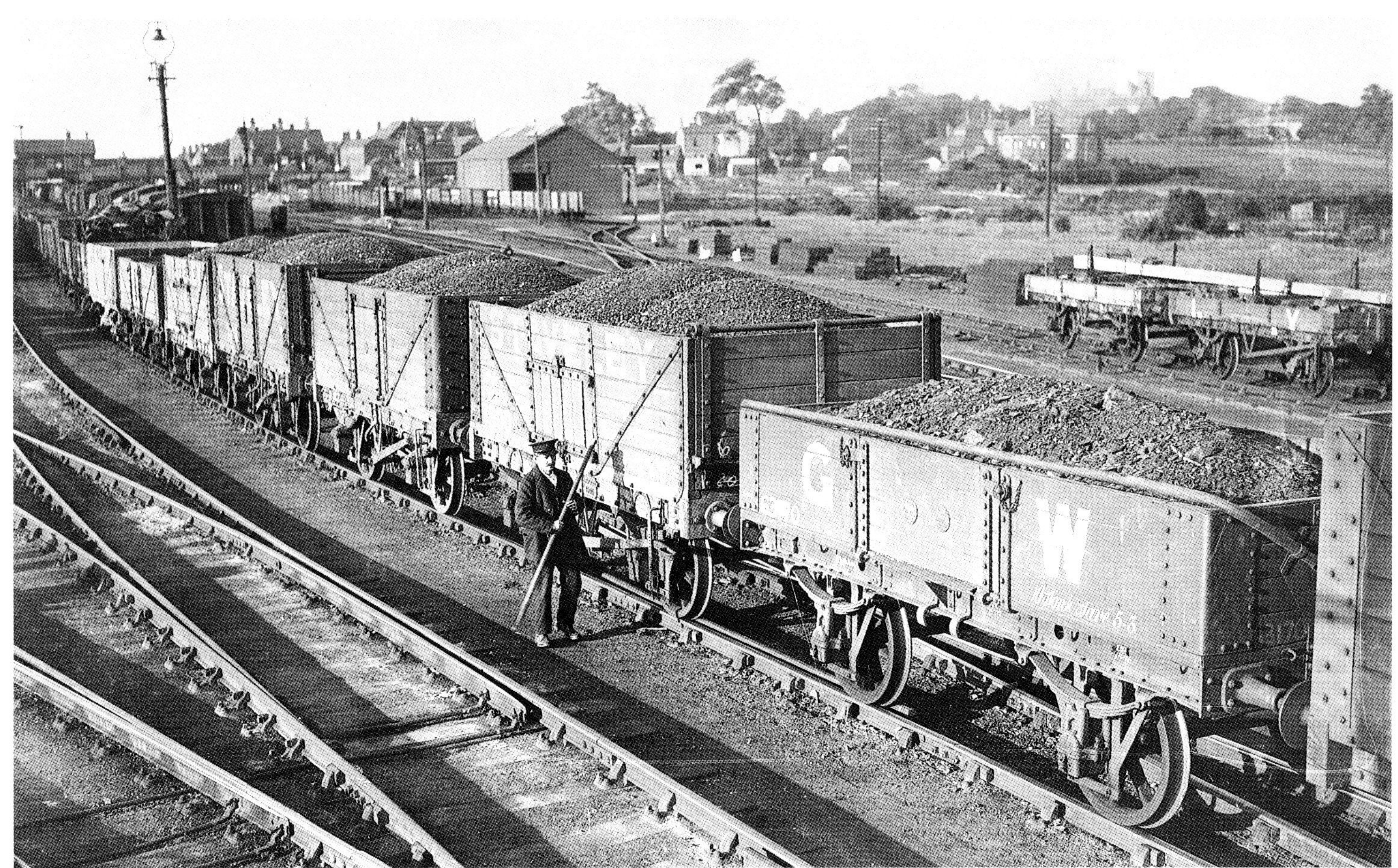

▲ **Mrs Cordery, the wife of a railway employee at Ascot station in Berkshire, is escorted along the platform by the porter. With her house standing between two tracks, this is her only way to the street.**

**Penalty of promotion**
As the first railway managers to be promoted from the ranks, stationmasters occupied a somewhat ambiguous place in the local community. They were often lonely people, feeling inferior to the better educated doctor, parson and other 'gentlemen' who ran the town or village, yet having to remain aloof from their staff because it was felt that familiarity might breed contempt.

Nor did they get much companionship from their colleagues at neighbouring stations. Indeed, relations between stationmasters on the same branch line were often marked by fierce rivalry, not least over demands for trains to be re-timed. This was hardly calculated to increase efficiency, and well before the days of area managers, it was being urged by some observers that stationmasters should be superseded by branch masters.

The wooden floor of the waiting room echoes to the tread of his mirror-bright boots as he crosses to unlock the booking office. For most of the time, the porter keeps an eye on the office, but the Stationmaster usually sells the tickets himself. This allows him to follow all the comings and goings at first hand, as well as keep an up-to-the-minute reckoning of the station's takings.

Today, there are 23 passengers for the first train – 11 noisy youngsters going to school, and a dozen adults, including a young man on the way to London, his one-way ticket bought in advance.

## Unknown destination

Dressed in his Sunday suit and carrying a cardboard suitcase, the young man hopes to make his fortune in a city he has seen only once – as the background to last year's Armistice Day parade on Pathé News.

If the worst comes to the worst, the young man says, he can always join the Army. The Stationmaster wishes him luck and the young man promises to send a postcard – if not from Piccadilly Circus or Trafalgar Square, then perhaps from Cairo or Bombay.

The passenger trains are made up of 2-6-2 Prairie tanks and three carriages – one corridor

and two non-corridor – the corridor added following a suggestion by a parish councillor with a weak bladder.

The 'short', however, is an autocar working – one carriage and a small engine – introduced last year in an attempt to cut down operating costs and compete more effectively with local bus services.

It arrives at 7.48, discharging its usual eight quarrymen (there used to be more, but several have bought motor cycles). As they hurry down the platform, several items are unloaded, mainly empty market gardeners' crates, but also some farmyard equipment, as well as cakes, tobacco and newspapers for several of the local traders.

## Right away

The departing passengers scramble on board and, fob watch in hand, the Stationmaster gives the right away at precisely 7.53. The engine reverses out of the station and gives off a piercing whistle that resounds throughout the valley.

Following time-honoured routine, the Stationmaster brews himself a mug of tea in his small sanctum beside the booking office, then strolls to the signalbox to greet the early duty man and sign the train register.

**▲ Animals are loaded up for a farm removal from a Welsh to a Surrey village. Such removals are a common feature on country railways – the farmer, his tractor and his livestock travelling by a special train that has to make occasional stops for the animals to be fed and watered.**

**▼ Building work being carried out at this branch station in the West Country in the 1930s suggests that business is running at a healthy level. Note the passenger platform, which is long enough to accommodate a maximum of only two or three carriages.**

The Stationmaster was once a signalman, and he casts an approving eye over the signalbox's well-ordered interior. When the next box up the line indicates that the autotrain is out of section, the Signalman rises from his chair to answer, at the same time using the plunger on the red Tyer's single line instrument to release a token for the down goods.

Ten minutes later, their chat is interrupted by the junction box giving 'the train entering section' signal. The Signalman responds and asks for a token release from the next box down the line. Having extracted the token from the machine, he pulls off. Within minutes, the down goods comes into view.

This is the only down train that does not stop here, but it dawdles through to allow safe exchange of tokens between driver and signalman. This particular driver is a bit of a wag, and he and the Signalman swop several good natured insults. The Stationmaster smiles, but does not join in.

## Dealing with paperwork

After a quick visit to the parcels office, smelling, and often sounding, like a farmyard, with its regular cargoes of small animals and chicks, the Stationmaster retires to his sanctum to grapple with the day's paperwork.

There are several letters. One, from the parson, identical to last year's, thanks him for making the recent Sunday school outing to the seaside run so smoothly. Another, from the Company, warns him that swine fever has broken out again and that all pigs are to be refused until further notice.

He notes what has been taken so far today in a large ledger, then unlocks a cast-iron safe and places the money inside. At the same time, he transfers the takings from Saturday – just under £23 – into a stout leather bag for district office. Most of the cash came over from the goods office on Saturday lunchtime, passenger takings being only about £9.

**▼ The stationmaster-cum-porter-cum-signalman of a small station near Swansea takes time off for a spot of gardening in 1938. One of the 'perks' of the country stationmaster is a large garden, or some land rented from the railway, on which he can grow his own food and raise his own livestock.**

The bag goes up with the first train from the terminus, due in at 10 o'clock. This is usually the busiest of the day and by 9.45 there are more than 40 passengers waiting on the platform.

The train arrives promptly, and the Stationmaster hands his bag over to a guard, who gives him an empty one for today's takings. Half an hour after the first passenger train has departed, the first up goods arrives headed by an elderly 2-6-0 Mogul. There are eight trucks, including two for the quarry reception siding, to be detached and 21 to pick up, and one hour 50 minutes are allowed for shunting.

Meanwhile, the Stationmaster pays his daily visit to the quarry manager's office. The quarry is big business for the railway – well over £1,000 a month – and the Stationmaster is careful to keep on good terms with the quarry manager. Although the blasting is very audible, the quarry cannot be sighted from here. It is about 1.5km (one mile) away and the stone is carried to the sidings over half a dozen fields and two roads by an aerial ropeway.

Satisfied that the shunter is coping in the goods yard, the Stationmaster disappears briefly to see the first down passenger on its way. An elderly woman clutching an umbrella gets on, but no one gets off this morning.

## Using the passing loop

By now, the Mogul with its complement of trucks is wheezing on its way, and the crossing of the down passenger with the up goods is one of the two times in the day when the passing loop is used. The other is when the down train bringing the schoolchildren home crosses the up train carrying the returning quarry workers and most of the day's parcels traffic, including flowers, fruit and vegetables from the market gardens.

But that is at 5.12 p.m., and time hangs heavy until then. Although the number of trucks to be cut out of the afternoon down goods is perhaps the day's most important figure – it will, of course, govern how many are left in the yard and quarry siding overnight, and on Saturdays, over the weekend – the detaching takes only ten minutes.

▲ Watched by the Stationmaster, a Drummond 4-6-0, No 14676 *Ballindalloch Castle*, hauls its coaches into The Mound on Scotland's Highland Railway. At a small station, the stationmaster is usually on hand to supervise the arrival and departure of all trains.

The afternoon down passenger is seldom busy, and the Porter is frequently left to sell the few tickets which are requested. So the Stationmaster takes a leisurely lunch and a modest half-pint of cider in the lounge bar of the station pub. Members of his staff also call into the pub as their duties permit, but they patronize the public bar, and there is virtually no contact between them and the Boss.

## Selling the services

After lunch, the Stationmaster walks up the footpath across the fields, ostensibly to canvass for business among any farmers or market gardeners he meets, but really just to stretch his legs. Not that he misses an opportunity to sell the railway's services; it is just that there are not many openings, for most of those who need to transport their produce are already using the railway. Nor is there much hope of increasing passenger traffic, since few people wander far from town. Indeed, the majority have never even been on a train, and most of those that have were soldiers on their way to the front line in August 1914 or children on a Sunday school outing.

The particularly worthwhile days are those when specials use the station – one a month for cattle, two a year for sheep and several during the summer for horses when fairs are being held. These are the times when passenger business also becomes much more profitable.

The Stationmaster recalls an exceptional day years ago when five specials were lined up at his station at once, stretching the layout to the limit. Once a month in summer there is a non-stop Sunday excursion, up in the morning, down in the evening, giving the signalman two welcome overtime periods. However, there is no need for the Stationmaster to turn up. And even if he attends the arrival of an occasional Sunday engineer's train, he does not get paid extra.

## Rewards of the job

Money is not his primary concern, however. His house is provided by the railway rent-free, and his salary of £165 is more than adequate for his needs. His real reward is the job itself – ensuring that the station runs like clockwork; the signal oil lamps are changed daily and the oil drum is replenished as necessary; the water tower never runs low; the signalmen read the weekly traffic notices and are not absent on a fishing expedition when an occasional special is due to come through; every train arrives with the appropriate headlamp and departs with all doors closed and tail lamp shining; the quarry never runs short of trucks; and the market gardeners bring their produce in early enough.

With the evening train crossing completed, the Stationmaster locks the booking office, says goodnight to the Porter, who is already climbing on to his bicycle, and walks out of the station. Again, he counts the wagons in the goods yard and in the quarry siding. Reassured that everything is in order for the next day, he strides back along the footpath to home.

▼ Coal trucks are unloaded at a station near Birmingham. The stationmaster has to cope with the requirements of both passengers and goods traffic, ensuring, for example, that rolling stock is sufficient.

# The Beeching axe

**Few public figures have been more vilified than Dr Richard Beeching. He was Chairman of British Railways for only four years – from 1961 to 1965 – yet his impact on passengers was greater than that of the German bombing in World War II.**

The 1960s saw the most dramatic changes on Britain's railways since the 'Mania' years of the mid-nineteenth century. When the decade opened, British Railways (BR) was still a steam-hauled system (in spite of the initiation of the 1955 Modernization Plan), with long trains of loose-coupled, hand-braked wagons clanking their way between marshalling yards.

In 1960, there were still 16,108 steam locomotives at work; by the end of 1968, all had been replaced by diesel or electric traction. The total route mileage of 18,565 was 95 per cent of the mileage inherited at nationalization in 1948. By 1969, the percentage had fallen to 62.

## Unenviable reputation

At the heart of this transformation was the so-called Beeching Plan, drawn up by BR Chairman Dr Richard (later Lord) Beeching. Although Dr Beeching held the appointment for only four years – from June 1961 to the end of May 1965 – he became a national personality whose name still provoked anger and derision some 30 years later. The phrase 'doing a Beeching' became part of the national vocabulary. It was a synonym for ruthless cost-cutting, and many who never knew him talked of 'Butcher Beeching'. The positive side of the policies that he sponsored tended to be ignored or overlooked.

The way in which Beeching, with no previous transport connections, became BR Chairman was fortuitous. The Conservative government, deeply concerned at mounting BR deficits, decided both to break up the huge British Transport Commission (BTC), of which BR was the largest single component, and to straighten out BR's finances through more efficient management.

The Minister of Transport, Ernest Marples, set up an Advisory Group of businessmen, chaired by Sir Ivan Stedeford, Chairman of Tube Industries Ltd. Sir Ewart Smith, Deputy Chairman of ICI, was asked to join the Group, but Sir Ewart declined; he suggested, instead, Dr Beeching, then Technical Director of ICI – a recommendation which Marples followed up. Impressed by Beeching's contribution to the Advisory Group, Marples concluded that he was just the man to preside over the restructuring of the railways.

▲ A smiling Dr Beeching flourishes a copy of his explosive 140-page report, *The Reshaping of British Railways,* at a London press conference in March 1963. Described by one MP as 'the most staggering report ever presented to any government', the document sparked off a controversy that reverberates to the present day.

◀ The Waverley route between Carlisle and Edinburgh was one of the main lines listed for the axe in the Beeching Report, but approval for closure was not given until 1968. In spite of vigorous opposition, it was shut the following year. The line had carried heavy goods and parcels traffic like this up train of parcels and tanks at Galahiels behind a St Margaret's (Edinburgh) B1 4-6-0, No 61191.

Beeching was then under 50, and strongly tipped as a future Chairman of ICI. He was greatly interested by the challenge which Marples's offer posed, but insisted that he must retain his ICI salary level of £24,000. This hit the headlines and created a sensation – Beeching's predecessor, Sir Brian (later Lord) Robertson, had been paid only £10,000. The Treasury was persuaded by Marples to bite on the bullet, and Beeching duly became Chairman, first of the BTC for the last six months of its existence and then of the new British Railways Board (BRB).

## Statistical deluge

Beeching's immediate impact upon BR senior managers was favourable. They encountered a relaxed, cigar-smoking figure, very different from the rather austere Sir Brian Robertson. Beeching was masterly at chairing a meeting; he asked penetrating questions and was good at listening just as long as necessary, and no longer.

He soon remarked that, when he called for data, he was deluged with statistics of operations, but was given no indication of the profitability of the work being carried out.

An early decision was to inaugurate 'traffic studies' under the energetic and abrasive Stanley Raymond, Traffic Adviser at BR's headquarters at 222 Marylebone Road. Raymond set up a kind of Operations Room covered with charts which illustrated the traffic volume and type over every section of line, and the expenses and receipts at every station.

These traffic studies formed the groundwork of what may be called the Beeching philosophy. This argued that the railway was doing far too much that could be done more economically by road transport, and that it should concentrate on what it could do best – the movement of bulk passenger and goods traffic, usually in block trains.

## The chief lieutenants

Beeching's main lieutenants in developing this theme within the railway were Raymond himself (soon promoted to BRB membership) and Fred Margetts, also on the Board, who had been General Manager of the North Eastern Region and had attracted Beeching's attention by calling for a more 'business-led' railway.

Beeching also brought in several 'outsiders' from the world of business, the most conspicuous (and the least popular with railwaymen) being Philip Shirley of Unilever and Leslie Williams of Shell; neither would survive Beeching's departure. In addition, he recruited some younger managers from outside to work in the Regions, and a few of these would stay to make a lasting contribution.

Beeching's relations with his officials showed some contradictions. Cool and urbane himself, he

### Beeching broadsides

Dr Beeching was sociable and friendly in company, but he could produce the occasional devastating remark. Once, after a dinner with a group of senior railway managers, he observed that his stay with BR had at least taught him one thing – that the operating function was always considered to be paramount.

Smug smiles on the faces of the operators present vanished when he went on: 'I find that surprising, because you all seem to be so bad at it.' (Beeching lived on the Oxted line of the Southern Region, notorious for unpunctuality.)

On another occasion, one of his lieutenants, the unpredictable James Ness, made what seemed like a personal attack on the Chairman at a Board meeting, which Beeching completely ignored, proceeding calmly to the next business. At the end of the meeting he turned to Ness and said 'I hope, James, that your headache is now better.'

▶ **The extent of the closures proposed by Beeching were to come as a shock, yet the unions had sufficient inkling of what was afoot to hold a national protest strike on 3 October 1962. But its only real effect was to inconvenience passengers.**

▲ Few economies were made to reduce costs on the long cross-country line between Taunton and Barnstaple, and traffic was steadily diverted via Exeter. The end came in October 1966, since when much of the trackbed was turned into the A361 trunk road. Here, the signalman at Morebath Junction (where the Exe Valley line to Tiverton diverged) hands over the token to the fireman of a former Great Western Railway 2-6-0, No 7326, with an eastbound train.

almost seemed to relish the abrasiveness of Williams and Shirley. He was at his best when talking to the younger managers attending courses at the British Transport Staff College at Woking. But he gave short shrift to the verbose and rather woolly-minded David Blee, General Manager of the London Midland Region.

He liked the often rebellious Gerard Fiennes, then General Manager of the Western Region, and he once listened courteously to a junior officer who told him that the Beeching Plan was misconceived, because closing country branch lines would only save peanuts; the real loss-makers were the big depots, where restrictive practices flourished.

## Sending out shock waves

When Beeching felt that he had sufficiently grasped and diagnosed the problems, he published a document in March 1963 written largely by himself under the title *The Reshaping of British Railways* – very soon and ever since to be known as the Beeching Plan. Widely publicized in the newspapers and on television, it sent shock waves through the nation.

It revealed that half of BR's 7,000 stations produced only two per cent of the traffic. Just 34 stations produced no less than a quarter of the receipts. One-third of the mileage carried only one per cent of the traffic in ton-miles and passenger-miles. Half the system did not earn enough to maintain the infrastructure, let alone contribute towards the cost of movement.

Apart from the imbalance in earning capacity, rolling stock was poorly utilized; on an average, each wagon performed only 72.5km (45 miles) of revenue-earning movement *per week*, and out of 18,500 mainline passenger carriages, only 5,500 were in daily, year-round service.

The real shocks, however, were contained in an Appendix to the Report, which suggested that some 2,000 stations should be closed and 250 train services withdrawn as uneconomic. Protests and expressions of dismay from rail users were widespread, but Ernest Marples was delighted. In a letter to the BR Chairman he described the Report as 'a superb effort'.

Even though the Report reads persuasively and seems to demonstrate Beeching's clarity of thought, its publication was a commercial blunder. It led to a premature flight of traffic away from the railway, with many traders and passengers transferring to road transport in anticipation of closures that, in the event, were not allowed to take place. It also produced general public pessimism about the future of the railway. Unfortunately, the media concentrated on the threatened closures and paid scant attention to the Report's proposals for developing goods concentration schemes, 'Liner Trains' and improved intercity services.

## Beeching Part Two

The sequel to the Beeching Report, published in February 1965, failed to make an equal impact. Popularly known as Beeching Part Two, it was entitled *The Development of the Major Trunk Routes*, and was largely drafted, under Beeching's guidance, by James Ness, whom Beeching had brought on to the BRB with responsibility for planning.

▶ The former London & South Western Railway branches in north Cornwall and Devon were savaged by the Beeching cuts, in spite of heavy holiday season traffic. One of the most scenic was the line to Padstow, which ran beside the Camel Estuary for the final few miles. Here a West Country Pacific brings a train over one of the tidal inlets in April 1960. The line is now a foot and cycle path.

Ness had been General Manager of the Scottish Region, where he had been disliked for harassing his departmental officers, and his promotion surprised many at BR headquarters. His suggested trunk line network confined investment to about 4,828km (3,000 miles) of the existing mainline system totalling 11,265.25km (7,000 miles).

Although the backbone of the system was to receive investment, it was clearly implied that the remainder might be 'reshaped' into oblivion. This did not happen, partly due to the political storms that would have arisen, and also the election of a Labour government in 1964.

## Weighing the balance sheet

What effect did the closures have in improving BR's finances? By 1969, these were looking much healthier. Indeed, in that year there was actually a surplus on railway operating of £45 million. This arose, however, mainly from the working of the Labour government's 1968 Transport Act, which instituted specific grants for loss-making services which fulfilled a public need; it also transferred to the newly formed National Freight Corporation, BR's loss-making 'sundries' business.

All this coincided with gains in productivity from electrification and new working practices. Savings there were from station and line closures – over the whole of the 1960s, the total number of stations fell from 7,450 to 3,235.

However, small country stations had few staff; equally, many closed branches were single-track with low maintenance costs. Moreover, although many of the lines had fed valuable business into the trunk system, they had been closed with little attempt to find out if any savings could be made on their operation. Scaling down the system was not a magic formula.

As for Beeching himself, he was unwilling to go along with the Labour government's policies for public transport. So he left the BRB, with a peerage, after only four years of his five-year contract had run. He became Deputy Chairman of ICI for a short period, but did not become Chairman, and eventually moved on to other fields of public service and private business.

He had left an indelible mark on BR. Everyone who had met him agreed that he was deeply impressive; he attracted personal loyalty even from dedicated railwaymen who fought against his proposals, such as Gerard Fiennes, who called him 'the great and good Doctor'. However, in applying the logic of manufacturing industry to transport, he had not appreciated the subtle interconnection of services and costs, nor the crudity of the data on which he had based his costing exercises.

Asked in later years about his period with BR, Beeching said that his only regret was that he had been unable to carry out reshaping in its entirety. Few would share the feeling.

### Charge of suicide

The Beeching Report was greeted with a barrage of criticism, some of the fiercest from the Dutch-born traffic expert Professor Hondelink. Hondelink, a naturalized British citizen, was renowned for his practical experience and forthright opinions. He had restored the shattered railway services in the wake of the Allied invasion of Europe in 1944, and had gone on to work for the international community, becoming a senior transport and communications consultant with the United Nations and the World Bank.

'I have now digested the Beeching Report,' he announced soon after its publication in March 1963. 'My comment is as follows: analysis clear, concise and capable; the accountant's work well done; the conclusions rough and unrealistic; the proposed implementation ruthless to the point of being suicidal...'

# Dawn of the diesel era

**In the United States and Germany in the 1930s, diesel power sparked a revolution in rail travel. British railway companies were more cautious, however, and it was not until after World War II that diesel traction in Britain began to present a serious challenge to steam.**

In 1891, the first attempt to harness the internal combustion engine to the railways was made when Gottlieb Daimler constructed a small petrol-powered locomotive. Others took up the task, and a passenger coach equipped with an 80hp petrol engine was introduced in Britain by the North Eastern Railway in 1903.

The most spectacular example was built for the French State Railways in 1933 by the famous motor manufacturers, Bugatti. Powered by a 200hp engine, the streamlined Bugatti railcar took the French President from Paris to Chartres at an average speed of 114km/h (71mph). Before long, both Bugatti and lightweight Micheline railcars were providing regular services.

It was not the petrol engine, however, that was destined to challenge steam's supremacy on the railway. A highly refined fuel such as petrol was not only expensive, but also highly flammable. In the event of a derailment or other unfortunate mishap, this would be extremely dangerous. What was needed was an internal combustion engine which would work efficiently with an oil fuel requiring far less refinement and with a lower flash-point.

The answer was the diesel engine. While the German inventor, Dr Rudolf Diesel (1858–1913), is generally credited with being the sole originator of the engine that bears his name, it was a Yorkshireman, Herbert Akroyd Stuart, who first

**▼ The pioneer of diesel traction in Britain was the London Midland & Scottish Railway. This three-car unit worked on the Oxford–Cambridge line in the late 1930s, making the 124km (77 mile) run in 80 minutes – less than half the time taken by steam.**

◀ **Seen on display at Euston in 1934, this diesel railcar was one of three used by the London Midland & Scottish Railway for branch line services in Scotland and the North of England. Each of the cars was powered by a six-cylinder diesel engine with hydraulic transmission.**

patented an oil engine based on compression ignition in 1890.

However, as has happened so often, a British invention was then developed commercially elsewhere, and it was Dr Diesel's work with the firms of Krupp and Maschinenfabrik Augsburg-Nuremburg (MAN) which resulted in the building of the first successful diesel engine in 1897.

However, 16 years were to elapse, before the first application of diesel traction to a railway vehicle. In 1912, a 1,200hp diesel locomotive was supplied by the Swiss firm of Sulzer to the Prussian-Hessian State Railways in Berlin. A year later, the first diesel railcar went into service in Sweden, soon to be followed by seven more.

## Post-war breakthrough

The outbreak of World War I in 1914 impeded progress among the combatant nations, but with the end of hostilities in 1918, important developments occurred in Germany, North America and the newly proclaimed Soviet Union. The Soviet engineer Dr George Lomonosoff produced a design for a 1,200hp mainline diesel-electric locomotive, four of which were built for the German State Railways in 1925. The same year, eight diesel-electric railcars, each powered by twin British-built Beardmore engines, were placed in service on the Canadian National Railways.

To demonstrate the reliability of the new units, one of them was worked over the 4,715.25km (2,930 miles) from Montreal to Vancouver in 67 hours, without shutting down its engines. In 1926, the Long Island Railroad launched the first diesel-electric mainline service in the United States.

## German advances

It was in Germany that the most spectacular results were achieved. The big breakthrough came in 1932, when a twin-coach streamlined diesel unit was turned out from the Görlitz works of Wagen und Maschinenbau AG (WUMAG). It had two 410hp Maybach diesel engines of the airless injection type, driving generators which powered motors on both axles of the central articulated bogie. In May 1933, it entered service as the *Flying Hamburger*, averaging a speed of more than 124km/h (77mph) between Berlin and Hamburg – the fastest schedule in the world.

As can be seen from part of the prototype, which is on display in the Verkehrsmuseum in Nuremberg, the passenger accommodation was not particularly spacious. And with the motor and exhaust pipe so close to him, the driver must have had an uncomfortable ride. Nevertheless, the *Flying Hamburger* was a resounding success, and it was not long before similar high-speed business services were radiating from Berlin, some three-car sets supplementing the original two-car design.

### Road railers

The first three decades of the twentieth century saw many attempts to fit ordinary road vehicles with flanged wheels and run them on railway lines. On the 3ft (915mm) gauge railways of the American Rockies, a number of such hybrids were used for passengers and mail, being known as Galloping Geese because of their somewhat unsteady progress and the large wing-ploughs they carried for clearing snow during the winter months.

In Yorkshire, various similar vehicles were used. The Derwent Valley Light Railway tried a pair of Ford buses in 1924, coupled back to back so they could be reversed easily. In another part of Yorkshire, an Italia racing car was used for off-duty transport on the Spurn Point military railway. In 1922, the North Eastern Railway converted one of its road buses used in the Durham area to run on rails. For the next four years it operated a busy daily service from York and then Selby, until someone used an open paraffin lamp to check the petrol level while it was being refuelled for its next trip.

▶ **The first high speed diesel train to go into regular daily service was the two-car *Flying Hamburger*, which began running between Berlin and Hamburg in 1933. Weighing 77 tonnes (tons), the train achieved speeds of up to 160km/h (100mph).**

**▲ No 10000 was one of two prototype mainline diesel locomotives ordered by the London Midland & Scottish Railway (LMS) after World War II. No 10000 began running in December 1947, on the very eve of the LMS's extinction, while its sister, No 10001, entered service seven months later.**

These had improved accommodation for passengers and included a dining saloon.

Two rival designs of high speed trains with diesel-electric drives appeared at the Century of Progress exhibition in Chicago in 1934. Their two-stroke diesel engines, developed by General Motors, were far more compact and powerful than any internal combustion engine to date. Union Pacific's M1000 could easily reach and maintain blistering speeds of more than 160km/h (100mph).

But it was the Chicago, Burlington & Quincy Railroad's *Pioneer Zephyr* that stole the show, arriving at the end of a 1,633.5km (1,015 mile) non-stop dash from Denver in just over 13 hours – an average speed of 124.9km/h (77.6mph). Not to be outdone, the Union Pacific sent its second diesel train, the M1001, on a high speed cross-country run the following year. The six-car streamliner completed the 5,138.5km (3,193 miles) from Los Angeles to New York in a record time of 56 hours 55 minutes.

These pioneer trains obviously highlighted the potential of diesel traction for mainline rail services. But the response of the railway companies in Britain was less than enthusiastic. With ample supplies of good locomotive coal to draw on, and with their profits affected by economic recession and increasing competition from road carriers, they saw little reason to adopt the new form of traction. Only a few isolated experiments were carried out, the most important being those of the London Midland & Scottish Railway (LMS) and Great Western Railway (GWR).

In 1933, the LMS began operating a number of diesel shunters, which represented the first large-scale use of diesel power on British railways. The following year, the GWR introduced the first successful diesel railcar service in Britain. It was followed by three more powerful units for a new Birmingham–Cardiff service, and the fleet ultimately numbered 38. The first 18 were built by outside manufacturers and were of many different designs, but the final batch was built at Swindon by the GWR itself, the last four being fitted for multiple-unit operation.

Another company which now began to show an interest in dieselization was the London & North Eastern Railway (LNER). Impressed by the performance of the *Flying Hamburger*, it obtained a quotation from the train's builders, WUMAG, for a similar unit to provide a fast business service between Newcastle and London King's Cross. But

**▶ GWR diesel-mechanical railcar No 2 was one of three units built in 1934 for express services between Birmingham Snow Hill and Cardiff. Powered by two 121hp engines, each unit was able to reach speeds of about 128.75km/h (80mph), and a buffet service was provided for the seated passenger capacity of 44.**

the gradients and slacks on the 431.25km (268 mile) route presented a problem not faced by the German train and the manufacturers were not prepared to guarantee the average speed the LNER required. Moreover, the proposed catering facilities, which consisted only of drinks and snacks, fell far short of what the senior management of the LNER had in mind.

So the company asked its Chief Mechanical Engineer, Nigel Gresley, to produce a suitable steam locomotive for the London–Newcastle service. The result was the A4 Pacific, used to power a new streamlined train, the Silver Jubilee. The train made its demonstration run on 27 September 1937, racing from London to Newcastle in just four hours – 30 minutes less than the time estimated by WUMAG. The success of the Silver Jubilee confirmed steam's supremacy in Britain and pushed mainline diesel traction even further beyond the horizon.

## Cross-country set

The only significant development to occur in the aftermath of the Silver Jubilee's triumph was the introduction by the LMS of a streamlined, lightweight three-car diesel set, which operated for some time on the cross-country route between Oxford and Cambridge via Bletchley. It was later transferred to the LMS Midland main line, where it worked some suburban services, as well as a number of express duties between London St Pancras and Nottingham.

▲ In September 1913, Dr Rudolf Diesel set sail from Germany to England hoping to swop notes with British colleagues. He disappeared from the ship, however, prompting speculation that he had been thrown overboard by German agents to prevent him from passing on his research to a potential enemy.

However, although Britain's large private locomotive-building industry was not particularly successful in selling diesels at home, it managed to sell a good many abroad, in countries where oil was more plentiful than coal, or where the steam locomotive operated under severe constraints. In 1935, for example, the Tyneside firm of Armstrong Whitworth built two 1,200hp diesel locomotives for use on a new railway being planned between Bombay and Karachi, in what is now Pakistan, where the waterless terrain made steam traction extremely difficult.

## The balance shifts

It was not until after the war that British railway companies began to think seriously again about diesel traction. The LMS led the way once more, introducing two 1,600hp diesel-electric locomotives for mainline work in 1947. These were followed, in 1952 and 1954, by three 1-Co-Co-1 diesel-electrics, delivered to the Southern Region of the recently formed British Railways. By now, the balance had started to shift away from steam and in favour of diesel. Not only was good locomotive coal becoming increasingly difficult to obtain, but so was the labour for the manning and maintenance of steam locomotives.

Under its 1955 Modernization Plan, the British Transport Commission decided that all future building of locomotives for other than electrified railways in Britain would be of diesels. After more than half a century, the diesel era in Britain had finally dawned.

### A problem of size

There are three main ways of transmitting a diesel engine's power to the wheels of a traction unit – mechanical, hydraulic and electrical. The problem in the early days with electric transmission was the size of the traction motor. This was so large that it had to be housed in the body, together with the heavy diesel power plant itself. The result was a dramatic increase in the size and weight of locomotives. It was in the 1930s that traction motors finally became small enough to be mounted on the bogies, and since then most railways throughout the world have gone for the option of electric transmission.

RUSSELLS
WATCHES

# TICKETS, PLEASE!

*The rise of the major railway companies and stations*

# The London Midland & Scottish Railway

**The LMS was the biggest of the Big Four, with a railway network that encompassed much of Britain. It was also led for most of its existence by a man of outstanding ability. But internal rivalries inherited from pre-Grouping days proved a serious handicap.**

The London Midland & Scottish Railway (a clumsy title almost invariably abbreviated to the smoothly pronounced initials LMS) was not only the largest of the Big Four created by the Grouping of 1923, it was also the largest private transport company in the world.

It employed almost a quarter of a million people, operated some 11,265km (7,000 miles) of track, 3,000 goods depots and 2,400 passenger stations, and ran trains throughout the length and breadth of Britain, with a substantial system in Northern Ireland.

However, in spite of its vast assets, the LMS started life with a fundamental weakness. Two of the companies that had merged to form it were the London & North Western Railway (LNWR) and the Midland Railway (MR), which liked to be known as, respectively, the Premier Line and The Best Way.

They had been old and bitter rivals, and it should have been obvious that these victims of a shotgun wedding would take a long time to become good bedfellows. An easier marriage had been that of the LNWR and the Lancashire & Yorkshire Railway (LYR), which had been voluntarily arranged in 1922.

The rivalry between the LNWR and MR was repeated in Scotland, where the three constituent companies were the Caledonian Railway, the Glasgow & South Western Railway and the Highland Railway (HR). The HR had always been dependent upon its larger neighbours to the south

**Pages 88–89: Visitors to York station could not fail to be impressed with its magnificent arched roof.**

**▼ Princess Royal class Pacific No 6208 *Princess Helena Victoria*, with the down Royal Scot, waits impatiently for the right away at Rugby in the late 1930s.**

▶ **The LMS's pre-war experiments with diesel traction led to the production of this articulated three-coach unit, numbered 80,000. Measuring 55.5m (182ft) and capable of carrying 108 passengers, the unit was tried out on the Oxford–Cambridge line, making the 124km (77 mile) run in 80 minutes.**

for its most important traffic, and it came into the fold fairly quietly.

There was much bitterness, however, between the proud Caledonian and the small but doughty Glasgow & South Western. To the men of the 'Sou' West', the 'Caley' had long been 'the auld enemy', and they resented the enforced alliance.

## Locomotive inheritance

The LMS established its HQ at its principal London terminus, Euston, where its first General Manager, Sir Arthur Watson, a former LYR man, was already installed in charge of the combined LNWR and LYR. The first Chief Mechanical Engineer (CME), George Hughes, was also from the LYR. Hughes inherited a huge fleet of around 10,400 steam locomotives of varying type and condition.

The LNWR engines, small or large, were commonly thrashed to the limit of their power, hauling long and heavy trains. The Midland had a small engine policy, partly because of some weak bridges which restricted axle-loads. It cossetted its attractively liveried locomotives, rigidly restricting the loads that could be taken without resorting to double-heading.

Two engines on its principal expresses and, in particular, on its long mineral trains, were therefore common. In contrast, the North Western drivers took pride in dispensing with a pilot, though the sharp bark of their exhausts and the rain of cinders on carriage roofs often showed how hard the Crewe products were being worked.

The difference in management styles was equally profound. The LNWR had been a very gentlemanly railway, recruiting cadets with good educational backgrounds, while the Midland had relied more on men who had come up the hard way and had gained plenty of practical experience. At times, first one, then the other, of these two outlooks seemed to prevail in the LMS.

> **Record-breaking run**
> When a Great Western Railway passenger locomotive exceeded 161km/h (100mph) in 1904, the GWR authorities kept it a close secret for fear of alarming the public. In the 1930s, things were very different, however, with the London Midland & Scottish and London & North Eastern railways competing to break speed records.
> The LMS was delighted when its Coronation Scot reached 183.5km/h (114mph) on a demonstration run in July 1937, and it basked in the resulting publicity. What was kept quiet was the panic among the passengers and the breakages in the restaurant car as the train descended from Whitmore Bank and careered into the platform at Crewe station, travelling at more than twice the permitted speed.

◀ **This early poster showing a Hughes Dreadnought 4-6-0 overshadowed by a vast Cunard liner was indulging in a certain amount of poetic licence. At this time, the Cunard vessels sailed from Liverpool Riverside – a point which no 4-6-0 would have been able to reach because of weight restrictions.**

## Start of a new era

A new era dawned in 1924 when Sir Guy Granet, a lawyer and a former MR General Manager, became LMS Chairman. He was close to retirement, but this did not stop him from attempting to clear up the ''ell of a mess' – the name often substituted for the company's initials.

The sterile in-fighting between former constituents had to be sorted out under an impartial and effective chief executive. Granet decided that he must look beyond the railways for such a man and his choice fell upon Sir Josiah Stamp, an industrialist and taxation expert. A man of strong views – he was a teetotaller, non-smoker and lay preacher – Stamp was regarded with some suspicion by railway professionals.

The appointment also caused astonishment because Stamp was to run the LMS not as general manager, but as an American-style President, assisted by three Executive Vice-Presidents.

One of those who questioned the new appointment was the leader of the National Union of Railwaymen, Jimmy Thomas, soon to be a member of the first Labour Cabinet. 'I well remember the very serious misgivings...when it was announced that [Stamp] was to be the new

▲ **Locomotives in the repair shop at Crewe works in the late 1920s. Although part of the LMS, Crewe was traditionally associated with the old LNWR, and there was intense rivalry between it and the LMS works at Derby, which had served the former Midland Railway.**

president,' he wrote later. 'There was considerable shaking of heads in railway circles, and a feeling that Sir Guy Granet, who was his railway godfather, had made a big blunder.'

In 1927, following Granet's retirement, Stamp added the role of Chairman to that of President. He delegated extensively to his team of Vice-Presidents, and his policies soon percolated through the vast, straggling LMS system.

His main concern was cost-efficiency, and it was claimed that, following the reforms at Crewe Works, a heavy repair on a locomotive could be carried out in 46 working hours, compared with 60 days previously.

## Marvels of science

Initially, the LMS Vice-Presidents were all professional railwaymen, but in 1930 Stamp imported into their ranks an Oxford scientist, Sir Harold Hartley, who set up the company's first research establishment at Derby. One of the devices tested here was 'the mechanical bottom', which would thump up and down for hours on a carriage seat to determine its resilience.

The priority, however, was the overhaul of operating practices. Sir Henry Fowler, once CME of the Midland, had succeeded Hughes as CME of the LMS in 1925. Described as 'a great man for boilers', he was a production engineer rather than a locomotive designer, and his reaction to the problem of traction – now becoming acute because of the company's ageing fleet – had initially been to build some more standard Midland types.

As a result, the LMS found itself woefully short of up-to-date mainline express locomotives, in particular, for the West Coast route to Scotland. Stamp's committee of Vice-Presidents got to work, urging Fowler to abandon standard Derby practices and produce an appropriate engine for the company's prestigious new Royal Scot train, running between Euston and Glasgow.

The performance of a borrowed Great Western Railway (GWR) Castle had greatly impressed the LMS operators, and since time was short for preparing an entirely new design, they asked Swindon if they could borrow the drawings of these locomotives.

**London duo**

Although the London Midland & Scottish (LMS) was essentially a heavy goods and long-distance passenger railway, it inherited two important suburban systems in the London area – the North London Railway (NLR) and the London Tilbury & Southend Railway (LTSR).

The NLR had always been closely associated with the London & North Western Railway (LNWR), which took over its operation in 1909, though the line was not legally absorbed until 1922. The LTSR was snapped up by the Midland Railway in 1912. But both systems retained a strong individual character even in LMS days.

▲ **A Stanier 8F Class 2-8-0 forms the backdrop as blacksmith William Thomas King gets to work at Bletchley engine shed in Buckinghamshire in 1935. Bletchley was the only steam depot in the country where railway horses were shod.**

> **Settling old scores**
> The rivalry between the London & North Western and Midland railways persisted long after the two companies had become part of the LMS. The feud took on a literally tangible form at New Street station, Birmingham, which was divided into North Western and Midland sides.
> A porter on the North Western side was once asked by an old lady where the Bristol train started from. 'Down the road, mum, the Great Western station at Snow Hill.' 'But I was told Bristol trains ran from here'. 'Yes, mum, but you wouldn't want to go on the bloody Midland, would you?'

The GWR refused, however, and in the end, R.E.L. Maunsell of the Southern Railway lent them the drawings for his new Lord Nelson Class which, with suitable modifications, enabled the LMS to create what was to become one of the most famous locomotives in the world – the Royal Scot. The locomotive began operating in the summer of 1927.

A commercial drive to attract traffic, both goods and passenger, was launched in 1932 under the leadership of Ashton Davies, an extrovert personality from the LYR. Davies encouraged competition among LMS staff by featuring their achievements in two new house journals – *Quota News* for sales performance and *On Time* for operating performance.

At the same time, Stamp tried to safeguard the future of locomotive development by relieving Fowler of his post as CME and settling him upstairs as assistant to the Vice-President for Works. As a temporary measure, he was succeeded by E.J.H. Lemon, an efficiency expert, who had transformed much LMS workshop practice.

## Fear of fireworks

In his search for a permanent replacement, Stamp faced a familiar problem. 'If I'd put a North Western man in,' he recalled, 'they'd have had a banquet at Crewe followed by fireworks in the park. If I'd appointed someone from the Midland, all Crewe would have been in revolt. It had to be someone from outside.'

Stamp chose William Stanier, chief assistant to C.B. Collett, CME of the Great Western. Stanier introduced with modifications, the best features of GWR locomotive designs, culminating in the splendid Pacifics of the late 1930s.

Even more important was the proliferation of efficient work-horses, such as the Black Fives, the 8F Class for heavy goods and the excellent suburban tank engines.

In 1938, Stamp was able to announce that, 'The policy of standardization, coupled with the construction of more powerful types...has enabled the number of locomotives since the amalgamation to be reduced from 10,396 to 7,688...to perform no less work, while the reduction in the number of types has been from 404 to 162, and on the completion of work now authorized the stock will be 7,458 of 132 types, and of course the end is not yet.'

By the time World War II broke out a year later, the LMS presented the image of a great company under strong management. It had a prestige streamlined train, the Coronation Scot, matching the rival streamliners of the LNER on the East Coast route. And since 1937, it had maintained an average speed of 96.5km/h (60mph) for its express services between major centres.

There was, however, another side to the coin. Stamp, in spite of his brilliant mind, lacked an instinctive feel for the railway and what was happening at the grass roots. There was dirt and shabbiness in many places. Locomotives were not

◀ **A Garratt-type locomotive, No 4994, passes Elstree in Middlesex with a train of coal empties bound for Toton Yard, just north of Trent in 1931. By this time, the LMS was moving some 85 million tonnes (tons) of coal a year, of which $6\frac{1}{2}$ million tonnes (tons) was for its own use. The company's requirements were said to keep 26,500 miners employed.**

cleaned as they had been, while stations were obscured by ill-planned, small-scale commercial developments promoted by the Estate Department. There was talk of rebuilding Euston station – a mixture of muddled inconvenience and dilapidated grandeur – but the war intervened.

And although management was high-powered at the top level, it was strangely uninterested in developments on other railways. For example, it failed to emulate the GWR in promoting larger-capacity wagons for coal traffic, or in introducing Automatic Train Control (apart from a small-scale experiment).

Nor was its safety record particularly good, especially compared to that of the GWR. It had no enthusiasm for mainline electrification. And its centralized, autocratic style of management had a depressing effect on morale.

Stamp's tragic death in an air raid in 1941, which also claimed the lives of his wife and son, left a gap filled by the promotion to President (though not Chairman) of his Vice-President for Finance and Services, Sir William Wood.

Wood took over at a time when the railway was struggling with vastly increased traffic and insufficient maintenance – problems which persisted into peacetime. The LMS was still grappling with these when the government announced its plans for public ownership of the railways. The company played a leading role in the propaganda war against nationalization, but the campaign was doomed to fail. The English component of the country's greatest railway was merged in British Railways as the awkwardly named London Midland Region from 1 January 1948. The Scottish component dominated the Scottish Region of BR.

The LMS was big in its physical size; in the character of its top men; in its achievements; even in its mistakes. It may, indeed, have been too big – but it was impressive.

▼ **Immaculate in its blue and silver livery, the first of the Stanier streamlined Pacifics, No 6220 *Coronation*, emerges from Crewe Works in May 1937. A month later, on a press run from Euston to Crewe, *Coronation* notched up 183.5km/h (114mph), taking the world speed record for steam traction from the LNER.**

# The Great Western Railway

**Known as God's Wonderful Railway, the GWR enjoyed a unique reputation for style, efficiency and innovation. It groomed one of its expresses to become the fastest train in the world and started a revolution in locomotive engineering that made it the envy of its peers.**

When the Railways Act of 1921 set up the Big Four railway companies, the Great Western Railway (GWR) had already existed for 86 years. Its original 190km (118 mile) broad-gauge line from London to Bristol had been completed in 1841, and within five years trains were averaging speeds of over 96.5km/h (60mph) between Paddington and Didcot.

The broad-gauge line was extended further in the years that followed, but the problems of interchanging with standard-gauge lines were too great, and the final stretches were converted to standard-gauge in May 1892. This left the GWR poised to benefit from the railway boom of the next two decades.

Under the 1921 Act, the territories of the Big Four were divided into more-or-less separate geographical areas. Three of the new giants – the Southern (SR), the London, Midland & Scottish (LMS) and the London & North Eastern (LNER) – included several major constituent companies, each with its own traditions, structure and approach, and this made the coming together a difficult and painful process.

By contrast, the Great Western Railway was the single dominant company in its area. Even the six main Welsh railways which were classified as constituent companies were relatively small, and each of them provided only one director on the enlarged GWR board.

In the early 1900s, the GWR's Locomotive and Carriage Superintendent, George Jackson Churchward, had initiated a revolution in locomotive engineering that left the other British railways far behind. Indeed, at the Stockton & Darlington centenary celebrations in 1925, the LNER carried out some industrial espionage to discover the secrets of the valve gear used on the Great Western's Castle Class locomotives.

One of Churchward's rare failures had occurred in 1908 with the building of *The Great Bear*, Britain's first Pacific express locomotive. In the

**▼ A member of the 4-6-0 King Class, No 6011 *King James I*, storms past Gerrard's Cross on the way from Paddington to Birkenhead in 1946. The Kings, introduced in 1927 as the most powerful express locomotives in Britain, remained the flagships of the GWR until nationalization 20 years later.**

**◀ This poster extolling the virtues of Cornwall was an early product of the GWR's ever active publicity department. It promoted the company through a whole range of products, including books, postcards, decorative luggage labels and jigsaw puzzles. It even marketed Great Western Whisky, a special blend sold at the Great Western Royal Hotel at Paddington station.**

1920s, it was dismantled and many of its parts were used in the construction of one of the new Castles. Thereafter, the 4-6-0 wheel arrangement was employed by the Great Western for its main passenger and mixed-traffic services.

C.B. Collett, who succeeded Churchward in 1922, developed the four-cylinder Stars into the Castles and Kings for express passenger duties. He also converted one of the two-cylinder Saints into the first of the mixed-traffic Halls, with 1.75m (6ft) diameter coupled wheels. Other mixed-traffic 4-6-0s of the GWR were the Granges, the Manors and the Counties.

Although Churchward had adopted superheating in the 1900s, the heating surface used was relatively small. It took the company's main works at Swindon a long time to realize the advantages of large superheaters, and this deficiency was not rectified until F.W. Hawksworth took over as Chief Mechanical Engineer during World War II.

The GWR was also noted for the standard of its coaches, their broad-gauge origins giving several inches of extra width. In the 1920s and 1930s, their appearance was improved, with steel panelling being used to clad the wooden bodywork, which was itself mounted on a steel underframe.

In 1935, a pair of restaurant cars with air-conditioning was built, although the cooling came from a tonne (ton) of ice in a box on the underframe. Some excellent open excursion stock was also constructed and, on race specials to Newbury, a full lunch would be served at every seat during the 83.75km (52 mile) journey from London.

In 1933, the GWR introduced its first diesel railcar, its bodywork being streamlined to match the mood of the times. This particular example was intended for suburban work along the Thames Valley, but the next three were built for a fast business service between Birmingham and Cardiff, for which a supplement was charged.

Some later vehicles had transmissions which permitted trailing loads to be hauled on branch lines, while another was used for parcels services, one of its main duties being to distribute confectionery from Lyons's factory at Kensington. After the start of World War II, a batch of second generation cars was ordered, which set the pattern for most of the later British Railways designs.

## Publicity pays

The Great Western had always recognized the importance of publicity, and as early as 1903 it had begun promoting itself as the Holiday Line. In 1914, the GWR's own film, *The Story of the Holiday Line*, shown at the London Coliseum, had made one critic realize 'to what an extent the Great Western holds the key to the Empire's most celebrated travel shrines and places of pilgrimage'.

Later, the GWR produced its annual *Holiday Haunts* – a far more substantial publication than any of today's holiday brochures – listing the attractions of each resort covered by its lines, and the accommodation available. In the late 1920s, there were famous five shilling excursions from London to Swindon to see the King Class

**▼ Passengers bustle through the entrance of the GWR's newly rebuilt station at Newton Abbot, Devon in 1927. So pleased were local residents that they presented all the public clocks for the new station.**

locomotives being built, with the return trip being worked by one of the new engines.

Useful publicity was also generated by the quest for speed, and one of the GWR expresses – the Cheltenham Flyer – was groomed to become the fastest train in the world. This record was first achieved in 1929, with a booked average of 106km/h (66mph) from Swindon to Paddington. Two years later, the Canadian Pacific took the record, but in 1931 the GWR struck back, raising the average to 111km/h (69mph).

On the first day of the new timing, a special attempt was made, and *Launceston Castle* completed the journey at an average of 125.5km/h (78mph). A year later, there was a further cut of two minutes, which lifted the booked speed over the 112.5km/h (70mph) mark for the first time anywhere in the world. This was preceded by an all-out publicity run, during which *Tregenna Castle* reached Paddington in 56 minutes 47 seconds – an average of 132km/h (82mph).

▲ **A line of King Class locomotives poses outside the running sheds at Swindon in 1930. The Kings were often used to haul trainloads of holidaymakers to the seaside. Serving coastal resorts from the Irish Sea to the English Channel, the GWR fully justified its claim to be the Holiday Line.**

## The coming of the Kings

The Great Western operated a number of named expresses, the Cornish Riviera Limited being one of the best known. Introduced in 1904, it ran non-stop from Paddington to Plymouth throughout the summer, the slipping of coaches *en route* reducing the load so it could be worked over the steep south Devon banks without having to stop for an assisting locomotive. It was initially routed via Bristol until the Castle Cary cut-off opened two years later.

When the Kings entered service in the late 1920s, the time for the 363.75km (226 miles) was cut by seven minutes to an even four hours. In 1935, when the new Centenary coaches were introduced to mark the anniversary of the GWR's formation, the train was nominally non-stop to Truro on weekdays, though on Saturdays its first stop was as far west at St Erth. However, as Kings were forbidden to cross Saltash Bridge, a stop had to be made at Plymouth to change locomotives.

A new express, the Bristolian, was introduced the same year between Paddington and Bristol, and averaged over 108km/h (67mph) non-stop in each direction.

## Marine activities

Running trains was not the only activity of the GWR. After Grouping, it emerged as the largest dock company in the world, the installations on the Welsh side of the Bristol Channel taking pride of place. Although built mainly for coal export, they also handled vast quantities of imports, including cattle on the hoof, with express goods trains running to the Midlands and London.

Coal production declined, however, during the 1920s and 1930s, and the Welsh ports also lost

business to Southampton and London. But they were to come into their own again during World War II, receiving huge quantities of war materials from across the Atlantic, including many of the US S160 2-8-0s.

Like a number of the major pre-Grouping companies, the GWR operated its own shipping services. From Weymouth there were passenger and cargo sailings to the Channel Islands, while a subsidiary, the Fishguard & Rosslare Railways & Harbour Company, operated services from west Wales to Rosslare and Wexford. After Grouping, a number of new ships were built, and several of these were 'called up' at the outbreak of war.

The *St David*, serving as a hospital ship, was sunk off Italy in 1944. Earlier, others on the Irish services had been attacked by enemy aircraft, the *St Patrick* being sunk in 1941, with the loss of 30 lives, including the captain. Their post-war replacements had the GWR coat of arms prominently embossed on their hulls, a feature which remained after nationalization.

## Fortunes of war

World War II saw an enormous increase in rail traffic, not least on the GWR. During 1939, 84.5 million passengers travelled on the Great Western. Five years later, the total was more than 147 million. The kilometres run by its freight trains also increased by ten per cent at this time. Among the items transported were works of art from the National Gallery and elsewhere in London, which were stored at safe sites in the country.

There were several periods of exceptional activity, starting with the evacuation of children from London and five other areas in September 1939. On the first day, 58 trains, with 44,000 passengers on board, left London's Ealing Broadway station at nine-minute intervals. After the German invasion of the Low Countries in 1940, yet more people were evacuated, this time from Kent and East Anglia. All told, the Great Western ran over 500 special trains in the first 12

**▲ Headed by a King Class locomotive, the Cornish Riviera Express thunders along the coast between Dawlish and Teignmouth in 1936. According to a GWR publicity handout, the train had become 'the real live fairy tale of millions of holidaymakers...and given a world-wide prominence to some of the finest holiday resorts in the country'.**

**▶ In 1935, the GWR, anxious to enhance its modern image, streamlined two of its locomotives, a King and a Castle – the latter seen here outside Old Oak Common Shed in London. But the new design, with its bullet nose and flared cab, had few admirers, and both engines soon reverted to their original appearance.**

▶ **A luggage label proclaims the GWR's world-famous train, the Cheltenham Spa Express, more usually known by its unofficial title of the Cheltenham Flyer. The train made its first record-breaking run in 1929, when it travelled from Swindon to Paddington at a booked average speed of 106km/h (66mph).**

months of the war, conveying more than 285,000 evacuees.

When the flying bomb onslaught began on London in 1944, there was a further evacuation, while thousands of shelters were moved into the capital to protect those who had to remain. It was in the middle of this emergency that Paddington station was closed for the first time ever.

This unprecedented event occurred on Saturday, 29 July, when the station was besieged by thousands of people wanting to get away from London for the Bank Holiday weekend. It was only after the GWR's general manager, Sir James Milne, had intervened directly with the Ministry of War Transport that permission was given to use the extra locomotives and coaches available.

To help handle the wartime traffic, a sum of 16,000 women joined the Great Western's staff. This was roughly comparable to the number of men who left to join the forces, of whom almost 1,000 were killed on active service. Many of those remaining at work on the railway showed great bravery during air attacks, and one of them, Norman Tunna, who worked as a shunter at Birkenhead, was awarded the George Cross for extinguishing fires in wagons carrying high explosive bombs.

Although the end of the war signalled the end of danger, the country remained in the grip of austerity. Coal, steel, oil, and timber – all the ingredients essential for economic recovery – were in desperately short supply. Nevertheless, post-war shortages did not stop the GWR from developing new locomotives and rolling stock. These included the mixed-traffic 4-6-0s of the County Class, a batch of Castles with three-row superheaters, and the 94XX Class pannier tank, distinguished by its taper boiler.

Two gas-turbine engines were also ordered, but they proved costly to operate and were withdrawn. By now, the GWR and the other three giants of the Grouping had ceased to exist, their place taken by the even bigger giant of British Railways.

## Gone With Regret

In the course of its 112 year existence, the Great Western Railway had become an integral part of the community it served, being known to users and enthusiasts as God's Wonderful Railway. When it disappeared after nationalization in 1948, the railway's admirers saw its initials as standing for Gone With Regret.

▼ **A motor tractor bumps over the cobbles at Paddington station in 1931, pulling an old horse dray. The GWR replaced horses with these small tractors, which were more versatile for use in confined spaces.**

# The London & North Eastern Railway

**Stretching from Scotland to East Anglia, the LNER was a railway of contrasts and contradictions. Yet its line-up of express passenger trains was second to none, and its plan for the future of the railways had some uncannily prophetic elements.**

Each of the four companies which came into existence as a result of the 1923 Grouping had a marked individuality – none more so than the London & North Eastern Railway (LNER). It had, on the face of it, many difficulties. Its long and straggling system earned it the nickname of the 'London and Nearly Everywhere Railway'.

It paid its shareholders the lowest dividends. It was more dependent on freight than any of the other companies, and its main goods traffic – coal, iron and steel, agricultural products, meat and fish – were all hard hit by the long depression of the 1920s and early 1930s. On the other hand, its best passenger trains were second to none and its management morale was strong.

The LNER board, under the effective chairmanship of William Whitelaw, a Scottish landowner and industrialist (and grandfather of the present Lord Whitelaw), chose a decentralized organization. Below a Chief General Manager (CGM) were three Divisional General Managers who, in effect, ran three separate areas.

The Southern Area, with headquarters at London's Liverpool Street station, comprised the

**▼ A mixture of smoke and steam envelops King's Cross station at Easter 1933, as four Gresley Pacifics wait to tackle the East Coast mainline route. Centre stage is Class A1 No 2547 *Donovan*, while next to it is No 4475 *Flying Fox*, appropriately coupled to the Flying Scotsman train itself.**

◀ **A somewhat sceptical looking passenger collects a ticket for the LNER's cinema car, about to make its demonstration run between King's Cross and Peterborough in 1935. The coach, a converted bogie brake van, could seat 44, and had a sloping floor and back-projection screen. Admission price was one shilling.**

'Three Greats' of former days – the Great Northern (GNR), Great Central and Great Eastern. The North Eastern Area, based on York, was in effect the North Eastern Railway (NER), plus the Hull & Barnsley.

The Scottish Area, based on Edinburgh, comprised the North British Railway and (after a few years as an area in its own right) the little Great North of Scotland Railway, with headquarters at Aberdeen.

## Top brass recruitment

The whole enterprise was nevertheless effectively pulled together under the CGM's office at King's Cross. The first CGM was Sir Ralph Wedgwood from the NER, a distinguished and experienced railwayman. He was ably supported by a small, shrewd Scotsman, Robert Bell, also from the NER, who as Assistant General Manager personally recruited university graduates and a few selected staff into management training and planned their subsequent careers more thoroughly than was done in any other mainline company.

The system itself was full of contrasts – for example, between the finely engineered track of the East Coast main line and the straggling branches in East Anglia, or between the splendid ex-NER stations at York and Newcastle and the down-at-heel ex-GNR station at Peterborough.

Whereas the Southern electrified its suburban services as quickly as possible, the huge daily movement into and out of Liverpool Street was handled in cramped carriages hauled by ageing little tank engines – 'Gobblers' and 'Buckjumpers' – performing miracles of effort that belied their diminutive size.

But out of Liverpool Street also ran the Hook Continental, a more luxurious boat-train than any, except perhaps the Southern's Golden Arrow. King's Cross despatched the Flying Scotsman complete with a hairdressing salon and other comforts, and night sleeping car trains to Newcastle, Edinburgh, Aberdeen, Glasgow, Fort William and even little Lossiemouth on the Moray Firth.

**Royal bonanza**

Camping coaches were a popular form of self-catering holiday accommodation in the 1930s, with the railway companies placing old vehicles in attractive areas and equipping them with kitchens, toilets and washing facilities. The peak weekly rental charged by the LNER was around £2, and since its coaches could take up to six holidaymakers, this was a bargain price.

The company, however, was quick to take advantage of a sudden consumer demand. This occurred during the Coronation week in 1937 – George VI and Queen Elizabeth were being crowned – when London was invaded by thousands of sightseers. The LNER placed 52 camping coaches at various sites around the capital, charging £10 per coach – five times the normal rent.

▶ **Standing by *Sir Nigel Gresley*, the 100th Pacific to be built at Doncaster, the machine's designer (left) receives a special award in 1937. LNER Chairman William Whitelaw is presenting Gresley with a miniature silver replica of the engine.**

▲ **The LNER's new London–Edinburgh express service, Coronation, races over the Royal Border Bridge at Berwick in the late 1930s. At the end of the train is the 'beaver-tail' observation car, with its modernistic design and luxury seating. At dusk and dawn the car's interior lights were dimmed to give passengers a better view of the scenery.**

Like the other Grouped companies in 1923, the LNER had a legacy of overworked motive power from the World War I period, and an urgent need for replacements. But money was tight and plans to electrify the track between York and Newcastle had to be shelved.

However, in Herbert Nigel Gresley (Sir Nigel after 1936) from the Great Northern, the railway had the Chief Mechanical Engineer (CME) it needed. Grandiose schemes for building large numbers of new standard locomotives were not possible, nor did Gresley propose them: instead, he built small batches specially designed for a particular type of traffic or a particular district.

## Man of ideas

Gresley certainly enjoyed the admiration evoked by his splendid-looking Pacifics for the principal mainline expresses. Furthermore, he standardized the Great Northern type of bow-ended, teak-bodied carriages, the buck-eye coupling, the principle of articulation and the semi-rigid Pullman-type gangway connection.

Gresley's policies produced a mixed bag of types. His Pacifics were steadily improved from the A1 to the A3 Class and the final streamlined world-beaters, the A4s, including the famous 203km/h (126mph) record-holder *Mallard*. The B17 Sandringham 4-6-0s were satisfactory (if rough riding); but the Hunt and Shire 4-4-0s were much less popular with drivers, and the striking P2 2-8-2 giants designed for Scotland needed rebuilding to be really useful.

The V2 2-6-2 was the nearest to a successful general-purpose locomotive designed by Gresley, and it was to bear the main burden of heavy wartime duties between 1939 and 1945. Eventually, 184 of the class were built.

The LNER's famous trio of streamlined 'High Speed Trains' (anticipating BR's use of this title by 40 years) originated in a study by Gresley of the German high speed diesel train, *Flying Hamburger*, which led him to suggest that, with streamlining, similar speeds could be obtained with steam traction.

Accordingly, in 1935 the Silver Jubilee service started to run between King's Cross and Newcastle in four hours, followed by the Coronation to Edinburgh in six hours and the West Riding Limited to Leeds and Bradford in

▶ **Marking the 50th anniversary of the Flying Scotsman service in 1938, the Stirling single No 1, with a special from King's Cross, steams into Stevenage station in Hertfordshire. Here passengers transferred from the nineteenth century coaches to the new Flying Scotsman train hauled by No 4498 *Sir Nigel Gresley*.**

just over three hours. Norwich was later served by a less glamorous East Anglian express, with only the locomotive streamlined.

While the best express trains were much admired, the commuter services around London left a lot to be desired. But the LNER board could not be expected to invest large sums while the financial position was so difficult; for instance, the LNER net revenue fell from £13.1 million in 1929 to £7.2 million in 1932.

## Schemes for improvement

In 1933, the government offered cheap credit to the railways for modernization, mainly to stimulate employment. The LNER put forward two electrification schemes, one for the main Manchester–Sheffield–Wath freight route through the Pennines, and the other for the overcrowded suburban line from Liverpool Street as far as Shenfield in Essex.

At the same time, London Transport agreed to take over and electrify several LNER London suburban routes. Work on all these schemes was well under way when war broke out in 1939, and most of them had to be left uncompleted until after the war had ended.

However, because freight was the LNER's main business, money had been found earlier to build a pair of mechanized marshalling yards at Whitemoor, near March in Cambridgeshire, which were a model of advanced technology for their time.

In addition to being the largest dock owner among the Big Four railways, the LNER had a sizeable shipping business, the pride of which was the night service between Parkeston Quay (Harwich) and the Hook of Holland. There were also two cargo fleets, as well as a ferry service for freight trains between Harwich and Zeebrugge.

Another source of much needed revenue for the LNER was its hotels, though perhaps only the Great Eastern at Liverpool Street, the Royal Station at York and the North British in Edinburgh were grand enough to rival the biggest that the LMS was able to offer.

Some sections of the LNER were strong in the provision of restaurant cars. The King's Cross–Leeds cars were much appreciated by Yorkshire businessmen, as was the catering on the Anglo-Scottish services, especially the Flying Scotsman and later, of course, on the streamlined High Speed Trains.

Towards the end of the 1930s, the LNER leadership changed. William Whitelaw was succeeded as chairman in 1938 by Sir Ronald Matthews, a Sheffield industrial magnate, and Wedgwood as CGM in 1939 by Sir Charles Newton, an accountant by profession. In 1941, Gresley died, and a ex-NER man, Edward Thompson became CME. Thompson had often chafed under Gresley's domination, and he immediately began to rebuild his predecessor's earlier Pacifics – an operation which did nothing to improve their appearance.

During World War II, the LNER suffered heavily from bomb damage in London, Hull, Sunderland, York and many other places in the eastern half of Britain. The workshops were turned over to war production and the shipping fleet was requisitioned by the government, several ships being sunk by enemy action.

**▲ Elegance and sophistication are the keynotes of this 1930s poster publicizing the Flying Scotsman. Although freight was the lifeblood of the LNER, it preferred to project the idea that its main business was carrying people.**

**▶ A party of German railway officials watches coal wagons being rolled into sorting sidings at Wath marshalling yard, near Barnsley in Yorkshire in 1927. The LNER had the highest average wagon capacity of all the railways – rising from 11.25 tonnes (tons) in 1923 to 12 tonnes (tons) in 1932.**

The end of the war found all the railways tired to exhaustion, with heavy arrears of track maintenance and an urgent need for new locomotives and rolling stock. But threat of nationalization cast a cloud over the post-war planning that had been carried out by the Railway Companies' Association, and the LNER played its full part in organizing protests against a takeover.

However, the LNER made a decision which the other companies declined to follow: it produced a suggested 'landlord and tenant' scheme as an alternative to outright nationalization. Under it, the government would buy the infrastructure – track, stations and fixed equipment – but grant leases or franchises to the railway companies to run trains over the state network. (There was a curious, almost prophetic, hint here of some of the ideas on privatization that were to be current in the 1990s.)

However, the then Labour government was committed to full nationalization and the LNER, together with the other mainline companies, ceased to exist at midnight on 31 December 1947. It bequeathed to BR a detailed scheme for replacing steam on the East Coast mainline with diesel locomotives – a scheme vetoed by the new LMS-dominated mechanical engineers in BR.

But no one could deny the success of Robert Bell's recruitment policies, as was demonstrated by the number of former LNER officers who quickly assumed senior positions in British Railways. The traditions of the LNER were to leave a long-lasting impression.

**▼ Headed by a B12/3 Class 4-6-0, No 8517, the new Hook Continental boat-train waits at Parkeston Quay (Harwich) in 1938. The train, finished in varnished teak panelling, was sound-proofed throughout and incorporated the most up-to-date systems of heating and air-conditioning.**

# The Southern Railway

**To some, the Southern Railway was the vital link between London and its suburbs. To others, it was the gateway to the summer holiday resorts of the south coast. Either way, this smallest of the Big Four railway companies provided a unique blend of steam and electric power.**

The Southern Railway (SR) was essentially in the business of catering for people. Unlike the other three mainline companies created by the Grouping of 1923, most of its revenue came from passengers, although the port of Southampton, which it owned and managed, generated large quantities of freight.

Born of an amalgamation of the South Eastern & Chatham Railway (SECR), the London, Brighton & South Coast Railway (LBSCR) and the London & South Western Railway (LSWR), the Southern, with only 3,540.5km (2,200 miles) of route, was the smallest of the Big Four. However, it would also prove to be one of the most enterprising, as it accommodated and, indeed, encouraged the hectic between-the-wars expansion of the London suburbs.

Sensibly, the territories of the old constituent companies became sections of the new SR – Western, Central and Eastern. In the early years, this allowed the continuity of timetables and day-to-day running, although a serious mistake was made in not tidying up the overall management soon enough.

To begin with, the three general managers continued in parallel – they were each paid £7,500 a year, a veritable fortune in the days when a working man was lucky to get £150 – and their unanimous agreement was needed for every major decision. However, common sense eventually prevailed and in January 1924 Herbert Walker from the South Western was put in overall command.

## Sense of fair play

Born in 1868, Walker had joined the London & North Western Railway (LNWR) at the age of 17, eventually becoming outdoor Goods Manager for its southern area. In 1911, aged 43, he had been appointed General Manager of the LSWR. Although he had a reputation for being a disciplinarian, he was also known for his keen sense of fair play – as the LNWR *Athletic Gazette* put it, he was 'very just and ready to stand by his staff'.

It was this giant of a man who was to dominate the SR for more than a decade, welding it into the equivalent of a great family business. To most of his employees, Walker *was* the Southern.

**▶ This photograph of a young enthusiast chatting to the friendly driver of a towering King Arthur was the inspiration for one of the most famous railway posters of all time. The poster helped to establish SR's image as the Sunshine Line.**

◀ **A train enters Tolworth station in Surrey, inaugurating the latest phase of the SR's electrification programme, which began in 1925. In contrast to such modernistic stations as Tolworth – note the streamlined canopy roof and porthole lighting – most of the SR electric stock was formed from old coaches mounted on new underframes.**

▼ **A Dover-bound Bulleid Pacific, No 21C157 – it was later to be named *Biggin Hill* – hauls the *Golden Arrow* boat-train away from Victoria station shortly after World War II. Introduced in 1929, the train was withdrawn at the outbreak of war but began running again soon after the end of hostilities. In 1961, it went over to electric traction, making its final run in 1972.**

Prospects for the new company were hardly encouraging. From the 1920s all of Britain's railways faced growing economic difficulties. World War I had pushed up wages and run down the systems, with trams and, later, buses eating into the suburban traffic in the larger towns and cities. The situation was at its worst in London, where commuter lines, especially those inherited from the SECR, were the subject of music hall jokes.

The onset of the Great Depression in 1929 compounded the problem. Many rural lines lost up to half of their passengers within a few years. Walker believed that the Southern's salvation lay in electrification – not only of the London suburban lines, but also of those to the south coast. Using the third-rail system which he had introduced so successfully on the LSWR, Walker pursued the programme on the SR with his characteristic vigour. In 1923, the Southern had only 124km (77 miles) of electrified route; by 1939 it had 2,830.75km (1,759 miles).

The new services were quicker, cleaner, cheaper and more reliable than steam, and travellers responded accordingly. In 1923, the weekday average of kilometres travelled on the SR was 209,214 (130,000 miles); by 1938 it was 273,588 (170,000 miles).

**The Big Four**

With the end of World War I, a passionate debate broke out over the future of the railways. In 1914, the government had taken control of the 120 or so independent railway companies, and there were many, including the rail unions, who believed this temporary control should give way to outright public ownership.

The government accepted that, with the railways run down and costs escalating, a return to the cut-throat competition of pre-war days would be disastrous. It was opposed, however, to full-blooded nationalization, preferring instead to group the railway companies into larger units – a policy which came into effect on 1 January 1923, with the emergence of the Big Four.

## Suburban migration

The social implications of these improved services were enormous. As previously inaccessible places were brought within easy reach of the capital, thousands flocked to the leafy new housing estates of suburbia. This migration was actively encouraged by the Southern, which made commercial arrangements with several house builders. The company even published a popular *Residential Guide: The Country at London's Door*. The builders, for their

part, often helped to finance the construction of a station to serve their new developments.

The flagship station of the Southern, however, was Waterloo, the rebuilding of which had been completed by the LSWR in 1922, just in time to hand over to its successor. The terminus exuded an almost regal air, with its largely upper and middle class clientele moving off each evening to the new stockbroker belt of Surrey and north Hampshire.

Not that the SR's other London termini – Victoria, Charing Cross, London Bridge and Cannon Street – were inconsequential. From Victoria, for example, ran the Southern Belle (later renamed the Brighton Belle). From here, too, departed day-trippers to Ramsgate and Margate and boat-train passengers to the Channel ports.

Dover and Folkestone were well served by Southern ships, which sailed to France at frequent intervals. Each vessel could accommodate over 1,000 passengers, plus luggage, and there were lounges, bars, smoking rooms and restaurants for two classes of passenger.

## Cross-Channel luxury

The most luxurious of these cross-Channel steamers was the 3,000-tonne (ton) *Canterbury*, launched by the SR in May 1929. This plied between Dover and Calais and was reserved exclusively for passengers on the *Golden Arrow*, the company's newly inaugurated first-class only Pullman boat-train from Victoria.

▲ **Some of the men rescued from Dunkirk in May 1940 receive refreshments. The Southern Railway handled almost 300,000 troops during the hectic eight days of the evacuation, ferrying them in 567 special trains slotted in to cause minimal disruption to the normal timetable.**

For those passengers who wished to avoid the inconvenience of transferring from train to ship and ship to train, the Southern in 1936 offered a novel alternative – the *Night Ferry*. Consisting of six Wagon-Lits sleeping cars, this travelled the long distance from Victoria to Paris, crossing the Channel from Dover to Dunkirk aboard one of the company's specially built train-ferries.

But the Southern's main connection with the sea was Southampton, whose docks the LSWR had prudently acquired in 1892. To Walker, the port was the 'jewel in the crown' of the SR, and he was determined to add to its lustre. In 1930, the SR embarked on a massive £8 million extension – a bold gamble given the stormy economic climate.

The gamble paid off, however, and Southampton, with its newly expanded facilities, attracted the world's major shipping lines. Many famous passenger ships, including the newly built *Queen Mary*, called at the port, each being met by Ocean Liner specials from Waterloo.

## Getting up steam

At its formation, the Southern Railway was unquestionably a steam railway, with a huge stock of 2,285 elderly locomotives. This ageing fleet was not replenished during the 1920s because of

Walker's electrification programme, which severely restricted the scope of the SR's Chief Mechanical Engineer, Richard Maunsell, for developing steam locomotives.

Fortunately, during his years on the SECR, Maunsell had rebuilt in superheated form a large number of 4-4-0s, which made them particularly efficient machines for hauling the heavy Continental boat-trains and the Brighton and West of England line expresses. Useful work had also been done by R.W. Urie of the LSWR, whose rugged 4-6-0s Maunsell used as the basis for the renowned King Arthur Class, launched in 1925.

In 1926, the SR produced another express locomotive, the 4-6-0 *Lord Nelson* – the first in a class that would include 16 engines. It was instantly hailed by the Southern's publicity department as 'the most powerful passenger express engine in Britain', an honour which it lost barely 12 months later to one of the Great Western's King Class.

**▼ The grand frontage of Waterloo station, seen here in 1936, was very much in keeping with the station's high class clientele – civil servants, City gents, Army officers – who commuted between the capital and the Home Counties. Other Waterloo regulars included passengers travelling on the Ocean Liner specials that served Southampton.**

Nevertheless, so impressed was the LMS with the *Nelson* that it borrowed the design drawings to use as a basis for its first passenger express engine, the *Royal Scot*, which went into service in 1927.

In 1930, Maunsell produced the first of his Schools Class engines, the most powerful 4-4-0s ever to run in Britain. Together with the Nelsons and Arthurs, these remained the SR's regular top express motive power until after the outbreak of World War II.

By then, the SR had a new Chief Mechanical Engineer, Oliver Bulleid. (It also had a new general manager, since Walker himself had stepped down in 1937, soon after Maunsell's departure.) Often described as 'the last giant of steam', Bulleid, in 1941, introduced the famous Merchant Navy Class of 4-6-2s, with their air-smoothed casings and Bulleid-Firth-Brown Boxpok wheels. These and the smaller West Country Class 4-6-2s were to stay in service until the end of steam.

## Casualties of war

The Southern made a vital contribution to World War II, helping not only in the evacuation from Dunkirk and the D-Day landings at Normandy, but also in the movement of non-essential civilians

from the Kent coast area. Being closest to occupied France, Southern installations and trains suffered badly from Luftwaffe attacks.

The Maunsell Schools locomotives were especially vulnerable, since they worked the hard-hit lines between London and the Kent coast. One hundred and seventy Southern railwaymen were killed by enemy action while on duty.

Despite the disruption of war – over 100 of its 800 stations were damaged and ten per cent of its coaching stock was put out of action – the Southern soon resumed the activity for which it was best known, the conveyancing of seaside holiday makers. By August 1947, it had reinstated its Bank Holiday specials, with Waterloo handling 72 mainline departures carrying an average of 812 passengers.

## New Pullman service

In April 1946 came the return of the *Golden Arrow* and the reopening of the sea route to France. This was followed by the reappearance of two other stars of pre-war days – the Bournemouth Belle and the Brighton Belle. In June 1947 a new Devon Belle Pullman service was introduced, offering reserved seats and an observation car – a dramatic contrast with the jam-packed corridors endured by most travellers on the railways of post-war Britain.

By October 1946 the Southern had restored over 80 per cent of its pre-war timetable; although this was reduced during the fuel crisis of the following winter, the company had good reason to feel pleased with itself. There was little time for self-congratulation, however. At midnight on 31 December 1947, the nation's rail network passed into the control of British Railways. SR and the other three mainline companies were suddenly a thing of the past.

**▲ Spectators line the quayside at Southampton docks in 1936 to watch the *Queen Mary* begin her maiden voyage to the United States. Owned and operated by the Southern Railway, the docks underwent dramatic expansion in the 1930s. By 1939, Southampton had become the premier passenger port in the country, handling almost 50 per cent of the traffic.**

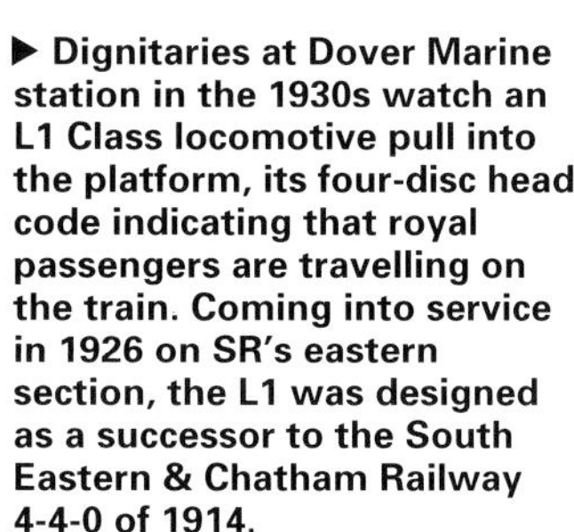

**▶ Dignitaries at Dover Marine station in the 1930s watch an L1 Class locomotive pull into the platform, its four-disc head code indicating that royal passengers are travelling on the train. Coming into service in 1926 on SR's eastern section, the L1 was designed as a successor to the South Eastern & Chatham Railway 4-4-0 of 1914.**

# The Metropolitan Railway

**Running beneath the streets of London, the Metropolitan was the world's first underground railway. Yet it was this same line that also opened up the Home Counties, encouraging thousands of city workers to take up residence amidst the rustic charms of Metroland.**

London, in 1850, was too successful for its own good. As the undisputed hub of the industrial world it drew people in vast numbers. During the preceding two decades over one million new arrivals had crammed themselves into the capital; by 1850, its population stood at 2.5 million – a level unprecedented for any city in history. And far from reaching saturation point, the expansion seemed set to continue indefinitely.

Housing the multitudes had never been a problem. Developers could – and did, vigorously – create new accommodation. But transport was another matter altogether. As they had done for centuries, people and goods moved across the city by horsepower, a method that was inefficient at best, dangerous at worst and unsanitary to say the least – the average fall of manure stood at 18kg (40lbs) per horse per day. For the present, this rudimentary infrastructure could cope. But soon, unless something better could be found, London would grind to a standstill under the sheer weight of its numbers.

Trains were the obvious solution. But where could they run? Overland was an impossibility: clearing the approach for London Bridge station alone had involved the purchase and demolition of £1.5 million worth of slum dwellings. The answer lay underground.

It was not a new concept. Since the 1830s, John Hargrave Stevens, an architect, and Charles Pearson, a solicitor, had been campaigning for an underground railway. At first, their proposals were greeted with derision. However, as the city became more and more congested, the idea of a transport system running beneath its streets began to make headway. By 1860, a detailed plan had

**▼ An artist's impression of Baker Street station, completed in 1860, three years before the MR's opening, shows a smokeless locomotive and pristine tunnel. The reality of travelling underground proved rather different, and an MR report of 1865 spoke of 'the very impure state of the atmosphere at some stations.**

▲ The 670.25m (733yd) long Clerkenwell Tunnel, bisected by a bridge carrying the 1863 tracks, was opened in 1868. But serious faults soon appeared through large quantities of drainage water building up behind the brickwork.

been debated and approved by Parliament, and in March of that year work started on the world's first underground line.

The Metropolitan Railway (MR) was to run 6km (3¾ miles) between Paddington station (Bishop's Road) and Farringdon Street in the City of London, with five intermediate stations, one serving the London & North Western Railway terminus at Euston, and another the Great Northern Railway (GNR) terminus at King's Cross. The tracks were to be mixed-gauge, to allow the passage of the Great Western Railway (GWR) broad-gauge trains which came in at Paddington. The whole project was to be built by the cut-and-cover method – in effect, a deep trench was to be dug and then covered over.

By following the course of existing roads, the planners were able to keep costs and overground obstructions to a minimum. However, below ground they faced a logistical nightmare. The soil was riddled with gas mains, water mains and sewers – set 'as close together as the pipes of a church organ' – the accumulation of decades of haphazard, cost-cutting construction. And at King's Cross they faced the fearsome prospect of the Fleet Ditch, a Stygian canal of sewage that flowed from Highgate to the Thames, carrying the effluent of 50,000 houses. In adverse conditions, its level could rise 2m (6ft) in one hour.

The mains were painstakingly diverted, which allowed the tunnellers to cut their way 'with the delicacy of a surgical operation'. And the Fleet was eventually channelled into a vast metal tube. But even when all the tunnelling was done, there remained one further problem: Parliament insisted that the locomotives emit neither steam nor smoke.

Such a thing was unheard of. But the engineers duly set to work. John Fowler of the MR produced a prototype, a broad-gauge 2-4-0T, which used white hot firebricks instead of coke to maintain steam pressure in the tunnel sections. Emissions were to be further reduced by condensing the steam through a cold water tank under the boiler.

A trial run was arranged for 24 May 1862, carrying a group that included the Chancellor of the Exchequer and future Prime Minister, W.E. Gladstone. But it was a dismal failure, and Fowler's Ghost, as it became known, was consigned to the scrapyard. In its place came a design by Daniel Gooch, Locomotive Superintendent of the GWR, which had accepted a contract to work the MR.

## Air and water leaks

Gooch did not try to repeat Fowler's experiment with firebricks. But his engines, again broad-gauge 2-4-0 tanks, did incorporate two large cold water tanks under the boiler to condense the exhaust steam. Although an improvement on Fowler's Ghost, the new engines had their problems. The exhaust pipes leaked both air and water, and the tanks soon overheated. Nevertheless, Parliament was satisfied, and the GWR commissioned 12 of the new locomotives, six of them named after insects, and six after foreign potentates, which arrived in time for opening day on

▼ Anxious to promote itself as a mainline railway, the MR introduced two Pullman cars on the run from London to the outer suburbs in 1910. They last worked in October 1939, after which they were converted into portable dwellings.

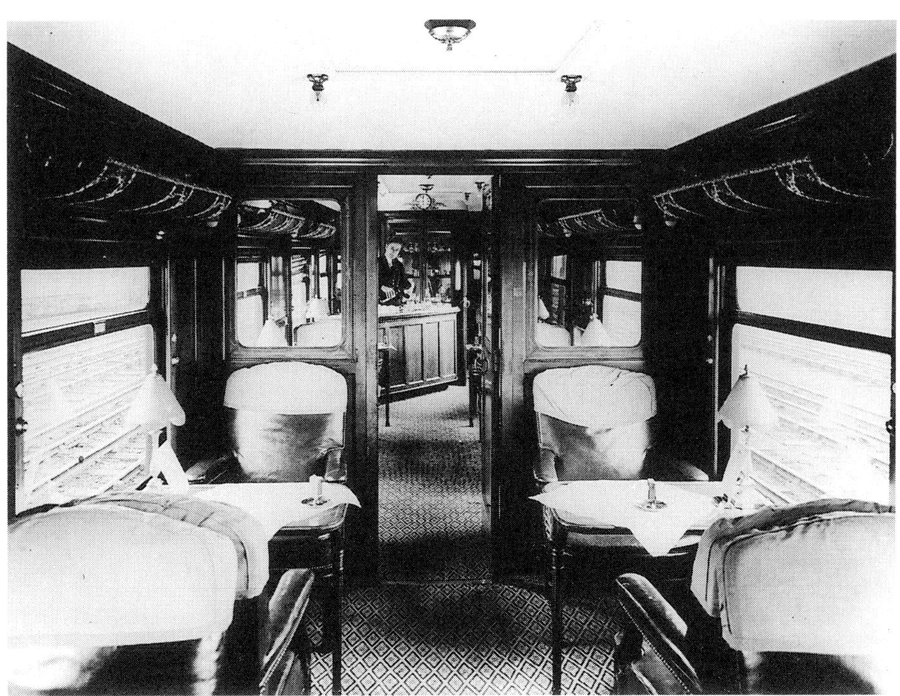

**▲ An A Class locomotive, No 23, waits at Quainton Road in Buckinghamshire in June 1933. Transferred to the London Passenger Transport Board later that month, the MR handed over 36 steam locomotives, 21 electric locomotives and 211 electric motor cars.**

10 January 1863 – almost three years after digging began.

There had been much scepticism about the enterprise. The MR's detractors called it 'the Drain' – there had been a worrying moment when the Fleet Ditch burst into the Farringdon Street works – and *The Times* claimed it was 'an insult to common sense' to suppose that people would ever give up cheap open air rides by horse bus in order 'to be driven amid palpable darkness through the foul subsoil of London'. Indeed, shortly before the MR's opening, Gooch, after spending a day in the tunnels checking on his engines, had been so overcome by fumes that he had fainted and had been unable to return to work for several weeks.

But the response of the public was rapturous. Forty thousand tickets were issued that first day, and so fierce was demand that King's Cross closed its ticket offices for an hour. In its first three weeks of operation, the MR averaged ticket sales of 29,000 per day. In March 1864, the railway felt confident enough to begin extending east to Moorgate. It was clear that the underground was here to stay.

But already there was trouble. The MR wanted its GWR contractors to run more trains, while the GWR, with a £175,000 investment in the MR, wanted priority access to shares in the profitable Moorgate extension. Neither side would budge,

**Class structure**

From its inception, the Metropolitan Railway (MR) followed standard practice by providing first, second and third-class carriages. There was, indeed, considerable suspicion of working class passengers, who were widely regarded as dirty, dangerous and dishonest. It was perhaps in the hope of weeding out such undesirables that in 1864 the MR became the first railway company in London to offer cheap fares to workmen. They could use two early morning trains at 2*d.* for the full journey, with the option of returning by any train after midday.

A worker on the Metropolitan District Railway has left a vivid picture of the average turn-of-the-century second class male railway traveller in London. He was 'generally a fine fellow', who 'smoked Guinea Gold, drank bottled beer, read Marie Corelli, bet on favourites, worshipped a fox terrier, believed Britain was a Democracy and held a commission in the Volunteers. On Saturday afternoons he fired at Wormwood Scrubs and gathered teaspoons as prizes.'

so, in August 1863, the GWR had played what it thought was its trump card. It removed all its engines from the Metropolitan.

The smaller company was uncowed. It borrowed locomotives from the GNR and LNWR, at the same time ordering 18 standard-gauge 4-4-0Ts, complete with condensing equipment, from Beyer Peacock of Manchester. These locomotives were to be the MR's mainstay from 1864 until 1905, when electrification of its city and some of its suburban services was introduced.

The new machines were certainly sturdy – one was still being used by the South Hetton Coal Company in 1948 – but they had their disadvantages. Without a cab, the driver and fireman were exposed to the elements whenever they left the tunnels. And the control of emissions fell short of Parliament's expectations. 'In the tunnels, steam and sulphur were the order of the day,' said one underground worker. Another observer described the underground railways as 'sulphurous tunnels, their stations merely holes in a grimy flute'.

## New man in the driving seat

In 1872, the MR acquired a considerable asset in the shape of its new Chairman, Sir Edward Watkin. An energetic individual, who controlled railway companies across England and even as far afield as Canada, Watkin was 'gifted with a superb imagination which made light of difficulties'. But even he winced at the many problems encountered in his latest venture.

**▶ The MR published a plethora of leaflets, brochures and postcards promoting Metroland – 'London's nearest countryside'. The name is said to have been coined by James Garland, an MR copywriter. Away with influenza in 1915, Garland claimed to have jumped out of his bed with excitement when the word came into his head.**

**▼ A party of top-hatted dignitaries, including W.E. Gladstone with his wife and the engineer John Fowler (in light coat and hat), reaches Edgware Road station during the first trial run on the MR on 24 May 1862. The train was hauled by a 2-4-0T, known as Fowler's Ghost, after its designer, but so poor was the engine's performance that it was withdrawn from service and later broken up.**

When the extension of the Metropolitan was made to Bishopsgate, for example, the company was obliged by Parliament to make good all damage incurred by its tunnelling under a Roman Catholic chapel in Moorfields. 'Altogether', Watkin reported angrily in 1875, 'we have to spend £14,500 for dealing with one structure only in the completion of this short piece of railway of about 600 or 700 yards [548.5 or 640m] between Moorgate Street and Bishopsgate Street [now Liverpool Street] stations.' The result, in his estimation, was that 'the worthy gentlemen and ladies worshipping there have a brand new edifice at the entire cost of the Metropolitan Railway.' As he told his backers, 'I hope you will be well prayed for, for, I assure you, you deserve it.'

One of the MR's greatest triumphs during this period was the completion – jointly with the Metropolitan District Railway (MDR), another cut-and-cover line – of the Inner Circle in 1884. Curiously, it succeeded in spite of Watkin himself. Having formed a dislike for his opposite number at the MDR – James Staats Forbes – he did all he could to thwart the project, even pulling strings to block the independent raising of capital. It was due in part to this feuding that a projected merger between the MR and MDR never materialized. So bitter was the feeling that for many years the

▲ **Baker Street station as opened in 1863. Note the globe gaslights and mixed-gauge tracks, both characteristic features of the early MR. The line carried 9.4 million passengers in its first year – a figure that had more than quintupled by 1870.**

**Watkin's dream**

In the eyes of its dynamic Chairman, Sir Edward Watkin, the Metropolitan Railway was no mere commuter service. He saw it as a vital link between two other railways of which he was Head – the Great Central (as it was later called) and the South Eastern. The result, he hoped, would be a much-needed north-south trunk line covering the whole of England. Moreover, he envisaged a Channel Tunnel extension which would allow trains to travel from the North of England 'to Paris and the entire continent of Europe'.

It was to be over a century before technology made possible the fulfilment of Watkin's grander plans. But he lived to see at least one of his ambitions realized. In 1899, thanks largely to his endeavours, the Great Central Railway (later to become part of the London & North Eastern Railway) arrived at London's Marylebone station, using the Metropolitan tracks south of Quainton Road in Buckinghamshire.

Metropolitan would employ no-one whose father worked for the District.

Nevertheless, both companies continued to thrive. The District went south to Richmond and Wimbledon, and east to Barking and Upminster. The MR, meanwhile, plunged north-westwards into the Home Counties, to Uxbridge, Watford, Chesham and Wendover, hauling freight as well as passengers. At one point it reached Verney Junction, 80.5km (50 miles) outside London, and ran luxury Pullman coaches to the Chilterns.

A reporter from the *Middlesex & Buckingham Advertiser* who travelled along the MR's new line to Uxbridge in 1904 was clearly enthralled by the experience: '...bathed in glorious sunshine and scented with new mown hay, the countryside was at its best. Here stretches of meadowland, with herds of sleek cattle grazing lazily, there the clink and rattle of grass-cutting machines.'

The description was a foretaste of something the MR was to make uniquely its own. In 1919, it set up a subsidiary company, Metropolitan Railway Country Estates Ltd, to purchase land and promote housing estates in Buckinghamshire, Hertfordshire and Middlesex. Posters, magazines, and even songs extolled the virtues of a rural existence within easy commuting distance of London.

Metroland, as it was dubbed, seized the imagination of wealthy professionals, and by 1930 the MR had constructed 4,600 houses. As private developers followed suit, the process gathered momentum, turning outlying towns like Uxbridge, Stanmore and North Harrow from sleepy coaching stops into architectural showcases of their day.

The poet John Betjeman, for whom this inter-war paradise held a compulsive fascination, described the scene:

'Houses deliberately "quaint"...stood in ample gardens of flowering trees bordering commons where well-worn footpaths traversed the bracken...Large country houses were built, sometimes escaping into a mythical past, in a style more antique than the oldest timber manors in the country; sometimes escaping into a mythical future of fresh air...and everlasting sunshine.'

Metroland was the MR's swansong. In 1933, the Metropolitan was taken over, together with the rest of the London Underground system, by the London Passenger Transport Board, and soon after World War II it was nationalized. The changes brought modernization, but at the cost of the MR's essential character.

The last through trains beyond Amersham ran on 9 September 1961, and three years later the final MR steam locomotive was withdrawn from service. The Metropolitan now became a faceless entity amidst the web of lines spanning London. But its place in history was assured: abbreviated to Metro, its name had become the international synonym for urban rail transport.

# King's Cross & St Pancras

**No two buildings standing side-by-side, built in the same period for the same purpose, could be more disparate than King's Cross and St Pancras stations. One is boldly functional; the other is the quintessence of High Victorian Gothic.**

As the London terminus of the East Coast main line, King's Cross is the older of the pair. It was designed by Lewis Cubitt, nephew of Sir William Cubitt, Engineer-in-Chief of the Great Northern Railway (GNR), and opened in October 1852. The temporary terminus at Maiden Lane was showing signs of weakness, so King's Cross had to be built quickly.

Several iron-arched roofs had already been erected successfully, giving greater height and wider spans than the early pitched-roof trainsheds, but possibly because time was short Lewis chose laminated timber arches, in two 32m (105ft) spans, following principles well established in bridge-building and a number of smaller stations in the north of England, although nowhere on this scale.

The newly constructed Crystal Palace provided a precedent in its wooden transepts, so the experience and technology enabled the design to be executed quickly and economically. The ribs were fabricated on site, using large chocks to obtain the correct radius before the rib sections were hoisted into place, where they were supported by brick side walls and a central wall running down the middle of the station, pierced by elliptical arches. It was the final arched station roof to be constructed in timber.

The roof's profile was mirrored in the buff brick facade in the form of a pair of giant arched lunettes above two arcades, between which rose a charming Italianate clock tower forming a delicate foil to the otherwise somewhat austere design. Lewis himself proclaimed that his station depended for effect on the largeness of some of its features, fitness for its purpose and its characteristic expression of that purpose. Later, the timber arches had to be replaced by iron ribs of identical shape; on the east side in 1866–7, followed by the western arches 20 years later.

At first, there were only two platforms, one at each side, that on the west for departures flanked by the main entrance and offices, and the eastern one for arriving trains from which passengers could step straight into waiting cabs. The rest of the space was occupied by carriage sidings which were gradually replaced by additional platforms.

More were progressively added on the west side, outside the main roof, in effect forming a separate station with its own entrance, confusingly called King's Cross (Local), and yet another

**▼ The site of King's Cross had been a 'waste, howling wilderness' in the shadow of the Fever Hospital before the Great Northern Railway cleared the area for Lewis Cubitt's terminus. Later the elegant simplicity of Cubitt's facade and Italianate clock tower was ruined by the growth of what railwaymen referred to as the 'native village' – a disordered cluster of buildings for ancillary station functions.**

◀ **The approach lines to St Pancras were built on the site of the Old St Pancras burial ground. The cavalier clearance of the graveyard by construction companies and stories of human remains being carted off to bone mills caused a public furore and fears of an epidemic. An inquiry was held before work was permitted to continue.**

beyond that called King's Cross (Suburban). They had separate designation letters to distinguish them from the main platform numbers, which themselves were even more confusingly in two sets for the arrival and departure sides. By 1926, there were 15 platforms, by which time sensible numbering had been imposed, although a sequential system from east to west was not adopted until 1972.

The trouble with King's Cross was that it was too short. Gas Works Tunnel was quite close to the platform ends, forming a bottleneck that, despite doubling and then tripling, hampered the efficient movement of steadily lengthening trains, so that trains waiting to depart often blocked the paths of those trying to get in.

Moreover, engines were continually trying to move into and out of the yard on the west side; rigid adherence to arrival and departure platforms caused criss-crossing of locomotives and trains immediately outside the station; and trains entering the local station were forced to cross the main departure tracks. So it is hardly surprising that at busy times delays were chronic.

**Tale of two tunnels**
The Great Northern and Midland railways' connecting lines to the Metropolitan Railway under Euston Road were in steep, sharply curved tunnels, the northbound one curving under the Great Northern Hotel on a 1 in 35 gradient, making it extremely difficult to operate in steam days. Conditions for enginemen facing the climb in smoke-filled darkness were appalling. In 1932, the engine of an ascending train started sliding backwards on the greasy rails. The crew, unable to see through the gloom, was unaware of what was happening until the rear collided with a following train. The tunnels have been disused since 1978.

St Pancras Tunnel was not quite so bad. To divide the block section, there was an underground signalbox reached by a spiral staircase from the station above. It was a lonely, eerie place, with the darkness outside broken only by the lights from passing trains whose smoke filtered in past the window frames. Fortunately, the signalbox was closed in 1958.

## Closures and improvements

There was no real improvement until the completion of the electrification of suburban services in 1978, which enabled five of the suburban platforms to be dispensed with (one was reinstated in 1989) and simplification of the entire track layout, including closure of the easternmost Gas Works Tunnel. At the same time, the two platforms on each side of the station on the lines leading down through tunnels to the underground Metropolitan Railway were also closed. They had been opened in 1863 to give the GNR access to the City and South London. In their place, City trains were diverted to Moorgate from Finsbury Park.

The introduction of InterCity® 125 trains virtually did away with locomotives at King's Cross, followed by IC225 electrics when the East Coast main line was electrified in the late 1980s. At last, the station was considered adequate for its traffic.

The station façade was for many years despoiled by a miscellaneous and untidy group of small buildings, huts and shelters dating from Victorian times. These were also swept away and a covered concourse built in front of Lewis Cubitt's arcade, enabling the long-inconvenient booking office on the west side to be closed.

Sir William Cubitt's main problem in planning the GNR into King's Cross was the crossing of the Regent's Canal. In 1837, Robert Stephenson had encountered the same barrier, resulting in the 1.5km (one mile) long incline at 1 in 72-112 down to Euston from the canal bridge at Camden. At King's Cross, the canal was only 183m (200yd) from the planned ends of the platforms and about 9m (30ft) higher, so Cubitt tunnelled under it. As a result, locomotives faced a fearsome start for the first few kilometres (miles) up a 1 in 107 gradient through Gas Works and Copenhagen Tunnels.

## Planning the line into St Pancras

When William Henry Barlow planned the Midland Railway (MR) extension to London in 1862, he faced the same difficulty at St Pancras, and was determined not to make the same mistake. Tunnels through the Northern Heights, further out, were unavoidable but, apart from three very short stretches, his gradients over the first 19km (12 miles) were no steeper than 1 in 176.

At St Pancras, there were also two other major problems; like the GNR, the MR wanted access to the Metropolitan line, although the station site lay over the River Fleet, which acted as a sewer for a great area of North London and was not to be disturbed.

To counter all these difficulties, Barlow devised the masterly plan of building his station above ground level, with a ramp up from the street, thereby allowing him to bridge the canal without creating a dangerously steep final descent into the terminus. At the same time, a space was created beneath the station for use as a huge warehouse for Burton beer, one of the MR's most lucrative traffics, with a hydraulic lift to transport wagons up and down.

To make maximum use of the space, Barlow built – instead of the customary brick arches – a grid of iron columns and girders to support iron plates carrying the platforms and tracks overhead. According to Barlow himself, he used the length of a beer barrel as the unit of measurement to determine the optimum spacing of the columns.

A further advantage of an elevated station was that the passenger deck formed a ready-made tie for the single-span arched roof, a daring concept never before attempted on such a scale, giving a clear, unobstructed sweep of 74.8m (245ft 6in) across the station and a maximum height of 32m (105ft) above the rails.

It was the first of the great arched roofs that dispensed with supporting columns, copied in Europe and America, but exceeded in width by only three others, all in the United States, and by none in height. This gigantic trainshed was 210m (689ft) long and the crown of the arch was slightly pointed to improve wind resistance and achieve a Gothic outline that matched the detailing of the station and the hotel that was built on the front.

The Fleet was channelled into an iron conduit, again made easier by the lack of columns which otherwise might have dictated special reinforcement where the river passed beneath them. The branch to the Metropolitan was built in a double-line tunnel which descended at 1 in 75 beneath the Old St Pancras graveyard and curved under the station to a second subterranean junction in front of King's Cross.

Horrific accounts appeared of graves being desecrated, bones being flung aside and men reluctant to work in the contaminated ground, causing public outcry. Work was stopped while an inquiry was held and the MR had to give guarantees before it could be resumed. Yet the company was commended as a public benefactor for clearing away the notorious slums which occupied the station site, with no thought given to its ruthless eviction of over 10,000 residents.

The station opened in October 1868. Thanks to the foresight of Barlow and the MR, St Pancras, unlike King's Cross, has always been adequate for its traffic. Initially, there were five platform faces and 11 tracks, six of them carriage sidings which, in 1892, gave way to two more platforms.

Overhead electrification was introduced to St Pancras in 1983. While King's Cross was wired in a particularly ugly fashion, with steel gantries ranged down the platforms, ruining the vista, the same job at St Pancras was done in exemplary fashion by suspending the catenaries directly from the roof. So unobtrusive are they that one is hardly aware of their existence.

## Hotels of distinction

A feature of both King's Cross and St Pancras is the railway hotel. At King's Cross, it was the station's architect, Lewis Cubitt, who also designed the Great Northern Hotel, opened in 1854, and still in business. Crescent shaped, it faces the west side of the station, in a modest Italianate style. It was the first hotel to offer bedrooms with en suite sitting rooms, and featured an early form of fireproof construction.

Much more splendid was the hotel erected by the MR at St Pancras. The MR was a provincial railway based on Derby, proud and highly competitive. It wished to proclaim its arrival in London with a flourish, and decided to build a sumptuous hotel in front of its new station. The design competition was won by Sir George Gilbert Scott, the leading architect of his day, who had a burning ambition to complete a really large project in the fashionable Gothic style.

He had designed the Foreign Office in Whitehall and the Albert Memorial, but the St Pancras hotel was his showpiece. Opened in 1873, the Midland Grand Hotel was a fantasy of towers, turrets, pinnacles and spires, with every conceivable form of Gothic ornamentation. (Scott also designed the elaborate booking hall on the station,

**The giant scaffold**

**The roof at St Pancras was erected with the assistance of two huge scaffolds on wheels, carrying working platforms and cranes, and weighing about 1,300 tonnes (tons). They were made from large timbers and put together in three sections. Each section ran on rails and was moved by a gang of men, one at each wheel with a pinchbar. Working to the foreman's beat of a hammer on an improvised gong, they painstakingly levered the whole thing along about 38mm ($1\frac{1}{2}$in) at a time.**

**▼ Holiday crowds throng No 6 platform at King's Cross in 1925. The scissors crossing in the foreground was reduced to a single release when in 1926, a new island platform was created where the clerestory coach stands on the right. An N2 0-6-2T stands with a set of Pullman coaches on the extreme right, and a pair of gas cylinders may be seen on a wagon to the right of centre.**

▲ **The old Midland Grand Hotel at St Pancras is one of London's best known buildings. Designed by George Gilbert Scott, the hotel opened on 5 May 1873, and was described as 'the most sumptuous and the best conducted hotel in the Empire'.**

**Casualties of war**

Both stations sustained extensive bomb damage in World War II, with 37 incendiaries falling on King's Cross in a single night. Worse followed on 11 May 1941, when Cubitt's station was hit by two 453.5kg (1,000lb) bombs, chained together. Part of the west side office block was destroyed, creating a gap, and 12 railwaymen were killed. A section of the main roof was also brought down.

St Pancras was hit three times during the Blitz in October 1940 and was closed for five days. The trainshed roof was damaged and the roof of the booking office was destroyed. It was replaced unsympathetically after the war, but when restoration took place in 1983, a false ceiling was installed which matches Scott's interior.

with its figures of railwaymen in stone, and the oak linenfold panelling to the ticket office.)

By 1935, however, it was old-fashioned and the MR's successor, the London Midland & Scottish Railway (LMS), converted it into offices. For a number of years it remained empty. However, at present, discussions are under way to transform it into the new front door for Eurostar services, with possible hotel and flat facilities.

King's Cross is synonymous with the Flying Scotsman, probably the world's most famous train, which has left London for Edinburgh daily since 1862, although the title was not officially recognized until after the formation of the London & North Eastern Railway (LNER) in 1923. The train took part in the 1882 races to Scotland against the West Coast mainline companies, and in 1928 started running non-stop, the longest ever passenger run of that kind. But it never became a streamliner, like the Silver Jubilee and Coronation which, in 1935 and 1937, brought King's Cross renewed glory.

The station was also the departure point for a number of other LNER named trains, such as the Night Scotsman, the Scarborough Flyer, the Yorkshire and Harrogate Pullmans, and the Aberdonian, which was the lineal descendant of the East Coast competitor in the renewed races to Scotland of 1895.

Across the road, St Pancras served as the main departure point from London to the East Midlands. Beyond, the MR had strong competition for

▶ **This picture of St Pancras station in around 1912 shows Barlow's tremendous trainshed. There were then seven platforms (including the short No 1 on the far left), the wide expanse of carriage roads on the west side having been broken by the insertion of a wooden island platform in 1892.**

**▲ A busy scene at King's Cross in spring 1949, with A1 Pacific No 60133 (later *Pommern*) heading the Flying Scotsman and a trio of N2 0-6-2Ts on suburban services. Most of the suburban platforms were closed with electrification of such services in 1978.**

Manchester, Liverpool, Yorkshire and Scottish traffic. The station now has only two named trains, the Master Cutler to Sheffield and the newer Robin Hood to Nottingham, a far cry from LMS days, when it saw the Palatine and the Peak Express to Manchester, the Thames-Clyde and Thames-Forth expresses to Glasgow and Edinburgh via the Settle & Carlisle line, and the Yorkshireman to Sheffield and Bradford.

At present, King's Cross caters for over 34 million passengers each year, but exciting future developments will ensure that both King's Cross and St Pancras see an even greater number.

The existing King's Cross Thameslink station is to be replaced by a new low-level station adjacent to St Pancras station, as part as the works for the Channel Tunnel Rail Link. It will offer more platforms which, in turn, are to be made wider, and will allow interchange with St Pancras and King's Cross mainline stations, London Underground and Eurostar.

This £800 million investment is estimated to take five years to complete. The proposed benefits include more trains running through Central London; more trains continuing their journeys into London; the operation of longer trains with up to 12 carriages; and the expansion of the Thameslink service. Thus, journeys are likely to be quicker and more comfortable.

**Resignalling schemes**

St Pancras was resignalled in 1957 and 1982. The earlier scheme entailed the replacement of three signalboxes with one, and the introduction of colour light signals. The 1982 resignalling accompanied electrification, with a new power box at West Hampstead.

At King's Cross, a new power box was opened in 1971 and enlarged six years later to cover the routes from the terminus and Moorgate to Sandy.

# Euston station

**With its famous Doric Arch, Euston was once a national landmark. But re-development was necessary in the 1960s and resulted in its demolition, causing an outcry. It was considered a high price to pay for a new and improved station.**

Opened by the Queen in 1968, the new Euston, with its spacious concourse, immediately attracted criticism. 'Impersonal...too much like an airport...too far to walk to the trains.' Despite such strictures, it was a huge improvement on the confusion, dirt, draughtiness and sheer inconvenience that after more than a century and a quarter of piecemeal extensions and additions had come to characterize the old station.

The Euston of the steam era became a curious combination of the splendid and the seedy. When the London & Birmingham Railway (LBR) completed the world's first trunk line in 1838, the directors decided that they should symbolize their remarkable achievement. They chose to commission a triumphal entrance for their new London terminus.

A well-known architect, Philip Hardwick, designed a huge classical arch to form this 'Gateway to the North', together with a corresponding entrance to Curzon Street station at the other end of the line in Birmingham.

## Magnificent gesture

In 1849, Hardwick, together with his son Philip Charles, designed the equally spectacular Great Hall that the LBR's successor, the London & North Western Railway (LNWR), erected behind the Doric Arch.

It had an elegant cornice, a gallery along all four sides and a colonnade of Ionic columns. Twin staircases, on either side of a statue of George Stephenson, led to the splendid dignity of the Board Room and Shareholders' Meeting Room, which could seat 400 people and was the scene of many an official banquet. It was as magnificent a gesture as the Doric Arch had been, and marked the formation in 1846 of the LNWR – then the world's largest railway company.

The public was suitably impressed. 'When Euston was first built,' wrote one Victorian observer, 'it was regarded not as a railway station but as a spectacle. Visitors used to flock to it in omnibuses and examine it with the careful scrutiny of sightseers.'

However, beyond the Doric Arch and along one side of the Great Hall lay anti-climax. Low iron sheds, partly glazed, covered two platforms and four tracks. They were partly prefabricated, which made them cheap and easy to erect.

**▶ Carol singers gather in Euston's Great Hall during Christmas 1960. Erected in 1849, the edifice, with its graceful columns, four-sided gallery and imposing statue of George Stephenson, was 37m (121ft) long, 18.5m (61ft) wide and 19m (62ft) high. The ceiling was said to be the largest unsupported structure of its kind in the world.**

**▼ The great arch at Euston station, seen here in 1900, incorporated four giant fluted columns, each 13.5m (44ft) high and 2.5m (8ft 6in) in diameter. The columns were hollow, and one of them contained a spiral staircase to a room inside the pediment which served as an office and store room.**

True, they had a degree of elegance imparted by the gracefully curved spandrels between the columns, although with both ends and one side open they did little more than keep out the rain, while insufficient height made them a trap for fumes and steam, a problem that became worse when locomotives started to burn coal instead of coke. There was little alleviation until 1872, when the shed roofs were raised by 1.75m (6ft).

## Power to impress

Nevertheless, whatever its faults, Euston still retained its power to impress. A visitor to the station in November 1848 wrote:

'No sound is heard in the cold air but the hissing of a pilot engine, which, like a restless spirit advancing and retrograding, is stealing along the intermediate rails, waiting to carry off the next down-train; its course being marked by white steam meandering above it and by red-hot coals of different sizes which are continually falling from beneath it.

'In this obscure scene the Company's interminable lines of gaslights (there are 232 at the Euston station), economically screwed down to the minimum existence, are feebly illuminating the damp varnished panels of the line of carriages in waiting, the brass doorhandles of the cabs... and while the blood-red signal lamp is glaring near the tunnel to deter unauthorized intrusion, the stars of heaven cast a faint silvery light through the long strips of plateglass in the roof above the platform.'

The approach of a train was announced by the ringing of a bell, at which sound 'every gaslight on and above a curve of 900ft [274.25m] burst into full power. The carriages, cabs &c. appear, comparatively speaking, in broad daylight, and the beautiful iron reticulation which sustains the glazed roof appears like fairy work.'

After the roof columns were raised in 1872, further extensions followed, increasing both the height and the size of the train shed, and by 1891 Euston had a total of 15 platforms of varying lengths.

## Railway hotel

Euston had one of the earliest railway-owned hotels, the first in London. Opened in 1839, it comprised two buildings, one on each side and forward of the Doric Arch, hiding two of Hardwick's flanking lodges.

In 1881, the two hotel buildings were linked by a bridge block which effectively masked the arch and utterly destroyed the original concept. New office blocks were built on each side of the arch itself about this time, destroying one of the lodges and hemming in the arch more completely than ever. Euston was now a labyrinth.

In general, arrivals used the east side of the station and departures the west, the latter including some wooden platforms that were to give an air of incongruity in the 1930s, when streamlined trains were introduced.

## Major destinations

Euston was – indeed, still is – the main point of departure for Birmingham, Liverpool, Manchester and Glasgow, and for Ireland via Holyhead, although for many destinations there was strong competition from other railways.

In its heyday, as many as 72 major towns could be reached from Euston station. Their names were

**▼ A passenger stands by the information bureau in the Great Hall in 1930, under the stern gaze of George Stephenson. The 3m (10ft) high marble statue is now on display at the National Railway Museum in York.**

**Camden incline**

One problem for the grand new Euston of 1837 was the gradient up to Camden. This was too steep for locomotives, so the trains had to be hauled up by a continuous cable driven by two stationary winding engines at the top of Camden Bank. Once at the top, a train would be coupled to its locomotive.

Incoming trains had their engines detached at Camden and rolled down to Euston by gravity under the control of 'bankriders' – brakesmen who perched on a seat on the roof of the leading carriage.

An organ pipe operated by compressed air was installed at each end of the incline, and its 'wailing whistle' warned of approaching trains. A bell was then rung at the station to alert porters and cabmen.

displayed in gilt letters on the two stone entrance lodges built on Euston Road in 1870, although only 37 were on reasonably direct routes. They include such unlikely places as Burton-on-Trent, Stamford, Swansea and Tenby.

The 2 p.m. Corridor – it was the first of the company's trains to consist entirely of corridor coaches – was one of the LNWR's best known expresses, with sections for Glasgow, Edinburgh and Aberdeen. In 1908, it received a set of new 12-wheel coaches that turned it into one of the finest trains Britain had ever seen.

But the most famous of all Euston's trains – and one that still runs today – is the Royal Scot, launched in 1927 to work the West Coast route between London and Scotland.

## East-West racing

Euston has been the starting point for a number of record-breaking attempts. In 1888, and again in 1895, the companies making up the West Coast and East Coast routes to Aberdeen competed to run the fastest train, arousing intense national interest.

The 1895 contest was the more dramatic. Night after night, the rival trains left Euston and King's Cross, steadily clipping minutes off the journey. The winner was the West Coast train, which raced the 869km (540 miles) from Euston to Aberdeen in an astonishing eight hours 32 minutes – an average speed of 101km/h (63.3mph), including stops.

Then, in 1936, the London, Midland & Scottish Railway (LMS) Pacific locomotive *Princess*

**▼ Pacific No 46232 *Duchess of Montrose* rests at Euston's Platform 1 with the Royal Scot from Glasgow.**

◀ **The demolition of the old Euston, including its famous Doric Arch, began in 1962. The leading architectural historian, the late Sir Nikolaus Pevsner, described the arch as the finest classical monument in London, and condemned its destruction as the greatest act of corporate vandalism.**

*Elizabeth* set a new non-stop record of five hours 44 minutes for the Glasgow–Euston run, and in the following year the Coronation Scot train, hauled by the Pacific *Coronation*, set the British steam record of 183km/h (114mph) on a demonstration run from Euston, only to lose it to *Mallard* of the London & North Eastern Railway (LNER) in 1938.

From the 1860s, various rebuilding schemes were put forward, but it was not until 1935 that the LNWR's successor, the LMS, decided on positive action. Designs for an entirely new station were drawn up, including a multi-storey hotel with a helicopter pad on the roof.

World War II intervened, however, and it was left to British Railways to rebuild Euston as a direct consequence of the decision to install overhead electrification on the West Coast route.

## Demolition protests

The plans for the new station called for the demolition of the Doric Arch, sparking off a series of protests that received their final rejection by the Prime Minister, Harold Macmillan. The work was beset by delays beyond the builders' or BR's control. In 1963, the government imposed a ban on new office building in London, which meant deferral of the four tower blocks and hotel planned for the station forecourt, and loss of rental income which had been intended to help offset the cost of rebuilding.

Three office towers and a raised link block were subsequently built in the 1970s. At one side of the station piazza stands a bronze statue of George Stephenson's son, Robert, who built the LBR. This, together with the two Euston Road entrance lodges and the LNWR war memorial that lies between them, is all that remains of the old Euston.

The concourse itself is spacious and bright. As at many redesigned terminals, you cannot see the trains, which some think is a pity and gives rise to the airport analogy. There are 18 platforms, the central ones being generally reserved for outer suburban, Northampton and Birmingham stopping trains, and for the suburban service to Watford.

Completion of the new Euston and electrification of the West Coast main line in 1966 enabled train services to be dramatically improved in speed and frequency. However, this is set to be enhanced further by Railtrack's £5.8 billion upgrade. Work already undertaken has involved the closure of a 1960 power signalbox which has been replaced by a new signalling centre at Wembley. The project intends to increase line speeds to 201km/h (125mph) by 2002, with an additional increase to 225.25km/h (140mph) south of Crewe from 2005.

▼ **Passengers wait in the gallery of one of Euston's two booking halls in the 1850s. Both halls – one for the London and Birmingham traffic, and the other for the branch lines – were lit by overhead glass domes.**

# Liverpool Street station

**A recent £150 million refurbishment ensures that Liverpool Street station is one of London's most attractive railway stations. The development stands in dramatic contrast to the original station, once regarded as one of the worst of the London termini.**

Liverpool Street station had already seen major refurbishments in the 1980s which took seven years to complete. In December 1991, some 116 years after it was first opened to the public, Her Majesty the Queen officially reopened the station. British Rail considered the new Liverpool Street to be its flagship station, though the terminus had its admirers long before the facelift.

It was the poet John Betjeman, writing in 1972, who paid tribute to the qualities of its lofty, almost cathedral-like roof – qualities that have been subtly enhanced in the various stages of transforming it into a modern, convenient terminus.

The story of Liverpool Street starts almost half a kilometre (quarter of a mile) away at the site of the old Bishopsgate goods station, where the Eastern Counties Railway (ECR) built its Shoreditch terminus in 1840. In 1862, when the ECR became part of the Great Eastern Railway (GER), the need for a larger terminus was given urgent attention – one sited in the City of London, convenient for the commuter traffic that was beginning to flow from the expanding eastern suburbs, which the GER wished to exploit.

## Parliamentary go-ahead

In 1864, Parliament sanctioned a new station in Liverpool Street, next to the North London Railway's Broad Street terminus, then under construction. The Act authorized new approach lines descending at 1 in 70 to platforms below street level, enabling a connection to be made through a tunnel to the Metropolitan Railway.

But the connection was used on a regular basis for just a few months, thereafter seeing only occasional special workings, and was last used in 1904. It was an expensive mistake, not only entailing the high cost of excavating the station site, but

**▶ Shafts of spring sunlight pick out the stolid figure of a railway policewoman on duty at the Bishopsgate end of Liverpool Street station in 1952. The latticed footbridge seen above the Underground signs joined the west and east suburban groups of platforms, which were separated by the two mainline platforms.**

**▼ A 4-6-2 Britannia Class Pacific, No 70036 *Boadicea* – note the grime-caked nameplate on its smoke deflector – arrives with a train from Norwich under the new electric overhead gantries at platforms nine and ten in 1960. Liverpool Street's electrification programme began in 1935, but was not completed until 1992.**

resulting in difficult starts for heavy mainline trains up the incline to Bethnal Green, which hampered operations throughout the age of steam. Bishopsgate was closed, and reopened in enlarged form as a goods depot in 1881.

Since an estimated 7,000 people were to be displaced from their homes, the 1864 Act required the GER to run two 2*d.* return trains daily – one from Edmonton and one from Walthamstow. However, the government's aim of encouraging displaced families to move out to better housing in the suburbs misfired, as in many similar cases elsewhere, and it simply made worse the already chronic overcrowding in the surrounding slums.

Designed by the GER's engineer, Edward Wilson, the new station, occupying an area of ten acres (four hectares), was opened in 1874–5. The four-span, 23.25m (76ft) high iron and glass roof covered 12 platform faces, the easternmost pair for mainline trains being considerably longer than the others. An L-shaped headquarters office block fronted on to Liverpool Street itself, flanked by an approach road sloping down to the concourse.

Wilson's design for this building compared ill with his magnificent trainshed; the undistinguished Gothic styling incorporated lancet windows and a low clock tower, surmounted by a dumpy turret that was destroyed in World War II. Inside, the boardroom and senior officers' rooms were equally restrained. Not for Liverpool Street were the costly splendours of Euston.

## New extension opened

Increasing traffic, particularly suburban, soon made Liverpool Street too small, and in 1894, an eastern extension was opened alongside Bishopsgate, providing eight more platforms. This time the GER was required to rehouse displaced inhabitants, which it did by building tenement blocks. The extension, or eastern trainshed as it became known, was designed by John Wilson, nephew of Edward, and W.N. Ashbee, the GER's architect.

The roof was lower and less impressive than the western trainshed, although it was still light and airy. The extension backed on to the Great Eastern Hotel, built alongside the Liverpool Street offices in 1884 by Charles E. Barry. Its mixed Renaissance style overpowered Edward Wilson's offices, and in 1901 it was extended around the corner into Bishopsgate in an Edwardian Tudor-Dutch style by Robert Edis, who also designed the Hotel Great Central at Marylebone.

The station now formed two distinct parts, bisected by the two long mainline platforms stretching back to the hotel, where sidings extending under the hotel were crossed by a footbridge. To avoid the long trek around, an elevated walkway from the side entrance in Bishopsgate

**▼ A pre-war poster advertises the LNER's luxury boat-train, the Hook Continental, which left Liverpool Street for Harwich every night at 8.30. With its handsome appearance and well-heeled passengers, the train brought a touch of unaccustomed elegance to the gloomy station.**

Northern Railway from King's Cross, but it did offer some useful cross-country connections.

A number of named trains ran from Liverpool Street. In 1897, the GER started the Cromer Express, later renamed the Norfolk Coast Express. After the 1923 Grouping, when the GER became part of the London & North Eastern Railway (LNER), there were few changes until 1937, when the LNER introduced a new luxury train, the East Anglian, for the service to Norwich, Cromer, Yarmouth and Lowestoft. A year later, it introduced a second, the Hook Continental boat-train, for passengers travelling to the Hook of Holland via Parkeston Quay (Harwich).

However, by far the greatest number of passengers using Liverpool Street were commuters from east London suburbs and the towns of southern Essex that eventually formed a semi-urban area extending to Hertford, Ongar, Brentwood and Southend. They were the travellers who, twice a day, made the station one of the country's busiest, riding five-a-side in cramped four-wheel coaches that in the third-class had wooden seats and lower than shoulder height partitions in what passed as compartments.

Various attempts were made to alleviate the overcrowding, including the construction of what

**▲ Two early morning commuter trains, their passengers already deposited and dispersed, wait amid the murk of Liverpool Street station in the 1950s. 'Here,' wrote the poet John Betjeman in 1952, 'the old London sulphur smell pervades and even red bricks receive a black coating.'**

**The Jazz Service**
In July 1920, Liverpool Street's superintendent of operation, F.V. Russell, introduced a scheme to reduce chronic overcrowding on the Enfield and Chingford lines. By altering the tracks and signalling, Russell was able to run steam trains on these routes at maximum possible intensity.

Nicknamed the Jazz Service, after the distinctively coloured identification stripes over the first and second-class compartments, the new scheme allowed peak hour turn-round times of only four minutes. Because the engine of each incoming train took the next one out, the locomotive on the front could be uncoupled while another was being attached to the rear for the return journey.

zigzagged across the head of the station, connecting the two concourses and crossing the mainline platforms *en route*.

The walkway also gave access to the three charming little Edwardian bow-windowed tea rooms which so enchanted Betjeman, two situated on the west side and one on the east. Unfortunately, they had to be demolished during the station's modernization.

In spite of its lofty roof, Liverpool Street in the days of steam was a gloomy, smoky place – hardly surprising given its traffic flow. In 1912, it was used by 1,250 trains a day, carrying a total of 200,000 passengers. In 1921, it was used by only 14 more trains a day – but carrying almost 230,000 passengers.

The principal mainline trains served Cambridge, Colchester, Norwich, King's Lynn and the ports and resorts of East Anglia. At the same time, the GER enjoyed a virtual monopoly of the boat-train traffic to Holland, Germany and northern Europe, which went from Liverpool Street via Harwich.

## High speed service

In the 40 years up to the turn of the twentieth century, the mainline services underwent a steady transformation. At first, the GER wisely concentrated on reliability and punctuality rather than speed. Then, in 1879, it ran a train from Liverpool Street to Norwich via Ipswich inside three hours – a reduction of no less than 70 minutes on the previous fastest time.

In 1892, a thrice daily service was begun to York via Cambridge and Ely. It did not attempt to compete with the direct route over the Great

**▼ Promenaders stroll past the London terminus of the Great Eastern Railway, opened in 1875. By the 1920s, Liverpool Street had become the focus of the most intensive suburban steam service in the world and was being used by over a quarter of a million passengers a day.**

was probably the country's first suburban train to seat six-a-side. However, such stratagems provided only a temporary solution. By the 1920s, Liverpool Street commuters were increasingly aware that their daily discomforts were not being shared elsewhere, particularly on the Southern Railway, where electrification was showing the way.

Eventually, in 1935, the LNER was forced to accept that steam trains could no longer adequately cope with the Liverpool Street traffic, and a start was made on electrifying the mainline out to Shenfield. However, with the outbreak of war in 1939, the scheme was suspended, and Liverpool Street entered a new and lethal phase.

## Surviving the blitz

Bombs fell on platforms 1, 4 and 18, and on one of the engine sidings at the end of platform 10. The Liverpool Street offices were also badly damaged. In January 1941, Hamilton House, the big block on the east side, lost one of its two wings, and three months later the block on the west side and part of the clock tower were destroyed. As one commendably restrained Liverpool Street driver later observed, 'working trains under such conditions is very trying to the nerves'.

With the end of the war, the electrification scheme was resurrected – this time, under the management of British Railways – and trains using the overhead system began running in September 1949. In 1950, electrification was extended to Chelmsford and Southend, and later the wires reached Enfield Town, Chingford, Hertford East, Bishop's Stortford and, in 1963, Clacton-on-Sea.

▲ **Nine o'clock on an August morning in 1928 sees Liverpool Street station undergoing its daily invasion of office workers from the suburbs. Overcrowding on the Liverpool Street commuter lines was intense, and the advertisement for the LNER's much vaunted Flying Scotsman service from King's Cross would have provoked some hollow laughter.**

Steam workings were further reduced by the advent of diesel traction, and the last steam train left Liverpool Street in 1962, to be followed by a thorough cleaning of the station. Meanwhile, electrification, applied at first only to suburban services, was gradually extended to the main lines out of Liverpool Street.

In spite of progress with electrification, Liverpool Street's two-part layout continued to be a great inconvenience, so eventually, in 1975 BR decided to build an entirely new terminus that would incorporate the few remaining services using Broad Street, the site of which would be used for commercial development.

## Modern terminus

The ensuing controversy caused more than ten years' delay but ultimately ensured the retention of the western trainshed, part of the office block and the Great Eastern Hotel. Broad Street disappeared, covered by Broadgate, which, together with the office blocks built over the eastern side of Liverpool Street and the station throat, formed the then largest single office development in Europe.

The revenue it generated paid for a revived Liverpool Street that was light, attractive and spacious, with longer platforms, a fine single concourse across the whole of the station and splendid period-style towers and entrance gates.

In 1992, the station that was once described by journalist and MP Tom Driberg as 'this hell hole' won two awards for its contribution to the environment. Recent developments have boosted the prestige of the station and surrounding area, with restaurants and shops – one notable feature being the Great Eastern Hotel bought by the famous restaurateur, Terence Conran.

### Assassination victim

June 22, 1922, was a sombre day for the Great Eastern Railway (GER). Its directors gathered at Liverpool Street station to watch the former Chief of the Imperial General Staff, Field Marshal Sir Henry Wilson, unveil a memorial to the staff of the GER who had fallen in World War I.

But Wilson was soon to have his own Liverpool Street memorial. The former soldier, later an Ulster MP and chief military adviser to the recently created government of Northern Ireland, was shot dead by two IRA gunmen as he stepped from the cab which had brought him back to his house in Belgravia. Both assassins were caught, and having been tried and found guilty of murder, they were hanged at Wandsworth gaol within a few weeks of Wilson's funeral.

# Waterloo station

**For years, the chaos of Waterloo station was the butt of music hall jokes. It was not until the 1920s, after more than two decades of building work, that a modern terminus emerged. With the Channel Tunnel development, Waterloo is Britain's busiest station.**

By 1885, Waterloo, with 16 platforms, was the largest station in London. It was also the most inconvenient, housed in a warren of piecemeal extensions and additions that had sprung up around the original wooden trainshed of 1848 – itself dismissed by *Building News* as the meanest structure of its kind in the capital.

The station was opened as the terminus of the London & South Western Railway (LSWR) when it extended its line from Nine Elms, to which its predecessor, the London & Southampton Railway, had opened ten years previously. (Nine Elms was given over to goods traffic until its closure in 1968.) By 1885, Waterloo had already undergone four enlargements. The original part, containing two arrival and two departure platforms, was called the Central station. Along one side was the South station, on the other side was the Windsor station, and beyond this was the newest sector, completed in September, known as the North station.

Each had its own entrance and, to complicate matters further, a track ran out across the small concourse of the Central station, through the front wall and over Waterloo Road on a bridge to join the South Eastern Railway (SER) line from London Bridge to Charing Cross. Passengers could cross it by a moveable bridge, which was drawn back to enable a train to pass – an event of merciful infrequency.

Inevitably, Waterloo aroused ridicule. There was a well-known joke about trains getting lost in the platforms, while one writer called the station 'a mighty maze without a plan'. A great amount of confusion was caused by the numbering of the platforms. The Central and South stations both had platforms numbered 1 and 2, while others had two faces yet only one number, so that when a train stood at each side, the unfortunate passenger had no means of telling which was the one he wanted.

Jerome K. Jerome parodied Waterloo in his comic masterpiece, *Three Men in a Boat*. Unable

**▼ An aerial picture taken in 1946 shows Waterloo station still surrounded by great swathes of bomb damage. The station itself was hit by enemy planes, but the horizontal ridge-and-furrow roof, with its 20 acres (eight hectares) of glass, remained surprisingly intact.**

◀ The Waterloo 'A' signalbox, seen here in 1903, was the largest in the country. At its maximum, the box contained 410 levers, worked by six men on each day shift and four at night, plus eight train register boys and three telegraph lads.

to discover where the 11.05 to Kingston is starting from – 'nobody at Waterloo ever does know where a train is going to start from, or where a train when it does start is going to, or anything about it' – the intrepid heroes slip half a crown to the driver of a stationary train to take them to their destination. It turns out that they have commandeered the Exeter Mail, which the distraught authorities at Waterloo spend hours looking for.

The chaos continued to grow, and by 1889 the station was handling 100,000 passengers and 700 trains a day, causing even the respected railway expert Sir William Acworth to declare that such heavy traffic rendered reconstruction impossible. But the impossible happened. In 1900, the LSWR started clearing 6.5 acres (2.5 hectares) of land for a new station.

## Station rebuilding saga

The company's Chief Engineer, W.J. Jacomb-Hood, examined at American termini before drawing up plans for a new Waterloo under one roof. In the event, the North station roof was retained, as it was the newest and quite sufficient, and 21 platforms were provided. Although some parts of the new station were opened in 1909, the entire project took 21 years to complete, partly due to the intervention of World War I. Jacomb-Hood died in 1914 and the work was finished by his successor, A.W. Szlumper.

The great curved front, designed by James Robb Scott, contained the LSWR offices, later to become the headquarters of the Southern Railway (SR), into which the LSWR was incorporated in 1923. Unfortunately, the facade cannot be viewed in its entirety, because a viaduct blocks the scene. At the western end stands the monumental Victory Arch in Portland stone, which commemorates the LSWR men who were killed during World War I. The architectural style has been aptly named Imperial Baroque.

A series of noble public rooms led off the spacious, sweeping concourse, 36.5m (120ft) wide and 234.75m (770ft) long; it was, and still is, everything that a well-designed station concourse should be. There were five refreshment rooms of various kinds, as well as a restaurant, including two large buffets and the Windsor Room, which were the last word in Edwardian-style elegance.

Another notable feature of the new station was a subterranean gentlemen's convenience, 243.75m (800ft) long and 12.25m (40ft) wide which, besides the actual lavatories, offered bathrooms, a boot-cleaning service and a hairdressing salon. The *Railway Magazine* described the convenience as 'perhaps the finest in England'. The ladies' lavatories were poor by comparison and, unlike

### Going to the dogs

A number of stations were well known for dogs with charity collecting boxes strapped to their backs. At Waterloo, the most famous of these animals was London Jack, who daily trotted among the passengers seeking donations for the London & South Western Railway Servants' Orphanage, and later the Southern Railwaymen's Home for Children.

When he died in 1901, his body was stuffed and placed in a glass case on the station concourse, where it stayed for many years. His charity work was continued by London Jack II.

▼ Two trains stand at their platforms in the original Waterloo, the so-called Central station, in the early 1900s. Signs direct passengers to two newer sections – the North and South stations. The track in front of the barrier joined the South Eastern Railway line from London Bridge to Charing Cross.

**Morning missile**
Before carriages were steam heated, passengers were provided with footwarmers – metal canisters filled with hot water. Early one morning around the turn of the twentieth century, a foreign visitor in a train leaving Waterloo found a footwarmer in his compartment.

Like now, this was a time when political extremists were planting bombs in public places, and the visitor, assuming that the still hot canister was an explosive device, threw it out of the window near Vauxhall. It crashed through the roof of a house and landed on a bed, though fortunately without injuring the occupant.

those for gentlemen, they perpetuated the division between first and third-class passengers.

The platforms and concourse were covered by a horizontal ridge-and-furrow roof containing some 20 acres (eight hectares) of glass. While it may lack the grandeur of great arched station roofs like St Pancras and York, a height of 18.25m (60ft) to the ridges ensures a fine sense of airiness and light. The opening ceremony was performed in 1922 by Queen Mary – standing in for King George V, who was ill – during which she inspected a guard of honour of nearly 100 LSWR employees who had been decorated in World War I.

Waterloo was now the largest and best laid out terminus in Great Britain, dealing with 1,159 trains a day. More than 700 were EMUs, for in 1915 the LSWR had embarked on a suburban third-rail electrification programme which the SR (and later the Southern Region of British Railways) continued. Waterloo's extensive suburban services cover south-west London, Surrey and Hampshire, while its mainline services extend to Portsmouth (for the Isle of Wight), Southampton, Bournemouth, Weymouth, and Exeter via Salisbury.

## Last train to Padstow

In pre-Grouping days, there was competition between the LSWR and the Great Western Railway for Plymouth traffic, although the LSWR had the longer and more difficult route. As part of this long-standing competition, the LSWR penetrated along the northern coasts of Devon and Cornwall as far as Padstow. In the Beeching cuts of the 1960s, however, almost the whole system beyond Exeter was closed, leaving only Barnstaple with a passenger service. The last train to Padstow ran on 30 January 1967.

**▼ Passing a guard of honour of London & South Western Railwaymen decorated in World War I, Queen Mary arrives to perform the official opening of the new Waterloo station on 21 March 1922. The work, partly delayed by the war, had taken 21 years to complete.**

One of Waterloo's best-known trains was the Atlantic Coast Express, nicknamed the ACE, which in summer months was the most multi-portioned train in the country. It comprised through coaches for the east Devon resorts of Seaton, Sidmouth and Exmouth, and for Exeter, Plymouth, Ilfracombe, Torrington, Bude and Padstow, all of which were detached at various points *en route*.

Waterloo's other best-known named trains were two Pullmans – the Bournemouth Belle, which began regular weekday running in 1936, and the Devon Belle, a relative latecomer, which started running in 1947 and divided at Exeter into two portions – one for Plymouth and one for Ilfracombe. From 1950, just a single section – the one for Ilfracombe – continued beyond Exeter. The train was famous for the observation car on the rear of the Ilfracombe portion.

The station has always been closely associated with Southampton where, in 1892, the LSWR took over the docks and commenced an extensive development programme aimed at weaning the transatlantic liner trade away from Liverpool. The policy was so successful that, by World War I, Southampton had become Britain's principal deep-sea passenger port, and boat-trains were a regular feature at Waterloo until airline competition led to the end of regular ocean liner business in the 1970s. The boat-trains ran through to the dockside,

▲ **Summer holiday crowds throng the concourse at Waterloo in 1946, anxious to flock to coast or countryside after six years of wartime deprivation. Note the 24-hour clock, which was probably installed for the benefit of passengers using the boat-trains to Southampton.**

and in 1950 a new Ocean Terminal was completed for direct services from Waterloo.

Waterloo could also claim strong military and naval connections. It served the many military establishments in Surrey, Hampshire and Wiltshire, including Aldershot and Salisbury Plain, and handled naval traffic for Portsmouth. In both world wars, it was the main station for troops embarking at Southampton for service overseas.

During World War II, the arches under the station were converted into air-raid shelters for some 6,500 local people. More than 50 bombs fell on the station, on three occasions closing it for several days. One raid destroyed the general offices that had remained from the old Waterloo. Another demolished the private station of the London Necropolis Company.

This had opened near to the terminus in 1854 and had been rebuilt in Waterloo Bridge Road in 1902. It consisted of two platforms – one for coffins and one for mourners – and the LSWR provided special funeral trains to the Necropolis Company's cemetery at Brookwood in Surrey.

However, the destruction of the Necropolis station still left three other Waterloos, in addition to the terminus. The first of them, Waterloo Junction, was opened in 1869 by the SER on its viaduct outside the LSWR station, to which it is connected by footbridge. In 1977, it was given a new name, Waterloo East.

The second was opened in 1898 by the LSWR as part of its Waterloo & City tube line. Known as 'the Drain' to its users, it ran from a station beneath Waterloo to another near the Bank of England. In 1994, ownership was transferred from British Railways to the London Underground.

The third was opened in 1906 by the Baker Street & Waterloo Railway – later known as the Bakerloo – with a separate entrance in York Road, as well as access from the concourse of the main station. One of the first station escalators was brought into service in 1919, linking the concourse and the subway which served both the Waterloo & City and Bakerloo lines.

## Foreign destinations

By 1981, Waterloo station was catering for 187,300 passengers daily. Now, as Waterloo International, it has become even busier. The international terminal was completed in May 1993, in readiness for Channel Tunnel traffic. It was designed by architects Nicholas Grimshaw & Partners to handle 45 trains a day and 15 million passengers a year.

Its five double-length platforms, which occupy the site of the six original northernmost platforms, required the demolition of the old North station roof. Its replacement is a spectacular arched roof of novel design in steel and glass. Each span comprises two banana-shaped bow-string trusses of unequal length, pinned at a central joint and forming a striking perspective of asymmetrical arches, gradually decreasing in width along the gentle curve of the platforms.

Beneath, three levels contain an airport-style passenger lounge and holding area, an arrivals hall and a basement car park.

▶ **Workmen finish off the approaches to Waterloo in 1848. Sited on an area of marshy ground just south of the Thames, the new terminus, with its three platforms and wooden trainshed, hardly seemed destined to become London's busiest station.**

# Crewe station

**When the first public train ran through Crewe in July 1837, it was still an obscure hamlet of less than 200 people. Over the next 20 years, it was to become one of the busiest railway junctions in Britain.**

As well as sitting astride the West Coast main line from Euston to Scotland, Crewe also has connections with the north-west of England, eastern England, the south and west of England via Birmingham New Street, and Wales and the borders, making it one of Britain's busiest railway junctions.

However, the station has a deceptively modest exterior. As a place where travellers often change trains rather than begin their journey, Crewe has never needed to impress with the kind of grandiose 'gateway' station boasted by, for example, its neighbour, Chester.

When the first public train ran through it on the opening of the Grand Junction Railway (GJR) on 4 July 1837, Crewe was no more than an intermediate stop on the journey between Liverpool and Birmingham. Some passengers had reached the station using the turnpike between Nantwich and Sandbach, busy market towns a few kilometres (miles) to the west and east, which the station had been built to serve. Accommodation was limited to a booking office, a general waiting room, a ladies' room and a urinal. There was also an engine house on the down side 'with a spare engine always ready for use', to quote a contemporary guide.

The station, named after nearby Crewe Hall, the residence of Lord Crewe, was enlarged when a line to Chester opened in 1840, followed by one to Manchester two years later. Strained relations with the GJR led to the Manchester & Birmingham Railway building its own platform on the up side just north of the GJR station. There was a single

**▼ With so many trains using the station, Crewe has long been a trainspotter's paradise. Here a group gathers on the lattice overbridge in August 1955 to await the departure of Ivatt 2-6-2T No 41229 with the 12.38 p.m. local service to Northwich.**

◀ **Crewe North Junction signalbox looking north and showing the 18in (457mm) gauge railway that ran between the station and the works. The signalbox was one of ten power boxes at Crewe created by the 1896–1906 remodelling.**

line connection between the two routes, but a gate was built across it.

Nevertheless, passenger and goods traffic grew rapidly, especially after the opening of the main line through to Carlisle and Glasgow in 1848. Crewe station underwent almost continuous expansion and improvement. In 1845–7, the main line was quadrupled with the laying of two extra tracks between the platforms. An impressive main station building was designed in Tudor-Jacobean fashion and the wooden Nantwich Road bridge, spanning the north end of the station, was reconstructed in iron.

This work was already underway when, in 1846, the London & North Western Railway (LNWR) was formed by the amalgamation of the London & Birmingham, Manchester & Birmingham and Grand Junction railways. (Six years earlier, the GJR had absorbed the Chester & Crewe Railway.) The North Staffordshire Railway – the 'Knotty' – opened a branch from Kidsgrove in 1848, and ten years later an LNWR subsidiary, the Shrewsbury & Crewe Railway (SCR), opened to provide an important through route to mid and south Wales. This was the only line to Crewe built by the LNWR.

It completed Crewe's six junctions and, together with the locomotive works and marshalling yard, made it the undisputed hub of the LNWR empire. By this stage, traffic was particularly heavy so improvements were vital to segregate long-distance expresses from local services and trains booked to stop. The LNWR Line Superintendent, George P. Neele, described traffic through Crewe as developing unceasingly, noting that blockades of trains from the south were not 'unfrequent'.

## Large-scale expansion

In 1867, the station was substantially rebuilt, with bays added for local services. More platforms and a new entrance followed in 1878, and the station was almost doubled in size in the three years from 1903, mainly by the addition of a third substantial island platform to the west. Again, bays were built at both ends and the total length of platform faces increased to 3,462m (11,358ft). The work followed completion of the so-called Independent Lines, the biggest expansion project since the junctions were finished, to keep goods trains clear of the station.

Few changes were made in the quarter of a century after 1906, operators being well able to handle the extra traffic generated during World War I. Traffic continued to increase after the war. Figures released in 1927 by the LNWR's successor, the London Midland & Scottish Railway (LMS), showed that at peak holiday times the number of trains dealt with at Crewe in a 24 hour period was upwards of 500. The volume of goods traffic was even more spectacular. By 1937, Crewe's three goods yards were handling some 47,000 wagons in a routine week.

More modern signalling was needed and large boxes with bomb-proof concrete roofs were being built at North and South Junctions when World War II broke out in 1939. They became operational during the Battle of Britain in 1940. The local railways escaped bombing, but workers were

▼ **Royal Scot 4-6-0 No 46164 *The Artists' Rifleman* pulls away from platform 5 at Crewe with a down Ocean Liner express bound for Liverpool docks in the summer of 1955.**

**▲ South Junction signalbox is seen here in 1916, after modifications to the layout and signalling. With 247 levers, the box controlled the junctions of the lines to Shrewsbury, Stafford and Stoke, as well as access to the South steam shed.**

### GWR connections

The Great Western Railway (GWR) reached Crewe through an 1863 agreement with the London & North Western Railway (LNWR), which gave the GWR running powers over the Shrewsbury & Crewe Railway line from Nantwich Junction. The GWR's goods trains were marshalled at Gresty Lane sidings and Basford Hall yard, while its passenger services used a bay at the south end of the station. Here the company had its own booking office, passenger agent's office, and lamp and porters' rooms. After the 1923 Grouping, fixtures were allocated to the LNWR's successor, the London Midland & Scottish Railway, and furniture to the GWR.

The GWR's staff of 27 at Crewe was headed by a stationmaster until 1915, when they were put in the charge of a yard master (class 2). The LNWR built one of its standard two-road engine sheds at Gresty Lane for use by the GWR, but the latter's locomotives were also serviced at North and South sheds.

killed in a raid on the Rolls-Royce aero-engine factory alongside the Chester line.

The war caused many alterations to express services. Some were cancelled and the journey times of others increased as paths were needed for troop trains and ever increasing goods traffic. An immediate casualty was the streamlined Coronation Scot, withdrawn after only two years in service.

Although the train was never booked to stop at Crewe, it did so just once – during its demonstration run from Euston to Crewe and back on 29 June 1937. North of Stafford it touched a record speed of 183.5km/h (114mph) and was still travelling at 91.75km/h (57mph) when it struck the first of three successive crossovers at Crewe station. Onlookers who had been watching from platform ends were still running for their lives as the express swayed across the third crossover before coming to a halt.

The Coronation Class streamlined Pacifics were among locally built locomotives that for years pulled the most prestigious of the LMS expresses, including the Coronation Scot, Royal Scot and Caledonian. An operating factor which made Crewe so busy, congested – and fascinating

– was that virtually every long-distance train that stopped there had either to be split or to wait while portions or vans were attached or detached. This could have its dangers, and there were times when, if football specials had to be split or change locomotives, the staff wore bowler hats as protection against missile throwers.

Electrification started at Crewe in the mid-1950s. This involved wiring more than 112.5km (70 miles) of track within a 1.5km (one mile) radius of the station and the lifting of Nantwich Road bridge to give 25kV overhead wire clearances. At the same time, a new station entrance, forecourt and booking hall were built, and a centralized booking office replaced three which had been situated on different platforms.

When electrification was completed in the mid-1960s, about 500 station staff handled almost 400 passenger and parcels trains a day. Each week, approximately 80,000 passengers changed trains at Crewe and another 20,000 arrived or departed on regular services. The heaviest traffic was of mail and parcels. Three million letters and 200,000 parcels a week were handled by the modern GPO sorting office built adjoining the east side of the station.

**▲ During the 1985 modernization of Crewe, the goods avoiding lines were vital for through services, such as this express. The relief lines enabled goods trains from all but the Chester route to the north to avoid the station.**

**▼ Crewe station in 1881 with the Crewe Arms Hotel on the left. The hotel was used by Queen Victoria on her way south from Scotland in September 1848. Drivers were warned to make the minimum of noise as they passed the Queen's quarters.**

## The new Crewe emerges

Today's station is the result of radical modernization started in 1984, including the construction of a new booking hall and travel centre. The main work, completed a year later, cost more than £14 million. The station and some approach lines were resignalled with a system controlled from a single-storey signalling centre built on the site of Crewe North locomotive sheds, and the track layout was remodelled and improved. Points and crossings were reduced from 285 to 110, which raised the speed limit for non-stop expresses from about 32 to 128.75km/h (20 to 80mph) and from 32 to 80.5km/h (20 to 50mph) for trains preparing to stop.

Some platforms were lengthened to handle longer trains and new ramps were built for mail and parcels traffic. But the biggest rationalization was the closure of all but the eastern face of the most westerly of the three island platforms, opened in 1906. The eastern face, now platform 12, was retained for occasional use.

During almost seven weeks of virtual shutdown in the summer of 1985, there was a concentrated attempt to improve passenger facilities. At the end of the operation, the BR chairman, Sir Bob Reid, congratulated the 1,200 people 'who formed the round-the-clock team that took to pieces the most famous railway junction in the world and put it together again in seven weeks'.

Passenger facilities were also improved in the 1990s. Waiting rooms, toilets, the lounge, the main footbridge, lifts, the information point and catering facilities were all refurbished, and following the cleaning and repainting of the concourse, a new shop unit was added in July1999.

The Basford Hall sidings have undergone major refurbishment, and at Crewe South, engineering facilities at the old carriage shed and a depot for the Venice Simplon Orient Express (VSOE) have been established.

# York station

**York station, opened in 1877 as a vital link in the East Coast route between London and Edinburgh, was immediately hailed for its stately grandeur – a quality that has endured beyond the end of steam.**

The North Eastern Railway (NER), which was one of the largest of the great Victorian railways, used to describe York as the centre of its octopus-like system, with lines radiating in all directions. Today, it is still the grand junction for the north, with the electrified East Coast mainline from King's Cross to Edinburgh as the backbone of its routes.

York's early railway history was complex and colourful, being dominated by one man, George Hudson, whose dubious financial dealings in the 1840s led to his disgrace and downfall.

He was Chairman of the York & North Midland Railway (Y&NMR), and it was at the company's terminal, a temporary structure just outside the city's historic walls, that the first railway passengers from London arrived on 11 July 1840.

But the need for a better station was urgent, and in 1841 the city's walls were breached so that lines could reach a more spacious station just inside them. This opened on 4 January 1841, and was shared with the Great North of England Railway (GNER), which reached York from Darlington on the same day, although it did not start passenger services until two months later.

However, a major shortcoming of the new station was that GNER trains had to reverse to get into it. That was still the situation in 1854, when the NER was formed from a four-way amalgamation of companies that included the Y&NMR. As more lines were built, including two running east to Scarborough and Hull, the pressure on York station increased.

It was the rapid growth of Anglo-Scottish traffic and the lobbying of the three companies involved – the NER, Great Northern Railway (GNR) and North British Railway (NBR) – that persuaded Parliament to give approval for York's third station.

▼ A famous landmark looms in the background as the locomotives of five companies sit at the southern end of York station's lofty train shed in the early 1900s. According to one admiring contemporary, York was 'a gentleman among stations', which 'seems almost to take its proportions from the grand old minster close by'.

**▼ With the sun glinting on its garter blue streamlined casing, LNER's A4 Pacific No 60034 *Lord Faringdon* sweeps through York station with the northbound Flying Scotsman in the summer of 1948. Launched in 1935, the A4s set new records in high-speed rail travel.**

**▼ The great arched roof of York station, with its elegant combination of iron and glass, bears striking testimony to the wealth and power of the Victorian railways. More than 243.75m (800ft) long, it consists of four spans of varying dimensions, the widest of which is 24.75m (81ft) and the tallest 14.5m (48ft).**

This was in 1866, but as the NER was by then in some financial difficulties, it was another eight years before work began on a grand design of the company's architect, Thomas Prosser. The most striking feature of the new station, opened in 1877, was its curved iron roof. There were 13 platforms to which the NER added two more in 1900, extending the total length of platform faces to 2,832.25m (3,097$\frac{1}{2}$yds) – just 274.25m (300yds) short of the total at Newcastle Central, which remained unchallenged as the longest on the NER.

The atmosphere of York station was captured by the historian John Pendleton in *Our Railways*, published in 1896, the year before Queen Victoria's Diamond Jubilee:

'The great station, with its bold sweep of main line and ample sidings, accommodates more than 200 trains daily, from The Flying Scotsman to the humblest stopper that crawls out Seamer way "to watch the corn grow". There is no station more interesting than that of York... It is lofty and spacious; handsome so far as a railway station can be, and attractive from its brightness, its light lines and the harmoniousness of its colouring.'

## Making changes

Changes have been made through the years, not all of them for the better. The original subway between the platforms, for example, was replaced by an ugly footbridge. But on the credit side there is the imposing Royal York Hotel (formerly the Royal Station Hotel), built soon after the completion of the station itself, and the delightful art nouveau tea room, dating from 1906, where passengers could sample 'true North Country "teas" at moderate rates'.

In addition to its own trains, the NER was also required to handle the so-called foreigners – the trains of the five other companies which had to run at least 32.25km (20 miles) over NER tracks to reach the city. These companies, which all played a part in the development of York as a junction, were the Great Northern (GNR), Midland (MR),

**▲ Travellers wait patiently by the graceful Corinthian columns of York station in the 1890s. As one observer wrote, 'The stately dignity of York is alien to hurry; if it hurries at all, its quickened step and bustle are associated with pleasure rather than trade.'**

Lancashire & Yorkshire (L&YR), Great Eastern (GER) and Great Central (GCR).

In 1923, with the onset of Grouping and the creation of the London & North Eastern Railway, the York railway scene lost some of its character and variety. Even so, it was still possible for years afterwards to see express trains arriving at the station behind the locomotive of one pre-Grouping company and departing behind that of another.

As for the expresses themselves, many were products of the exciting new era of streamlining. The Silver Jubilee, which ran non-stop through York on its journeys between King's Cross and Newcastle, was introduced in 1935. It was followed two years later by the Coronation, which made a three-minute stop at York *en route* between King's Cross and Edinburgh. Both expresses were always packed to capacity.

## Coaches set on fire

In 1939 came the outbreak of war and the imposition of emergency speed restrictions. However, unlike many other stations, York remained fairly unscathed. Its worst air raid was in 1942, when it was hit by a high explosive bomb and a shower of incendiaries. The attack occurred just as an express was pulling into the station, and the middle five coaches were set on fire. Station staff were quick to react. Hurrying passengers from the train, they uncoupled the burning coaches at each end, then hauled the front and rear sections clear of the station, leaving the blazing coaches to burn themselves out.

As the damage and dislocation of wartime receded, so normal services resumed. But the days of the steam train were already numbered. The

**◀ Passengers passing through York station in 1906 were able to sample homely northern fare amidst the oriental rugs and filigree Moorish arches of the new art nouveau tea room. By now, station refreshment facilities were being augmented by restaurant cars on trains.**

Coronation had run between King's Cross and York in 2 hours 37 minutes. Today's InterCity trains on the East Coast mainline, electrified at a cost of £550 million and officially opened by the Queen in the summer of 1991, make the same run in approximately two hours. Yet none of the modern trains has the charisma of the named expresses. One of these, the Scarborough Flyer, would change locomotives at York, a modest, if powerful, 4-4-0 of the Hunt or Shire Class sometimes taking over from a streamlined A4 Pacific for the 67.5km (42 mile) run through the quiet and lovely countryside to the coast.

Nowadays, the Scarborough branch is tied in with the Liverpool–Newcastle service and worked by the same express units, one example of the rather standardized pattern of InterCity and Regional Railways services running in and out of York. These routes have changed little over the years, apart from the closure of some of their wayside stations.

Non-electrified InterCity services between Scotland and southern England are worked by HST 125s. Trans-Pennine services between Merseyside and Tyneside, which all call at York, are maintained by Class 158 stock.

York has never had any intensive commuter services. The only stopping services are to Leeds via Church Fenton, and to Harrogate over a route from which the Beeching Report proposed the withdrawal of passenger services. But an associated economy did take place in 1967, four years after the Beeching Report was published, when expresses between Liverpool and Newcastle, which ran via Harrogate, were diverted to run via York and the line between Harrogate and Northallerton closed.

Local passenger trains running over the Yorkshire Wolds between York, Beverley and Hull ended in 1965, and passengers now have to travel via Selby.

Despite the euphoria of some writers for York station, the original buildings and concourse never matched the grandeur of the train shed. But improvements made by British Rail gave the entrance hall, concourse and adjacent platforms a spaciousness which made them more open and inviting.

The removal of ticket barriers swept away a sense of herding and passengers now have the freedom to stand on the concourse and view the great NER map made from glazed wall tiles. It is a good place to ponder on how much has changed, but also on how much has survived, of York's railway tradition.

**Prestige visitor**

Many expresses have steamed through York station, but none more prestigious than the Flying Scotsman. Introduced in 1862 as the Scottish Special Express, departing from King's Cross for Edinburgh at 10.00 a.m., it made a 30 minute stop at York for through passengers to take a quick lunch in the station's well-appointed refreshment rooms.

Today's Flying Scotsman still leaves King's Cross at 10.00 a.m. and still stops at York, though only for a few minutes, *en route* to Edinburgh. It covers the 632.5km (393 miles) to the Scottish capital in just over four hours – little more than one hour longer than it took for the fastest expresses of Victorian times to travel from London to York.

**▼ A2/3 Pacific No 60518 *Tehran*, built in 1946 and shedded at Gateshead, waits to leave York station with a northbound express in the 1950s, while a driver waits to relieve another crew. On the left, a wheel-tapper, hammer over his shoulder, walks past a rake of carriages.**

# ALL ABOARD!

*The role of the railway in everyday life*

# Showbiz specials

**Actors, pop stars, opera singers, circus performers – all used to travel regularly by train, providing colour and excitement for onlookers, but creating the occasional headache for police and railway staff.**

In the days before World War I, one of the most reliable sources of railway revenue was theatrical traffic. Often, several compartments or carriages would be hired by touring groups on the endless trek from one venue to another – Sunday journeys on slow, unheated trains between drab provincial towns, with poor lodgings and even worse food.

Basil Mercer, writing in the *Railway Magazine* in 1912, disclosed that on one Sunday in October during the previous year, the London & North Western Railway had carried no fewer than 112 theatrical companies – 'an average Sunday's business'. The number of passengers was 2,374, and the 30 special trains hired to carry them included 182 scenery trucks and eight horseboxes.

On board one of the specials, bound for various stations between Manchester and Carlisle, were the casts from six separate shows. As Mercer observed, 'When all the companies were together, this train must have been quite an interesting sight, representing as it did so many kinds of entertainment – musical comedy, repertoire, melodrama, farce and historical drama. All these were fair-sized parties, making up quite a big load for the engine.'

Most companies travelled separately, however, the number of passengers being determined by the type of show. 'There is a great deal of difference', noted Mercer, 'between a modern comedy or a melodrama, in which nearly every member plays at least three parts, and the musical comedy of the present day, which may travel any number from 40 to 80. Some companies are even larger. *The Land of the Golden Fairy Tales* – a Christmas production – travelled as many as 111 passengers, while the celebrated Beecham Opera Company had 100 passengers.'

For the big companies, which usually travelled between large towns, rail journeys were convivial and comfortable. But for the small entertainment companies, trooping back and forth from one provincial outpost to another, and unable to afford the luxury of being 'specialized', riding the rails was far from congenial.

▲ **Scores of photographers provide a welcoming committee for American Rock 'n' Roll star Bill Haley, whose arrival at Waterloo station in 1957 sparked a near riot. Waterloo, with its boat-train link to Southampton, was a popular alighting point for visiting celebrities.**

◀ **American entertainer Liberace, accompanied by his mother, chats to one of the thousands of adoring female fans who turned up to greet him at Waterloo station in 1956. On leaving the train, the idol and his entourage were overwhelmed by the mob and had be escorted out of the station by policemen.**

**Pages 140–141: A crowd of day-trippers and holiday-makers arrive at Scarborough station in 1913.**

The regular train service had to be used which, as Mercer pointed out, generally meant 'an early start and a late arrival, with a few "waits" in between'. A journey from St Albans in Hertfordshire to Colchester in Essex took almost 12 hours and went 'via Watford, Bletchley, Cambridge (4 hours' wait), Ipswich (1 hour wait), the party arriving at 8.55 p.m.'

Another nightmare trip was experienced by a company trying to get from Clacton in Essex to Margate in Kent. Having first been taken to London's Liverpool Street station, the wilting thespians were then hauled through Croydon, Tonbridge, Ashford and Canterbury, finally arriving in Margate at 4.45 p.m. – some nine hours after setting out. 'After this fatiguing experience,' wrote Mercer, 'the unfortunate actors had to amuse and interest an audience, the curtain rising at 7.30.'

The top stars – actors, singers, comedians, conductors – often hired a private saloon carriage, which was the most comfortable, as well as the most private, way of travelling. Futhermore, since the movements of such vehicles were rarely publicized, they offered a protection against the kind of unwelcome intrusion that befell the 1930s film star George Arliss.

Arriving one Saturday afternoon to catch a train at London's Charing Cross, Arliss found himself besieged by a mob of determined autograph hunters. He wrote:

'I couldn't retreat and leave the station because I should have lost my train. I couldn't seek refuge in the refreshment rooms, because my attackers would have no compunction in following me. So with the presence of mind worthy of a great general, I thought of the Left Luggage Office.

'It was just behind me and close to the platform from which I was to start. I turned to the man in charge and demanded the right to book myself in as a parcel. I paid my twopence and the man took me over the counter and I was saved. This method of retreat I confidently recommend to other picture stars in railway stations.'

## Welcoming committee

Not every star travelling by train was as self-effacing as Arliss. The Italian-born opera singer Adelina Patti made frequent and well-publicized 'final' tours in the years before World War I, setting out from the station near her great mansion at Craig-y-nos in the Brecon Beacons.

After completing a tour, the singer would return home in her private train, usually by the Great Western as far as Neath, where a little tank engine would be coupled on for the final leg of the journey to Craig-y-nos. At the station, a sizeable welcoming committee of servants and others from the great house would be lined up on the platform,

**▼ Liberace always stressed his family ties and the headboard of his train included a reference to his brother George. His Pullman had been specially fitted with antimacassars embroidered with Liberace motifs, and piano-shaped ashtrays – but these were all snatched by souvenir hunters.**

▲ **Elephants from Bertram Mills Circus trudge through Nuneaton (Trent Valley) station in Warwickshire in 1950 *en route* to a nearby show site. Such arrivals usually passed off peacefully, but on one occasion a circus elephant went berserk at Wolferton station in Norfolk and uprooted a gate.**

**A dash of drama**

For most theatrical groups, the rail dash from one venue to another was an inescapable fact of life. But few had to undertake a more hectic journey than Sir Herbert Tree's company in the early 1900s.

Having given a royal command performance at Balmoral Castle in Scotland one evening, the players set off immediately for Dublin, where they were due to appear the next night. They boarded the train at Ballater at 2.05 a.m. and, travelling via the West Coast route, reached Holyhead at 4.08 p.m.

Leaving the pier seven minutes later, they arrived at Dublin just in time to ring up the curtain – the successful climax to a feverish 965.5km (600 mile) Odyssey by land and sea.

the beetling crags of the mountains forming a suitably impressive backdrop.

For ordinary troupers, unable to afford the luxury of a private train, the most dire and dangerous time for rail travel was World War II. The Entertainments National Service Association (ENSA) performed at military bases all over the country.

Night-time journeys, sudden air raids, long delays, lost props, dim blue bulbs in blacked-out compartments – these are just a few examples of the problems faced by the ENSA parties, and they deserved medals for endurance even if the barrack-room wiseacres could claim that their initials really stood for Every Night Something Awful.

## Purpose-built train

On the other side of the Atlantic, where roads were abysmal and distances far greater, the fairs, peep shows, theatrical companies and circuses began using railways as early as the 1840s.

Phineas T. Barnum was the first maestro of the sawdust ring, and by the 1870s his road manager, William C. Coup, had persuaded him to invest in a purpose-built train of 61 cars to carry the assorted paraphernalia of what was rightly billed as the Greatest Show on Earth. This included 1,000 staff, 30 elephants and the big top, which when erected could accommodate an audience of over 5,000.

Half-fare excursions from a 161km (100 mile) radius brought in huge crowds to fill the marquee for two and even three performances daily. The whole circus would then board the train and travel overnight to the next venue – for another big parade and three more performances.

In 1889, the 80-year-old Barnum began a tour of England and the Continent, commencing with a Christmas show at Olympia in London which broke all records. Five more years of touring followed, with a special train built to European standards. This consisted of 67 cars, each 16.75m (55ft) long, which meant that it often had to be run in three sections.

Barnum died before the tour ended and he was succeeded by his partner, James A. Bailey, who promoted a second grand tour in 1899–1903. The Pullman coaches used by the star performers on this occasion were later sold off to the Alexandra Docks Railway Company in South Wales, where they spent their last years carrying miners and their families between Newport and Pontypridd.

A number of British circuses followed the Barnum and Bailey example – the best known was Bertram Mills – bringing a touch of the exotic to many a provincial siding.

## Broadcasting broadsides

With the end of World War II, the train began to be used not just for transporting showbiz personalities but as a way of publicizing them, too. An early example was the Irish Radio Train, one of whose stars was Eamonn Andrews, later to become a broadcasting celebrity in Britain. Popular beauty spots and places of pilgrimage were the regular destinations of the Radio Train.

A similar role was performed by the Television Train, which toured the West Country in 1961, publicizing the products and performers of the new ITV studios in Bristol and Plymouth.

▲ **Coupled to No 28 (an ex-GWR 0-6-0 tank engine), the two Pullman coaches used by Barnum and Bailey's Circus for their 1890s tour of Britain wait on the line at Newport in South Wales a few years later. Following the tour, the coaches were sold to the Alexandra Docks Railway Company.**

▼ **The actress Sarah Bernhardt, seen beside her private saloon at St Pancras station in 1894, was a demanding traveller. On a tour of America, she insisted that her driver should cross a bridge he knew to be unsafe. Sure enough, the train – 'half leaping and half rolling along' – had barely reached the other side when the bridge gave way.**

## Waterloo receptions

It was Waterloo station, with its stream of celebrities arriving by boat-train from Southampton, which gave the publicity seekers their greatest opportunities for staging dramatic entrances.

One of the most memorable receptions was that accorded to the American entertainer Liberace, whose candlelit piano recitals and extravagant attire had made him the idol of many middle-aged women, and some younger ones as well.

When the Liberace Special pulled in at Waterloo in September 1956, thousands of female admirers strewed a carpet of rose petals (mostly paper) for their hero to tread on first setting foot in London. Police, using a flying wedge formation, then escorted the star and his entourage through the thousands of screaming fans and out on to the carriage road, where a pair of Daimlers awaited.

Even wilder scenes greeted the arrival a few months later of the Bill Haley Rock 'n' Roll Special. The fans awaiting the King of Rock included both sexes and tended to be younger and more aggressive than the fans who had welcomed Liberace. In fact, the police were faced with a near riot and the conductor of the Rock King's Pullman described the affair as 'a frightening experience'.

But the age of rail closures, jet travel and larger road vehicles was about to dawn – and there was to be no place in it for touring circus trains or showbiz specials.

# Railway hotels

**Whether intended as a magnificent appendage to one of the mainline termini or as a remote holiday retreat, the railway hotel once appeared to be a reassuringly permanent part of the landscape. In fact, it was no more immune to change than the railway itself.**

An inseparable part of Britain's stagecoach system was the coaching inns, where passengers took a rest while the horses were changed, or where they spent the night. The coming of railways slowly killed this business. However, the idea persisted in the form of railway inns, because the railway network was still developing and many journeys took longer than a day.

When rail travel became faster, most of them declined into mere pubs, and many can still be seen plying their trade close to past or present stations. However, railways had already seen the advantage of providing their own hotels, and these soon became the last word in luxury. It is perhaps surprising, therefore, that the very first was a spartan establishment, described as a 'dormitory', for third-class passengers. This was provided by the London & Birmingham Railway (LBR) at its Euston terminus in London and was opened as the Victoria in 1839. Three months later, the LBR opened superior accommodation across the road, the Euston Hotel.

The Euston, with its ornate classical facade, was designed for first-class travellers and was the first of the railway *grande luxe* establishments. Other railways followed the LBR's lead, although a surprising number of the new establishments closed after only a few years, having made unbearable losses; the same optimism that had produced the railway boom and the railway crash evidently had its effect here, too.

Many not only survived, however, but went on to set new standards of luxury and comfort. They tended to be in city centres, close to the railway station, and relied on the railway for their clientele, with businessmen predominant. An early but

**Colourful clientele**

No railway hotel had a more colourful clientele than the Queen's in Birmingham. Opened by the London & North Western Railway in 1854 and closed on New Year's Eve 1965 prior to demolition, its long list of VIP guests ranged from Queen Victoria to the Emperor of Ethiopia, Haile Selassie. The Soviet leaders Nikita Khruskhev and Marshal Bulganin also stayed there, as did France's General de Gaulle. On one occasion, guests and staff were amazed to see a horse trotting up the stairs. This turned out to be Trigger, faithful mount of cowboy Roy Rogers, who was staying in a bedroom on the first floor.

Patrons of the Queen's well-stocked bars included Noel Coward, Ivor Novello, Gracie Fields, Danny Kaye and Laurel and Hardy. Many came just to be served by the hotel's famous barman, 'Flash' Battersby, whose favourite trick was to send cocktails skimming down the 6m (20ft) counter so that they came to rest exactly in front of waiting customers.

**▼ Opened in 1876, the Sandringham Hotel at Hunstanton on the north coast of Norfolk proved so popular that an extension was built in 1920, providing a total of 55 bedrooms. The hotel was sold in 1950 and demolished in 1967.**

▲ **Features offered by Manchester's Midland Hotel, opened by the Midland Railway in 1903, included a winter garden, seen here, five restaurants, a grand banqueting hall, and an 800-seat theatre which hosted England's first repertory company.**

**Adolf at the Adelphi**
Railway hotels have provided impressive settings for authors and film makers. MGM's 1939 version of *The Hound of the Baskervilles*, starring Basil Rathbone as Sherlock Holmes, was filmed at the Great Western Railway's Manor House Hotel near Moretonhampstead on the edge of Dartmoor, for a suitably spooky feel.

A story by Liverpool novelist Beryl Bainbridge, *Young Adolf*, features the city's former Midland Railway hotel, the Adelphi. One of its bell boys turns out to be the young Adolf Hitler, over here on a visit to his half-brother Alois. Alois did, indeed, run a café in Liverpool and the future Führer may even have visited him. It is unlikely, however, that he would have satisfied the Adelphi's rigorous staff requirements.

long-lived example was Cuff's Station Hotel, built privately but soon bought by the Midland Railway (MR); it was in the MR's home town of Derby and notable because it was architecturally identical with the main station building close by.

Unlike most of the old railway inns, the new city hotels were not built to fill an obvious need. Usually, there were enough hotels already. But in the optimistic decades before 1914 there was a feeling that, if a hotel was clearly more luxurious than its rivals, a regular clientele and reliable profit would be assured. And even if a hotel disappointed in its takings, it could still boost the reputation of the railway that owned it.

Non-railway hoteliers did not take kindly to the intruders. Soon after the MR built its new Midland Hotel in Manchester in 1903, complete with 800-seat theatre, Turkish baths and French cuisine, the chairman of hoteliers Spiers & Pond denounced the competition as 'unfair', declaring that every other hotel in the city 'was practically doing no business' as a result.

## Sense of security

In London, there were 11 railway hotels – one at every important terminus except Waterloo. The sense of security and well-being induced by these establishments was described in a memorable tribute published in *The Railway Age* in 1937.

The writer was particularly impressed by the Great Western Hotel, which the Great Western Railway (GWR) had opened at its Paddington terminus in 1854. 'Those like myself who knew it well, especially at Christmas when a child,' he wrote, 'will never forget its Victorian comfort, what it meant to lie in bed with the distant whistle of the trains outside: to feel that the bustle of the station was there when you had need of it, but that in the meantime it was none of your concern.'

There were more delights in store, for 'when through the heavily braided curtains the morning came with its yearly excitement of carols and pantomimes, was not the renewal of life on the platforms outside, and that familiar smell of trains that came gently in, a perfect prelude to the bacon and eggs downstairs under the great semi-draped allegorical ladies with their arms full of the good things of the earth?'

The Great Western was probably less grand than the London, Brighton & South Coast Railway's Grosvenor at Victoria, and it certainly palled beside the much later edifice erected in

Midland Hotel, Manchester

▲ **Opinion varied over the appearance of the four-storey Manchester Midland, with its polished red granite plinth, terracotta detailing and angle turrets. The *Manchester Guardian* hailed it as 'a novelty among Manchester's buildings', but a critic compared the 'vast and disordered mass to an ant heap'.**

MIDLAND RAILWAY.
Adelphi Hotel, Liverpool.
FORTH BRIDGE.
Midland Rʸ Cº Queen's Hotel, Leeds.
GLASGOW.
EDINBURGH.
Matlock.
Chatsworth.
BATH.
Cheltenham.
Buxton.
Midland Hotel, Bradford.
Clifton.
Bournemouth.
Midland Grand Hotel, Sᵗ Pancras, LONDON.
BEMROSE & SONS, PRINTERS, DERBY & LONDON.
GREENOCK PIER
GLASGOW
EDINBURGH
CARLISLE
NEWCASTLE
LANCASTER
BRADFORD
LEEDS
YORK
HULL
LIVERPOOL
MANCHESTER
SHEFFIELD
LINCOLN
DERBY
NOTTINGHAM
LEICESTER
PETERBORO'
BIRMINGHAM
WORCESTER
HEREFORD
BRECON
NORTHAMPTON
BEDFORD
CAMBRIDGE
CHELTENHAM
GLOUCESTER
SWANSEA
CARDIFF
BRISTOL
BATH
Sᵀ PANCRAS
LONDON
EXETER
BOURNEMOUTH
GEO. H. TURNER. GENERAL MANAGER. DERBY.

▶ For hotel-owning railway companies, postcards were an effective way of publicizing their establishments. This example, dating from 1904, plays up the cliff-top views and close proximity to the beach of the Great Northern Railway's hotel at Sheringham in Norfolk.

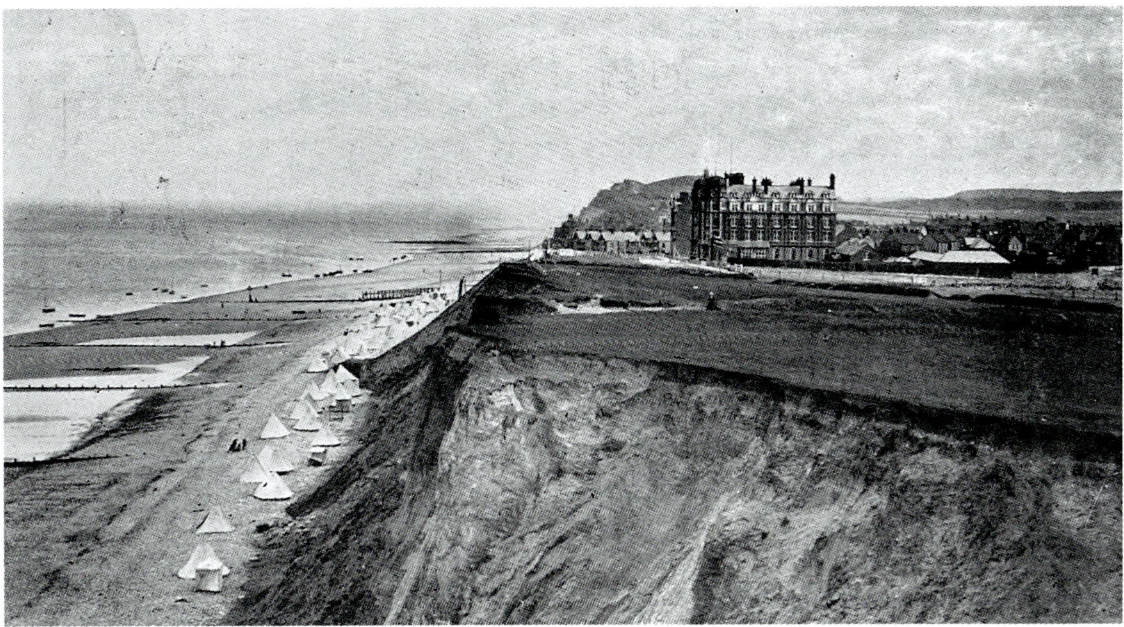

**Competitive spirit**

The Midland Grand at London's St Pancras station, opened by the Midland Railway (MR) in 1873, was the world's most celebrated railway hotel. But this distinctive Victorian-Gothic pile, applauded and reviled in more or less equal measure, came to be erected almost by accident. The architect, George Gilbert Scott, had not intended to participate in the design competition, but two months' enforced stay in a boring south coast resort when one of his children became ill there led him to change his mind and enter a drawing.

In his enthusiasm, he designed a far larger and more expensive building than the design specifications prescribed. Although the other ten contestants complained that he had broken the rules, the MR pronounced him the winner. Scott remained proud of his creation, writing later that 'It is often spoken of to me as the finest building in London; my own belief is that it is possibly *too good* for its purpose.'

◀ An advertisement produced around 1900 for some of the Midland Railway's hotels. According to Sir William Towle, Controller of the Midland hotel empire from 1885 to 1914, 'The nation owes a debt of gratitude to the railway companies for the provision of many good hotels which would certainly not have been built by other capital.'

1899 at Marylebone station, the new London terminus of the Great Central Railway (GCR). The GCR, being a late entrant to London, needed to impress and the Hotel Great Central certainly did that. It proved too expensive for the railway to complete or own, so a private company took over. Among the hotel's attractions were a winter garden and a cycle track on the roof.

Even the Hotel Great Central, however, could not compete with the massive Midland Grand Hotel at St Pancras station. Completed in 1876, and still one of the sights of London, this red-brick Victorian Gothic structure provides a more than fitting frontage for that other St Pancras spectacle, W.H. Barlow's enormous trainshed.

## Water-powered lifts

The Midland Grand was the creation of the architect Sir Gilbert Scott. Complete with its 30.5m (100ft) dining room and water-powered hydraulic lifts – reassuringly described as 'rising rooms' – it offered no fewer than 400 bedrooms, ranging from tiny rooms for servants just below the eaves to grand apartments on the lower floors. It took eight years to build and, although it did not have electric lighting, it did install some awe-inspiring 'gasoliers' (candle-less chandeliers).

Its dust chutes were also a novelty, as was the rubber surface on the cab roadway outside. On the lower and more public floors the hotel strove to be in advance of the times. In the 1890s it boasted a highly unusual, if not shocking, Ladies' Smoking Room, and in 1900 it installed London's first revolving door.

Staff discipline was strict at such establishments. Mrs Jean Robertson, who worked in late Victorian days as a housemaid at the Great North of Scotland Railway's Cruden Bay Hotel at Port Erroll in Aberdeenshire, recalled how 'Each evening waitresses received the head waiter's inspection. Each girl wore a navy-blue crepe de chine dress, small apron fastened at the waist with buttons, a little white cap, stiff collar and cuffs. General appearance was checked, but special note was taken of finger nails and shoes. No make up was allowed. This over, the head waiter sounded the dinner gong and into the blue and gold dining room trooped lords, ladies and gentlemen.'

While diners worked their way through the gargantuan meal, Mrs Robertson and her colleagues 'had to slop out the rooms, attend to wash bowls and ewers and remove the hot water cans that had been taken up to each bedroom before dinner'.

Although providing for intercity travellers remained the staple business of the railway hotel departments, they had other interests as well. One of these was catering for passengers using the cross-Channel and Irish Sea ferry services. The grandest of the ferry port hotels was the Lord Warden at Dover, built in 1853 by the South Eastern Railway.

One unimpressed guest was Charles Dickens. 'I particularly detest Dover for the self-complacency with which it goes to bed,' he wrote. 'It always goes to bed (when I am going to Calais) with a more brilliant display of lamp and candle than any other town. Mr and Mrs Birmingham, host and hostess of the Lord Warden Hotel, are my much esteemed friends, but they are too conceited about the comforts of that establishment when the Night Mail is starting. I know the Warden is a stationary edifice that never rolls or pitches and I object to its big outline seeming to insist upon that circumstance, and, as it were, to come over with it, when I am reeling on the deck of the boat.'

## Unfortunate incident

Another type of railway hotel was the one set up in a remote but scenic part of Britain and intended to generate new rail traffic. Such establishments were widely advertised; no traveller on the GWR, for example, could miss posters extolling the Tregenna Castle Hotel, an eighteenth century country mansion near St Ives in Cornwall. In spite of an unfortunate incident soon after its opening – a dog owned by one of the guests evacuated itself on a costly new carpet – the hotel flourished.

Scotland was a particularly fertile field for holiday hotels; it had no shortage of out-of-the-way tourist spots, and much of the clientele was prepared to travel long distances with first-class tickets. But the hotels had to provide more than mere comfort, and several of them included fine golf courses among their amenities.

Indeed, the magnificent Gleneagles at Auchterarder, near Perth, was able to boast two championship golf courses. (Two more were to be added later.) The 114-bedroomed hotel had been commissioned by the Caledonian Railway (CR) just before the outbreak of World War I, which delayed its completion until 1924.

By then, the CR had been absorbed into the post-Grouping London Midland & Scottish Railway (LMS), and the resources poured into the 'new Palace among the Scottish Mountains' were huge. In addition to the golf courses, there was a French restaurant – the first in Scotland – and a ballroom large enough to hold 200 couples.

Many of the railway hotels employed their own musicians, and guests at Gleneagles were entertained for some years by the distinguished bandleader Henry Hall. He had started as a stand-in pianist at the Midland Hotel in Manchester, and later worked as head of entertainment for all LMS hotels before becoming one of the BBC's greatest celebrities. In July 1924, he made his first broadcast from Gleneagles.

▼ One of the world's most famous golf hotels, Gleneagles in Perthshire was opened by the London Midland & Scottish Railway in 1924. No expense was spared in furnishing the new establishment, and 9,144m (10,000yd) of material were used for carpeting its 114 bedrooms, and 19.25km (12 miles) for carpeting its corridors.

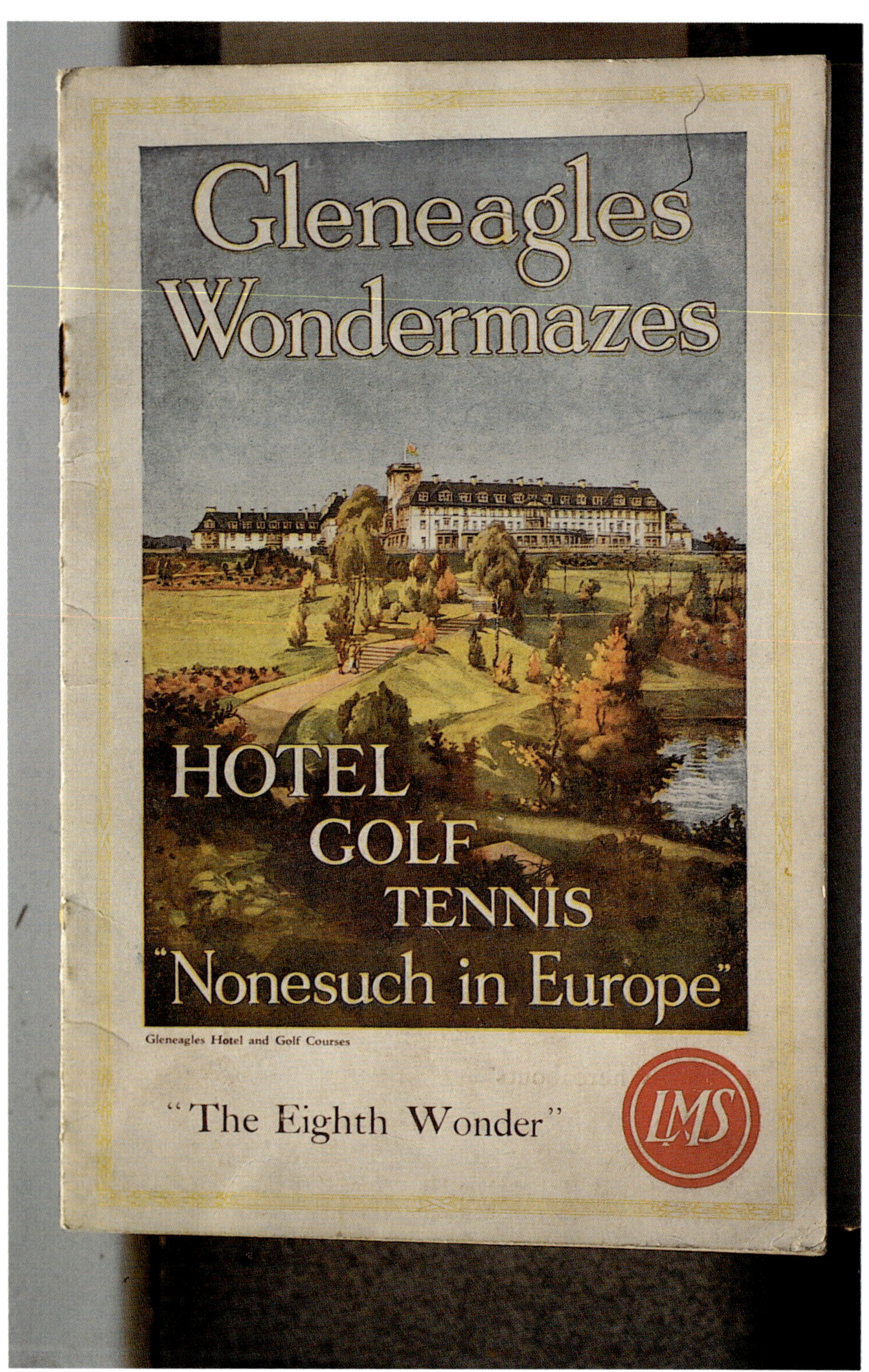


## Changing demand

With the dawning of the 1930s, the demand for Edwardian and Victorian styles of luxury declined. The old hotels' grandeur and solidity were selling points no longer. What customers now demanded were modern conveniences such as en suite bathrooms. But this was the time of the Great Depression and the railways were hard put to find the large sums of money needed for modernization schemes.

It did not help that so many of their hotels were constructed on a massive scale. As the Chairman of the LMS, Lord Stamp, observed, 'It is impossible to put in a new piece of heating apparatus, or anything of that kind, without meeting the same obstacles that would be encountered in modifying the Rock of Gibraltar.'

So a number were refurbished, while others were sold off. Some, like the Lord Warden at Dover and even the Midland Grand at St Pancras, became railway offices. One notable exception was the Queens in Leeds. The building, which dated from 1867, was knocked down and replaced with a new 200-bedroomed hotel – the first in Britain to be fully air-conditioned.

With the nationalization of the railways in 1948, the British Transport Commission made its headquarters at the Hotel Great Central, now known simply as 222 Marylebone Road. Also housed here was the new Hotels Executive (later renamed British Transport Hotels & Catering Services), one of whose tasks was to weed out those establishments with unhealthy profit margins. Over the next six years, no fewer than 13 were sold off, including the Lord Warden, the Cruden Bay and the Midland at Morecambe.

## End of the spiral

The final twist in this downward spiral began in 1979, with the election of a Conservative government committed to privatization. Gleneagles was disposed of in 1982 and the last of the railway hotels, the Queens in Leeds, was sold to a private chain in 1984.

Almost half a century earlier, the author of the 1937 tribute in *The Railway Age* had written: 'It would be a pity if the British Railways, the largest hotel owners in the world today, lost that subtle atmosphere, which in the past has made their hotels a temporary residence rather than a restaurant and sleeping place.'

# Holiday train excursions

**The railways well understood the public's desire for a day beside the sea or a walk in the country, and the normally cheap fares of the excursion train brought longer distance travel within the grasp of millions, opening up a whole range of new experiences.**

Credit for the idea of the first railway excursion has traditionally been given to the man whose name is synonymous with travel, Thomas Cook. The train which he organized ran on 5 July 1841 – a couple of Midland Counties Railway 0-4-0s hauling 500 temperance folk from Leicester to Loughborough.

However, this was not the first excursion. Supposedly, this honour belonged to the Bodmin & Wadebridge Railway, which in June 1836 carried 800 people in two trains from Wadebridge to the rustic charms of Wenford Bridge; 130 years later, British Rail ran a commemorative special over the then goods-only line.

Nor was Cook's train the first to be hired from a railway company by an outside organization; in June 1840, the marine and steam engine builder R. & W. Hawthorn of Newcastle chartered a train to give its workers, together with families and friends, a day in Carlisle.

The marked contrast between polluted urban areas and industry-free coastal resorts, with the restorative wonder of sea air, soon gave rise to excursions from towns to the seaside. In 1840, the London & South Western Railway (LSWR) offered a £1 excursion from Nine Elms in London to Southampton for a circumnavigation of the Isle of Wight.

The definition of exactly what constituted a holiday excursion is inevitably vague, particularly given the severe constraints on leisure time in Victorian Britain – at weekends, it was normal practice to work for at least Saturday morning, there was little or no paid vacation and Bank Holidays were introduced only in 1871. For many, the Sunday School outing or day visit to a London exhibition was the nearest they came to having a holiday. But once the normally cheap fares of the excursion train made longer distance travel a possibility, the public responded enthusiastically.

'There are thousands of our readers, we are sure,' declared *The Times* in 1850, 'who, in the last three years of their lives, have travelled more and seen more than in all their previous life taken together. Thirty years ago not one countryman in one hundred had seen the metropolis. There is now scarcely one in the same number who has not spent the day there.'

But even *The Times* was astonished by the vast influx of visitors to the Great Exhibition held in

**▼ Eager day-trippers, sporting their holiday boaters, pour on to the platform at Scarborough station in the early 1900s. Seaside resorts were the main target of the excursionists, with Blackpool in the north and Brighton in the south being the most popular. Fares would often be less than a third of the normal 'penny a mile' of the third-class rate, but stock usually consisted of bone-shaking four-wheelers, like the ones seen here.**

◀ **In the struggle to attract passengers, the Grouped railways resorted to some ingenious promotion schemes. Here William King, a London Midland & Scottish Railway porter at Blackburn, and an amateur artist, puts the finishing touches to his notice aimed at fans of Blackburn Rovers.**

the Crystal Palace in London's Hyde Park in the following year. During the 22 weeks the Exhibition remained open, 6.2 million people passed through the turnstiles, most of them having been brought to London by excursion train – 160,000 of them courtesy of Thomas Cook.

One of the excursions is described in a story by Thomas Hardy in which the heroine shares the discomfort of those going to the Exhibition:

'The "excursion-train" – an absolutely new departure in the history of travel – was still a novelty on the Wessex line, and probably everywhere...The seats for the humbler class of travellers in these early experiments in steam-locomotion, were open trucks, without any protection whatever from wind and rain; and damp weather having set in with the afternoon, the unfortunate occupants of these vehicles were, on the train drawing up to the London terminus, found to be in a pitiable condition from their long journey; blue-faced, stiff-necked, sneezing, rain-beaten, chilled to the marrow, many of the men being hatless; in fact, they resembled people who had been out all night in an open boat on a rough sea...'

## A nightmare return

Few suffered worse misfortune, however, than the participants in an early excursion to the Continent, organized by the Eastern Counties Railway in 1846. On the return from Rotterdam, the crew of the steamer were drunk, a gale blew the ship off course and on the journey back to London the locomotive's boiler burst near Ely.

Part of the problem of poor conditions lay in the ambiguous attitude of the railway companies to the whole idea of excursions, often reflected

Midland and North Eastern Railways.

GARIBALDI

DEMONSTRATION

AT THE CRYSTAL PALACE.

On SATURDAY, APRIL 16,

A Cheap Excursion Train will leave

HULL, SELBY, YORK

And the undermentioned Stations for

LONDON

(KING'S CROSS STATION)

FARES THERE AND BACK AND TIMES OF STARTING.

| Stations | | a.m. | FIRST CLASS s. | d. | COVERED CARR. s. | d. |
|---|---|---|---|---|---|---|
| Hull | dep. | 6. 0 | 25 | 0 | 12 | 6 |
| Howden | ,, | 6.54 | | | | |
| Selby | ,, | 7.20 | | | | |
| York | ,, | 7.15 | 21 | 0 | 10 | 6 |
| Church Fenton | ,, | 7.43 | | | | |
| Milford | ,, | 8. 2 | | | | |

LONDON (KING'S CROSS) ARRIVE ABOUT 4.45 P.M.

Children under Three years of Age, Free; above Three and under Twelve, Half-fares.

The Return Train will leave the King's Cross Station, London, on Wednesday, April 20th, at 10.15 a.m.

Tickets are not transferable, and will be available for returning by this Train only.

Luggage must be conveyed under the Passengers' own care, as the Company will not be responsible.

Ten Minutes will be allowed at Trent Station for Refreshments both in going and returning.

Derby, April 1864. BY ORDER.

Bemrose and Sons, Printers by Steam Power, Derby.

▲ **Excursion trains from the Midland, North Eastern, London & North Western and Great Western railways brought thousands of supporters to the capital to attend a rally addressed by the Italian patriotic leader, Giuseppe Garibaldi, at the Crystal Palace in April 1864.**

in the rostering of the oldest locomotives and carriages to such use. Sunday was inevitably the principal choice for excursion trains as it was not a usual working day; but many railway directors, particularly in Scotland, were opposed to running any services on Sunday, let alone ones that would tempt people from attendance at church.

And even if the directors had no scruples about making profits on the Sabbath, there were always members of the public keen to remind them, through the letter columns of newspapers, that railway travel on Sunday was 'a journey into hell'.

However, not every devout believer was prepared to forego the advantages of cheap Sunday travel. As early as 1842, the Preston & Wyre Railway carried 2,364 Sunday School teachers and pupils from Preston to Fleetwood, 'the whole multitude', according to the *Preston Pilot*, 'singing hymns throughout the journey'. A Sunday School outing from Winchmore Hill to Enfield seems to have been a somewhat more boisterous affair, with

**By public demand**

Excursion trains were laid on for a whole variety of events, from public executions to illegal prize fights. But few were more popular than the week-long Preston Guild, held every 20 years to celebrate the skills of Preston craftsmen, who began to organize on the lines of Friendly Societies in the eighteenth century. The week of parades and entertainment in 1922 attracted over half a million passengers in some 500 special trains.

Race specials also became big business for the railways, 82 trains running to Doncaster for the 1887 St Ledger Day, entailing a suspension of and clearing out of all goods traffic in sidings required for stabling the excursions. For the Grand National at Aintree in 1913, a train arrived and unloaded every two minutes.

a local vicar resolving 'never to allow such a dissipation under the name of a treat to happen again'.

Temperance organizations followed Cook's lead, often campaigning at seaside resorts, though how much good the Grand Teetotallers of Heslington may have done their cause by banging a drum all the way to the station at five o'clock in the morning is open to question. Congregations could be exceedingly loyal to a favoured resort: the Diss Methodists never deserted Great Yarmouth in 59 years for their annual excursion, which attracted 1,500 people in 1912.

Not everyone was as well-behaved as the temperance travellers, and a works outing to Southend in 1874 ended in a riot. Writing in the *Railway Magazine* in 1898, the stationmaster at Stonehouse on the Midland Railway's main Birmingham–Bristol line, cited Bank Holidays as 'our special *bêtes noires*. We can deal with any amount of extra traffic in reason, and get on tolerably comfortably, so long as we have a fairly decent class to deal with; but when it comes to a noisy, drunken, swearing mob – no uncommon element in a Bank Holiday excursion – it makes our work very hard and irksome indeed.'

## Brighton bonanza

Whatever reservations Sabbatarians and railway employees had about excursion trains were certainly not shared by seaside traders or boarding house keepers. In one summer weekend of 1859, the hordes of visitors descending on Brighton outnumbered the town's residents.

The demand for seats continually surprised the railway companies. Excursions were often late leaving because more carriages or extra engines had to be summoned. One excursion to Brighton in 1844 ended up with 60 carriages hauled by six locomotives. Even allowing for the shortness of early four-wheel carriages, the 82 vehicles of a Manchester & Leeds Railway excursion in the same year must have made a prodigious length.

Gradually, resorts came to be linked with particular inland manufacturing towns: the woollen towns of the West Riding went to Bridlington and Scarborough; Sheffield favoured Cleethorpes; Birmingham and the Black Country patronized the Cambrian and North Wales coasts; and Nottingham and Leicester took the train to Skegness, providing passenger traffic over the Great Northern and London & North Western Joint line for years after regular services ended.

Usually, local entrepreneurs responded by developing facilities at the resorts, but sometimes the railway played a role. The Carlisle & Silloth Bay Railway exceeded its statutory rights by buying over 200 acres (81 hectares) of land in Silloth for development and was even responsible for naming the streets. Hotels were built, usually for the top end of the market, though none went as far as the Stockton & Darlington Railway at Saltburn where the tracks ran right into the hotel.

The example of Hawthorn's in promoting an excursion for employees was quickly and widely followed. One of the great Victorian philanthropists, Sir Titus Salt, took 2,200 of his staff for a day in the country in 1848, the year of revolutions in much of Europe. The railway companies themselves joined in, the Caley Trip from the Caledonian Railway's St Rollox works at Springburn in Glasgow becoming an annual event, as did the Great Western Railway's outing from Swindon. Here 21,000 men, women and

### Organizational feats

The work of laying on a single excursion train has always been considerable. Once a path has been found for the train, suitable carriages have to be allocated and prepared, and, in some cases, catering facilities laid on. A locomotive and crew have to be rostered, details of the working included in the Weekly Traffic Notices and consideration given to the stabling of the empty stock before the return working – which could be a serious problem at a major resort like Scarborough. Here the solution was to build 6.5km (four miles) of siding beyond the tunnel on the Whitby line, which was easily reached from the separate Londesborough Road station for excursions.

All these requirements were in addition to the marketing of the train and the selling of tickets, tasks which many railway companies handed over to agents. Yet the flexibility and resourcefulness of the railways was often astonishing. When a coach company failed to show up for the Retford Baptist Sunday School annual outing in 1931, the organizers in desperation appealed to the stationmaster. Within 20 minutes they had been offered a trip to any station on the London & North Eastern Railway system. Doubtless on grounds of cost, they settled for the next station down the line.

**◀ Racegoers at Aintree station, near Liverpool, after the 1933 Grand National. The first railway race special was run by the Liverpool & Manchester Railway (LMR) to Newton-le-Willows for Newton races on 13 June 1831, with 26 cotton wagons fitted out for temporary use by second-class passengers. Anticipating trouble, the LMR asked for extra constables to supplement its own police, but the request was turned down – apparently without adverse effects.**

▲ **Children play outside camping coaches in Devon in 1959. Launched by the Grouped railways in the 1930s, this type of holiday accommodation was supplemented by more traditional inducements to travel, such as cheap day excursion tickets and special facilities for cyclists and walkers.**

**A chance encounter**
In September 1858, an excursion train organized by Thomas Cook of Leicester made an unexpected encounter. As it approached Dunbar, word spread that the Royal Train was approaching the station from the opposite direction. 'The next moment,' wrote the *Illustrated London News*, 'as the Royal train stopped, hundreds of men, women and children...joined in hearty cheer after cheer for every member of the Royal family; the young Princess gained laurels by her quick apprehension of the wishes of the people.'

After a few minutes, 'the excursionists withdrew, greatly delighted at this unexpected meeting with their Queen; and Her Majesty, equally pleased, no doubt, with such an impromptu outburst of genuine loyalty, proceeded towards her Highland home'.

children had to climb into the 500-odd carriages within the works since the station could not cope.

Possibly the best known of these feats of organization was the annual outing of the Bass brewery, which in 1893 required 15 trains from Burton-on-Trent and one from St Pancras to carry 8,000 passengers to Great Yarmouth. A 16-page programme was issued to participants, in which the Traffic Manager wrote: '...let me advise all to get substantial food and so be fitted for the fatigue of such a long day. Avoid messes and odds and ends, rather partaking of MEALS at proper hours as you do when at your ordinary employment.'

Industrialists also paid for children from deprived backgrounds to be taken on day trips. Sir Arthur Pearson set up the Pearson Fresh Air Fund for this purpose, and such was the response that in the first year 20,000 children were given a day in the country or by the seaside. The Quaker Reckitt family took 1,400 children from Hull to Beverley for the day, each child receiving a small envelope with 3*d*. in copper on arrival.

During World War I, all excursion traffic ceased, and when it was resumed the railways had to face increasing competition from growing car ownership and coach companies. It was not for some decades, however, that the railways' supremacy was seriously threatened – in May 1937, for example, they ran 4,079 excursions, albeit in a month that included the Coronation of George VI, an FA Cup Final, the Whitsun Bank Holiday and the Naval Review at Spithead.

Nevertheless, the threat did compel the Grouped railways to devise imaginative ideas, like evening excursions and circular tours, involving perhaps a coach and steamer ride, as well as the train journey itself. It also made the companies sharpen up their marketing, which most of them had begun to take seriously in the 1900s, producing such gems as the Great Northern Railway's bouncing fisherman to promote the bracing air at Skegness.

As in World War I, railway excursions were suspended during World War II. However, with the end of the war, the main lines to the popular coastal resorts again became packed with summer excursionists. But this was to be no more than an Indian Summer. The take-off in air travel, the spread of the motor car and the increasing truncation of the BR system ensured that the excursion train was doomed. Their profitability was probably never more than marginal, and some were almost certainly loss-leaders.

Although brave efforts were made to keep the business alive, the number of excursions run by the Special Trains sub-sector of InterCity was but a pale shadow of an institution that once seemed as permanent as Brighton Rock or the Blackpool Tower.

▶ **Derby day-trippers spill on to the platform at Tattenham Corner, one of three stations serving Epsom racecourse, in 1922. The running of excursion trains to race meetings was highly profitable, though the assembly of such vast crowds sometimes led to disorder. As early as 1838 a mob of racegoing excursionists bound for Epsom went on the rampage at Nine Elms when it became clear that there were not enough trains to carry them.**

# Railways & the cinema

**Film-makers were quick to realize the box-office appeal of the railway, and countless trains, stations and locomotives have been committed to celluloid. The end of steam in the 1960s was a problem, but producers then began turning to the preservationists.**

It may come as a surprise for many people to realize that the first railway film was made just over a century ago. In July 1895, the two French inventors, Auguste and Louis Lumière, were on holiday and decided to test out their new cinematograph for an 'action' scene. So they filmed the arrival of a train from Marseilles at La Ciotat, featuring an excellent three-quarter view of a Bourbonnais Class 2-4-2 locomotive and a highly polished line of little four-wheel carriages, followed by a bustling platform scene.

The Lumières exhibited their 15-minute film in Paris on 28 December 1895, as part of the world's first public cinema show. When the scene of the train steaming into the station was shown, a man sitting out of sight of the audience released a series of loud hisses from a compressed air cylinder. So realistic was the effect that people in the front rows leapt back lest they be mown down by the oncoming engine.

Two months later, the film came to London, appearing first at the Regent Street Polytechnic and then transferring to the Empire Music Hall in Leicester Square. Among those watching was a photographer from Hove, George Albert Smith, who was so impressed that, on returning home, he got a local engineer, Alfred Darling, to build him a camera and projector. In May 1896, Smith went to Hove station on the London, Brighton & South Coast Railway and filmed the arrival of the London Express, headed by a Gladstone Class locomotive.

## Opposition from the Alhambra

That same month, another film-making enthusiast, Robert Paul of Muswell Hill in London, using equipment he had evolved from Edison gear, went to a site alongside the Great Northern Railway at Wood Green and filmed trains coming up from King's Cross, including old Stirling singles and a North London Railway tank with a local going to New Barnet. This was later shown at the Alhambra Music Hall, also in Leicester Square, in direct opposition to the Lumière show.

It was not long before film-makers began featuring the railway in works of celluloid fiction. One of the pioneers was George Albert Smith, whose *Kiss in the Tunnel*, made in 1900, was among the first of the story films. The main influence, however, came from the US, with Edwin S. Porter's 1903 production, *The Great Train Robbery*. Shot in and around Paterson, New Jersey, and using typical American 4-4-0 locomotives of the day, this simple tale of crime on the iron road ushered in a whole new film genre – the railway melodrama.

The following decade saw hundreds of such films, not least in Britain, where audiences thrilled to productions such as *When the Devil Drives* (1907). Made by Robert Paul for Charles Urban, this included rare shots of the Dreadnought 2-2-2-2s bought by the London & North Western Railway.

The public's appetite for story films was whetted by the inclusion of a new and irresistible ingredient – the train crash. Again, the recipe was first tried in America, where the Vitagraph Company staged a collision between two old 4-4-0s for its film *The Wreck* (1914).

The first British film to include a crash was *The Wrecker* (1929). Based on a play by Arnold Ridley (better known for his playing of Private Godfrey in the television comedy series *Dad's Army*), and produced by Michael Balcon, it made considerable use of scenes shot on the Southern Railway (SR).

**▼ The British comedy *Oh! Mr Porter*, made in 1937, starred Will Hay as the incompetent stationmaster of a dilapidated and supposedly haunted railway station on the borders of Northern Ireland and the Irish Free State. In fact, the film was shot mainly on the abandoned Basingstoke–Alton branch line of the Southern Railway and the locomotive and carriages were former London & South Western Railway stock.**

▲ **Michael Redgrave, seen here armed with a revolver, made a suitably intrepid hero in Alfred Hitchcock's 1938 thriller, *The Lady Vanishes*, set on a train travelling to the Balkans. No director was more adept than Hitchcock at capturing the drama and excitement of a train journey.**

**Poetic licence**
One of the most famous of British film documentaries was *Night Mail* (1936), produced by John Grierson for the General Post Office Film Unit and following the journey of the Night Postal Special from Euston to Glasgow Central. The directors were anxious to create as authentic an atmosphere as possible, and a stenographer went along to record the conversations of railwaymen and sorters, for dubbing in later.

The film was made on a low budget and rumour has it that only about £25 was left for the sound track of the final reel. It was suggested that some verses might cover the absence of proper sounds, so a search was made for a poet who would do the job for a small fee. He was found teaching in a school in Wiltshire, and his name was W.H. Auden. But there was now hardly any cash left to pay for the music, so another search was launched, this time for an impecunious composer willing to work for practically nothing. The trail led to Benjamin Britten.

In the spectacular climax, a Stirling 4-4-0, heading a set of eight-wheel coaches, charges down a 1 in 40 embankment into a Foden steam lorry loaded with cement and explosives. The crash, staged at Spain's Crossing near Herriard on the abandoned Basingstoke–Alton line, still provokes gasps of astonishment. (Unfortunately, such realism was achieved at a high price – the destruction of the first bogie vehicles built by the South Eastern & Chatham Railway.)

As Balcon was completing his film in 1929, a new cinematic wonder arrived – the Talkies. *The Wrecker* was issued in a half-sound version and another railway film then being made at Elstree Studios was hastily converted to sound. It may, indeed, have been the first British Talkie, just pipping Alfred Hitchcock's *Blackmail* to the post. Directed by Castleton Knight, it was called *The Flying Scotsman* and featured a young and unknown Welsh actor, Raymond Milland, who was to find fame and fortune in Hollywood as plain Ray Milland.

But the real star of the film was the unbilled London & North Eastern Railway (LNER) Gresley Pacific No 4472 *Flying Scotsman*, whose exclusive use Knight was given for six weeks. He made the most of this advantage, deploying his skills as a newsreel director to overcome the deficiencies of a ludicrous script. He placed a camera on every available foothold of the engine, as well as building a special camera platform on one side.

However, no account had been taken of the fact that the locomotive might roll about at speed, with the result that half the platform was cut clean away in Ponsbourne Tunnel, leaving Knight and his cameraman clinging on for dear life.

There is excellent coverage of the run from King's Cross to Edinburgh, but the detailed action involving the stunt shots, the switching of points and the race through the countryside was staged on the Hertford Loop between Crews Hill, Cuffley and Bayford. Audiences were duly enthralled, although the scene of the villain uncoupling the locomotive from its carriages, which are then left to go racing on in pursuit of the engine, provoked a pained response from Sir Nigel Gresley.

Gresley objected to the implication that the LNER had not yet adopted the vacuum brake and demanded a special title pointing out that 'Dramatic licence has been taken in this film with the normal safety equipment of the LNER'.

## Channel ferry crash

In 1932, two years after *The Flying Scotsman* appeared, Alfred Hitchcock included some good

night shots of a Gresley Pacific on the run from Liverpool to Harwich in his film *Number Seventeen*. The final sequence shows a chase between a runaway goods train and a Green Line motor coach, climaxing with a crash into a Channel ferry. This was filmed with the help of a vast 0-gauge layout built at the once thriving Elstree Studios.

Over the next two decades, Hitchcock was to make a string of screen thrillers with a railway background, including such classics as *The Thirty Nine Steps* (1935), *The Lady Vanishes* (1938) and *Strangers on a Train* (1951).

A contemporary of Hitchcock's who also found inspiration in the railway, albeit of a rather different kind, was the French director Jean Renoir. In 1938, Renoir's *La Bête Humaine* (*The Human Condition*) exploded on to the screen. Based on a novel by Emile Zola, the story of an engine driver who murders for love is underlined by the railway background. For the final sequence, in which the driver, on the footplate of the Paris express, confesses to his fireman, the camera was mounted in front of the engine and the sound, instead of being dubbed in later, was recorded as the film's action unfolded.

The effect is stunning, with the torment of the driver's mind reflected, as one critic put it, by the recurring spectacle of 'trains tearing and screaming through the sunny countryside, trains burrowing through tunnels towards pinpricks of light with a muffled but redoubled roar, trains clanking and wheezing in the temporary repose of the junction'.

**▲ One of the most popular films with British audiences was the comedy thriller *The Ghost Train*, produced in a silent version in 1925 and remade twice as a talkie, in 1931 and 1941. In the 1931 version, not very convincing models were used to show a train plunging into a river from a swing-bridge.**

The celebration of various railway centenaries in the 1920s and 1930s led to a spate of commemorative films. First off the mark was Britain, with an LNER film of the Darlington centenary celebrations of 1925, which featured a parade made up in part of the best preserved steam locomotives in the world at that time, including Stockton & Darlington No 1 *Locomotion*.

In Germany, which celebrated its railway centenary in 1935, Willy Zielke produced an extraordinary film, *Der Stahltier* (*The Iron Horse*), which includes a superb replica of William Hedley's *Puffing Billy* (known in the film as *Puffen Wilhelm*) and an even better full-scale reconstruction of the opening of the Liverpool & Manchester Railway in 1830, complete with *Rocket*. There was also full credit given to the French for the first steam road locomotive.

It was only after providing this historical background that the film went on to show the opening of the first German railway in 1835 between Nuremberg and Fürth. The sequence included an accurate replica of the first German steam locomotive, *Adler* (*Eagle*), though it was made clear that the engine was built in England by Stephenson and driven by an Englishman, 'Mr Vilson' (William Wilson of Newcastle).

The first to see the film after it had been completed was Dr Goebbels, the Nazi Minister of Propaganda, who was outraged that it paid full credit to the real pioneers of steam railways and was not just a paean of praise to German industry and invention. Furthermore, Goebbels considered that it was shot in an extravagant *avant-garde* style not appropriate to the new German Reich.

**◀ A flag-draped 0-6-0 pulls into Oakworth station on the Keighley & Worth Valley Railway during the filming of *The Railway Children* in 1970. Some members of the film crew had been apprehensive about working with preservationists, but were delighted to discover how professional they were.**

**▶ It was a railway station that provided the unlikely setting for the classic 1947 weepie, *Brief Encounter*, which starred Trevor Howard and Celia Johnson as a middle-aged couple torn between love and duty. Although most of the film was made in the studio, some sequences were shot at an appropriately sombre Carnforth station.**

**Spot the difference**
Some film-makers showed scant concern for the realities of railway operation. In the 1941 version of the British comedy thriller, *The Ghost Train*, the express leaves Paddington hauled by a King, arrives at Teignmouth headed by a Castle, slows for a curve pulled by a bullet-nosed, streamlined King and comes to a halt with a Saint.

Even Alfred Hitchcock was not immune to error. In his 1935 film, *The Thirty Nine Steps*, the hero leaves King's Cross bound for Edinburgh on a London & North Eastern Railway train hauled by a Gresley Pacific. However, a later shot shows a Great Western Railway train bursting out of Box Tunnel near Bath, headed by a King. Hitchcock commented 'There is something more important than logic; it is imagination.'

Zielke was promptly whisked off to an asylum for the insane. He came out briefly to shoot scenes for Leni Riefenstahl's famous film of the 1936 Berlin Olympics, but was then returned to his cell. As a result, he survived the war (which is more than Goebbels did) and lived for many years afterwards. Goebbels had ordered the film to be destroyed, but a single copy survived, and this was smuggled to France and looked after during the war by the French Resistance.

The popularity of railway films continued well into the post-war years, with audiences enjoying such offerings as *The Titfield Thunderbolt* (1952), *The Train* (1964), *Von Ryan's Express* (1965) and *Murder on the Orient Express* (1974).

In *The Titfield Thunderbolt*, produced by Michael Balcon, a country line is saved by the villagers it serves. The writer of the screenplay, T. E. B. Clarke, was inspired by the Talyllyn Railway (TR) in North Wales. Clarke was amazed that the TR was 'a private line run through the summer months by railway enthusiasts from all parts of the country...Thus was born the idea of *The Titfield Thunderbolt*: the idea of a village with sufficient love of its little branch line railway to buy it up and run it with an amateur staff when it came to suffer the fate of so many pleasant but uneconomic lines in these materialistic times.'

## Life after steam

As mainline steam came to an end, film-makers looked increasingly to railways such as the TR. In Britain, a major-turning point was reached in 1970 with the making of *The Railway Children*, based on the novel by E. Nesbit. Steam had come to an end on BR two years before, so the film was made entirely on the Keighley & Worth Valley Railway (KWVR) in West Yorkshire, which was especially suitable, since Nesbit's book was set in the countryside around that area.

The film was a great success, generating an enormous amount of goodwill, not only for the KWVR in particular, but for preserved railways in general. These lines are still used by film and television companies, which realize that nothing is more evocative of years gone by than the sight and sound of a steam train.

**◀ The real star of *The Titfield Thunderbolt* (1952) was *Lion*, built by Todd, Kitson & Laird of Leeds in 1838 for the Liverpool & Manchester Railway. *Lion's* owners, the Liverpool Engineering Society, were reluctant at first to loan the engine, but agreed on seeing the script.**

# The home front

**From moving troops, supplies and vulnerable members of the population to defending the coastline, the role of the railways in wartime was immense. And during the years of conflict, as normal a service as possible had to be maintained.**

▼ In December 1939 a soldier stands guard as one of the new LNER Class V2 2-6-2 locomotives No 4826 steams north from King's Cross into Copenhagen Tunnel. Guarding the railways against Fifth Columnists and enemy agents was a vital part of the war effort and a prized duty for the train enthusiast if there was a chance of seeing something out of the ordinary. In later years, protecting the railways fell to the Home Guard.

The military importance of Britain's railways was first put to the test in August 1914 when the activities of 130 private railways were coordinated for the government by a Railway Executive Committee. Countless millions of rail miles were run, as the trains conveyed troops and supplies to the embarkation ports and on their return journeys handled a huge flow of wounded servicemen.

Between the two World Wars, Britain's railways benefited from a huge investment programme so that if Britain as a whole was not ready for mobilization in the summer of 1939, the railways certainly were. In the decade leading up to that September, over £315 million had been spent on the improvement of 59.545.5km (37,000 miles) of running lines and their associated infrastructure.

When war was declared against Germany, the Railway Executive Committee immediately took over control of the Big Four railway companies (GWR, LMS, LNER and Southern) and many of the independent and joint lines. The committee, formed from a group of railway managers, once again introduced state control on the railways. Many of its members had been involved in railway management during World War I, and their experience was to prove invaluable in the years which followed.

## Troops on the move

The committee's immediate priority was the movement of the British Expeditionary Force to its ports of embarkation. In many regards the

**'Who goes there?'**
In February 1942, legend has it that some Polish soldiers on their way to a training camp in Devon headed towards a small Great Western station to ask about trains. The station-master and his staff were just going on Home Guard duties. Though both groups of men were wearing uniforms and carrying rifles they could not see clearly because of a thick mist and the blackout. Such was the disparity in accents that each thought the other to be enemy paratroopers. Only after an hour of the two friendly forces holding each other at gunpoint was the issue resolved.

**▲ German troops go up to the front during World War I. Light railways like this could be laid quickly and over ground damaged by artillery fire to move men and equipment where they were needed most. But such lines were vulnerable to air attack and were rarely used in World War II.**

**▶ Although armoured trains had first been used by the British as far back as the Boer War, few would have considered running one on the 15in (381mm) gauge Romney, Hythe and Dymchurch Railway. For years it had been a tourist line, but with the threat of invasion it was the ideal way to protect the Romney Marshes.**

initial effect on the railways was minimal and, at first, it was very much business as usual as the last of that summer's holidaymakers made their way home. The only immediate evidence of any inconvenience was the withdrawal of almost all the restaurant and sleeping car services from the first day of war.

With reservists and conscripts making their way to camp, the farewell scenes that were to become commonplace during the next six years were seen at most mainline stations. As servicemen waved goodbye to families and friends, the railway's precautions against enemy attack were clearly evident in the background. The Air Raid Precautions (ARP) Department had been alerting civilians to the danger of gas as early as 1935 and the railways had been one of the first major institutions to implement the recommendations, with every member of staff receiving ARP training.

## Trains to the rescue

With the threat of bombing and gas, it was felt advisable to remove the most vulnerable elements of society from the major centres of population, and therefore the evacuation of children, expectant mothers and the sick commenced. From all the

**Southern up north**

Rolling stock was moved all around the country in the war years. Tiny shunters from Glasgow found themselves at the Welsh docks and ten Southern Railway King Arthur Class N15 4-6-0s ended up on Tyneside. Although meant for freight work, a few were used on passenger turns, one of which took No 751 *Sir Redivere* on a run from Harrogate to Leeds in 1943. As it pulled into Wetherby, one Cockney wit recognized the green livery and called out at the top of his voice, 'Anyone for Bognor?'

major cities, the flow of passengers began. Most carried their entire worldly possessions in battered suitcases, along with gas masks in small cardboard boxes. Luggage labels, bearing children's names, were pinned to coats. Trains came and duly loaded their passengers, taking them away to rural areas and safety from the bombs.

In railway terms it was a well-organized operation, but it was marred by bureaucratic bumbling which resulted in some passengers being sent to the wrong destination. A year later the railways had to relocate many evacuees from the south and east coasts, as the threat of invasion placed these areas in the newly created defence zones.

The next major assignment for the railways was to convey from the Channel ports the British Expeditionary Force in its retreat from Dunkirk. The Southern Railway ran 620 trains from the seven main Channel ports in just eight days. As the tattered remnants were moved to regrouping points, the London Midland & Scottish (LMS) and

**▼ Maintaining the permanent way was a vital part of keeping the railways running. Here a London Transport gang rehearses track laying while clad in full gas masks and protective suits.**

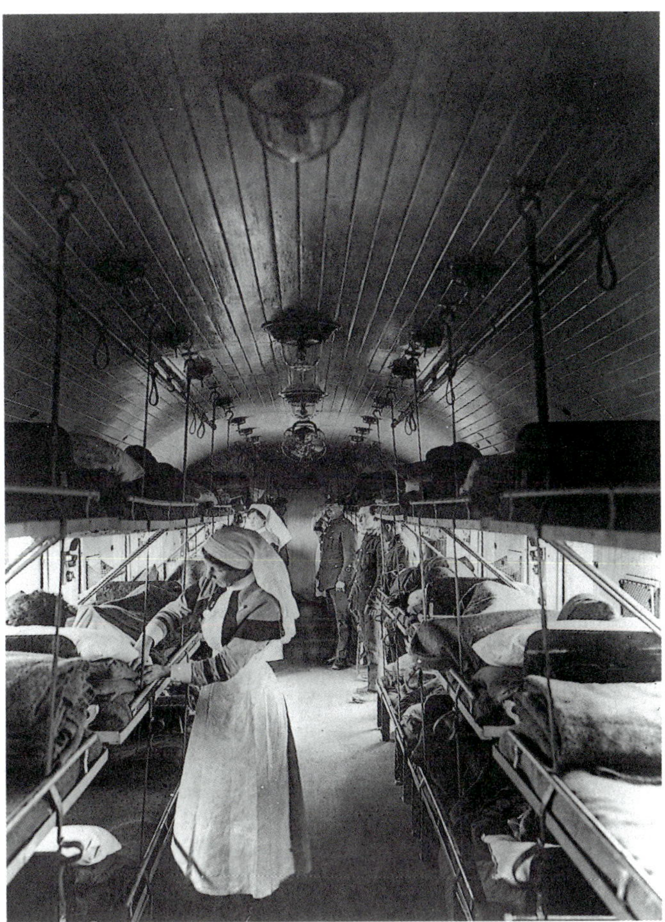

**▶ During World War I, seven British railway companies supplied 822 coaches for ambulance train service, with the LNWR's Wolverton works producing the most. In 1939, the whole process began again when companies were asked to provide a new generation of coaches for ambulance work.**

Great Western Railways (GWR) were running trains to ports like Cardiff, Liverpool and Glasgow to meet ships carrying the Commonwealth Forces.

The railways were also to play an important role in defence, and trains were kept at readiness in order to rush troops to any places where an invasion might be attempted. No invasion came, but the Battle of Britain now began. Despite its air raids on almost every major industrial target, Germany failed to make a concentrated attack on the nerve centre of the British transport system – the railway marshalling yards. This was a significant mistake on Germany's part.

## On the move

As every farm and factory went over to 'working for the national effort', it fell to the railways to move supplies and workers. The Atlantic convoys provided huge volumes of additional traffic for onward shipment by rail.

In 1942 the tide of war turned, and the First Army was taken to various ports for embarkation to North Africa. This assignment involved the movement of 1,120 trains carrying 185,000 men, 20,000 military vehicles and 250,000 tonnes (tons) of supplies. Yet, substantial as this traffic was, it was nothing when compared to that which built up in 1944.

When the opportunity for opening up a Second Front became a reality, the railways moved men and equipment into the strategic assembly positions. By this time, Britain no longer stood alone and, as the countdown to D-Day began, foreign uniforms and accents abounded. So great was the traffic that trains carrying less essential supplies sometimes queued for days on the approach lines.

**▲ LNER Class B12/3 4-6-0 No 8556 simmers in London's Liverpool Street station as its driver chats with a group of children awaiting evacuation. This massive railway operation spanned the nation and was a huge administrative task.**

**▼ As the war continued, and maintenance work was deferred, jobs like cleaning were virtually forgotten. Then, in 1943, a volunteer cleaning scheme was introduced. In this LMS roundhouse, a group of women workers spruce up Class 5MT No 5280 and its stablemates.**

The movement of heavy stores was the next phase, and this began on 10 May. These two types of traffic involved huge numbers of trains being sent from depots in Scotland and the north, a situation which resulted in the cancellation of many Anglo-Scottish expresses and severe overcrowding on other services.

Another extensive traffic flow just prior to D-Day was caused by the ferrying of supplies to the RAF and USAAF bomber bases. These were not the easiest loads to handle and there were three train explosions – the most notable was at Soham in Cambridgeshire.

During the early hours of 2 June 1944, flames were seen in a wagon loaded with 18,370.5kg

(40,500lb) bombs. Despite the heroic action of the train crew who uncoupled the wagon, it exploded and the station was razed to the ground. In a three-quarter kilometre (½ mile) radius, over 800 houses were damaged by the blast. The driver and signalman were both killed, and six others badly injured. Engineers quickly repaired the line and within 24 hours ammunition trains were once again running through Soham.

## Counting the cost

When the war ended, the slow process of repatriation began. Prisoners of war, injured personnel and servicemen from many nations were carried the length and breadth of Britain, as they moved to and from transit camps, demob centres, repatriation ports and the like. This extensive traffic all placed an extra burden on the railways, at a time when they were still heavily involved in moving military freight, leave trains and so on. All of this was over and above the essential freight and passenger traffic, which was vital to the country's economy as it made the transition back to peace.

Unfortunately, the valiant effort of the railways had not been accomplished without the payment of a heavy price. The abuse and over-use of the railway network, along with repeatedly deferred maintenance work, had left the Big Four companies in a terrible condition. Of immediate concern was their financial state, a position which could be addressed only by huge investment.

**▲ Many locomotives were built especially for the Ministry of Supply to help the war effort. After the D-Day landings, most were sent to Europe and performed vital work supporting the invasion. At the end of the war, 2-10-0 No 73788 was sold to British Railways and later became No 90764.**

**◀ Suburban carriages show their wounds at platform two after London's Liverpool Street was hit by enemy action in September 1940. Repair teams frequently had full services running again in a matter of hours but could never be sure when the next bombs might strike.**

The vast majority of locomotives in service were almost worn out, and many should have been scrapped a decade earlier. In addition, track conditions sometimes strained the limits of safety.

However, the ultimate price which had to be paid was nationalization. Just as the grouping of most private railways was a result of World War I, the formation of British Railways in January 1948 was a direct consequence of this second major conflict. Under the terms by which the Railway Executive Committee had taken control of the Big Four companies in 1939, the government was obliged to spend several million pounds to bring the railways back up to an acceptable standard.

Yet, despite the role the railways played from 1939 to 1945, all the major post-war transport funding went on road improvement. Politicians continued to withhold the cash, until yet another conflict – the Suez Crisis of 1956 – finally forced the Macmillan government to institute the British Railways Modernization Plan.

# The vital artery

**The coming of the railways in the nineteenth century revolutionized military planning. For the first time, it became possible to mobilize millions of men and keep them supplied hundreds of kilometres (miles) from home. The era of Total War had begun.**

It is not a matter of chance that the Railway Age coincided with the age of Total War. Without the high-volume transport that railways provided, huge citizen armies supplied with mass-produced munitions could not have been successfully deployed. The use of the steam railway by the military was tentative at first but, as the realization dawned that it could be the road to victory, there was a rush to exploit it.

Fast mobilizations became a possibility, and so did the advance of armies in areas where the need to live off the land would previously have held them in check. Until the Railway Age, an army's supply line depended on horses or mules, which themselves needed to be supplied with forage.

Indeed, armies never became completely independent of animal transport – in World War II, both German and Soviet troops were heavily dependent on the horse – but for supply over medium and long distances, reliance was placed on the steam railway.

The first railway purpose-built to supply troops in a campaign was only 9.75km (six miles) long. Laid by British navvies during the Crimean War of 1855, it expedited the movement of supplies from the harbour of Balaklava to the Allied troops encamped above the Russian-held town of Sebastopol.

Locomotives were used only at the harbour end, the wagons being pulled by horses elsewhere. Even so, use of the railway meant that hundreds of

**▼ A light railway laid by the Royal Engineers is used to transport British troops through one of the shell-shattered towns of north-west France during World War I. So great were the demands of the military that several British branch lines were closed and dismantled and their rails sent across the Channel.**

◀ **Work begins on the Balaklava railway, the line used for supplying British and Turkish forces in Russia during the Crimean War of 1855. The first railway built for purely military reasons, it was 9.5km (six miles) long and proved capable of carrying some 700 tonnes (tons) of traffic a day.**

animals could be dispensed with, and it is unlikely that the Allies would have been able to launch their assault on Sebastopol without it.

Already, in the 1840s, the Prussians had become interested in the use of railways for war. At first, it was thought that they would be useful only for sending supplies, with troops continuing to march to their destinations.

In 1850, however, the Prussians were surprised by their Austrian rivals, who unexpectedly moved 75,000 troops by train to the Prussian frontier. This sudden appearance of fresh forces obliged the Prussians to acknowledge – at least, for the time being – Austrian dominance in central Europe.

## Steaming to Bull Run

It was the American Civil War, however, which convinced the world's war ministries that the railways had become decisive. Outnumbered in population and out-produced in munitions, the Southern states fought as long as they did – from 1861 to 1865 – because they were able to send their troops by rail to threatened sectors of the enormously long front. In the first major battle of the war, at Bull Run, they turned the tide by bringing in 10,000 fresh troops by train.

At first, the local military commanders assumed control of the railway lines in their areas, and gave orders to the civilian railwaymen. It soon became clear, however, that army officers had no idea how to handle supply trains, being unable to grasp the concept that future supplies depended on empty wagons being promptly sent back.

The victorious Northerners solved this problem by calling up railway managers, granting them military rank and putting them in charge of transport. The general staffs of many countries took note of the American experience, and when the first of the big European wars broke out in 1870, both belligerents, France and Prussia, had detailed mobilization plans based on timetables of meticulously scheduled military trains.

As far back as 1843, while still a young officer, the Prussian Chief of Staff, General Helmuth von

**Steaming into battle**

In World War II, the British Army was at first provided with the Class 8F 2-8-0, designed by the London Midland & Scottish Railway. Later, the Ministry of Supply (MoS) ordered the Austerity 2-8-0 for service abroad. A few 2-10-0 variants were also built. In addition, the MoS acquired hundreds of 0-6-0 saddle tanks.

The US Army brought its own 2-8-0s for use in Europe, and prior to the D-Day landings at Normandy the engines were used by the British railways. But the most numerous war locomotive was the German Kriegslok 2-10-0, of which thousands were built for use in German-occupied territory. Like the British Austerities, the Kriegslok was designed for easy assembly and maintenance.

▶ **British Prime Minister Winston Churchill, seen here seated with his wife Clemmie, relaxes on board his special train during World War II. The train, known at first as *Cutlass*, was later renamed *Rugged*.**

◀ **Gun-trailers and rolling stock are lined up ready for shipment to the British Expeditionary Force (BEF) in France in May 1940. Between 9 September and 5 October the previous year, 261 special trains had travelled to the docks with reinforcements for the BEF – a total of more than 100,000 men, together with their equipment, armoured vehicles and artillery.**

Moltke, had written that 'Every new railway development is a military benefit, and for national defence it is far more profitable to spend a few million on completing our railways than on new fortresses.'

Von Moltke's view was triumphantly vindicated more than 25 years later, when in the first two weeks of the war with France, 350,000 German troops, together with horses and guns, were moved by train to their assembly points. The French, although they mobilized almost as quickly, were handicapped by feuding between the civilian railway administration and the military authorities, and it was the resulting chaos that contributed in large measure to their defeat.

## Colonial campaigning

For the British, with a small volunteer army and no land frontiers, mobilization by rail was less critical. They sometimes used field railways in colonial campaigns, and General Kitchener's victory at Omdurman in the Sudan in 1897 was won by troops transported over several hundred kilometres (miles) of new track laid by the Royal Engineers. There was a spate of military railway building in India, especially after the 1857 Mutiny, and in the mountainous and turbulent North West Frontier region, where Anglo-Russian rivalry was intense.

Much of the railway expertise in these remote places was provided by units of the Crewe Volunteers, a battalion of part-timers from the railway town of Crewe in Cheshire. They went into action again in South Africa during the Boer War campaigns of 1899–1902. In spite of Boer commando raids against the railway lines, British supplies moved from the ports to the campaign areas with little interruption.

A similar pattern emerged during the two world wars. Indeed, in World War I, British railway troops managed not just field railways, but shared the operation of mainline trains between the Channel ports and the Western Front.

From 1914, the South Eastern & Chatham Railway had its locomotives and men in Boulogne docks, and in 1915 the Railway Operating Division (ROD) of the Royal Engineers, composed mainly of railwaymen in uniform, began to take over the services, including French local trains.

In Britain itself, the railways had played an indispensable part in the mobilization. The main tasks, ensuring the flow of reservists to the Fleet and of the British Expeditionary Force (BEF) to Southampton, were fulfilled ahead of time. During the eight days starting 9 August 1914, 334 trains arrived at that port, bringing some 70,000 troops, 22,000 horses, 2,400 guns and 2,550 tonnes (tons) of supplies. By 18 August, the entire BEF had been landed safely in France.

Reinforcements soon followed and continued arriving until the end of the month, by which time 670 troop trains had arrived at Southampton and more than 118,000 troops had been sent across the Channel.

World War II, with its heavy bombing of lines and junctions, increased the vulnerability of the railways at a time when their importance in many battle areas had been diminished by the development of road and air transport. One important exception was Russia, where the lack of tarred

### War by Timetable

For two weeks in August 1914, a seemingly unending succession of German military trains rumbled westwards across the Hohenzollern Bridge over the Rhine at Cologne. There could hardly have been a better demonstration of the dominance of the railway timetable in military strategy. Mobilization plans had been drawn up months before and, once begun, the process took on a life of its own.

Historians subsequently described this as War by Timetable. It was especially important for the Germans, because they had to mass their troops on the French frontier, cripple the French Army, and then whisk their own forces to the Eastern Front before the Russians, with their great distances and inferior railway system, could properly mobilize.

But the Russians mobilized quicker than expected, thanks partly to French money invested in longer sidings and double tracking, so Germany failed to win its quick victory.

▶ **By 1918, more than 1,287km (800 miles) of 2ft (600mm) light railway had been laid by the British Army in France. Although this was worked by some 680 steam and petrol driven locomotives, many machines were the result of improvisation. Here a Ford motor car mounted on flanged wheels stands ready to haul an ammunition train.**

roads and the severe climate created a logistical nightmare for the invading Germans.

Hitler had assumed that his motor trucks would be sufficient to keep his armies supplied in Russia. Somewhat belatedly, this was discovered to be a mistake and the Germans made an enormous effort to rehabilitate and re-gauge the Russian railways in conquered territory.

This done, they were able to supply their troops, but not as regularly or securely as they wished. Thousands of the German war service locomotive, the Kriegslok 2-10-0, were sent to Russia, but the early failure to plan rail transport, plus attacks by Russian partisans, caused problems. It was said that delayed delivery of anti-freeze for their tanks was largely responsible for the Germans' failure to capture Moscow in 1941.

The Russians, for their part, received much needed Western munitions via the Trans-Iranian Railway, running for 1,392km (865 miles) between the Persian Gulf and the Caspian Sea. This line, built before the war, was taken over by the British and Russians in 1941 – the British operating the southern half, and the Russians the northern half.

On the British section, operated by the men of the Royal Engineers, 40 new passing loops were blasted out of the rocks – some on 1 in 66 gradients – and many new sidings, crossovers and shunting necks installed.

The arid terrain, which included both desert and mountains, and the scarce and impure water supply, made the line exceptionally difficult to work. Locomotives soon went out of service, and scores of drivers and firemen collapsed from heat-stroke. In 1944, the Americans took over the southern section and solved some of the physical problems by introducing diesel locomotives.

Only a few years after World War II, in the early 1950s, war broke out between the two halves of Korea – the Communist North and the anti-Communist South. The Americans, backing the South, made one of their primary targets the destruction of the North Korean rail system.

However, although the American attacks were intense, the North Koreans managed to carry out enough repairs to keep the system functioning. As one of the US commanders ruefully recalled, 'We dive-bombed and skip-bombed, we shelled with heavy naval guns, we cannonaded with ground artillery, we strafed with rockets and machine guns, we organized sabotage and guerilla attacks. But we never stopped the Red railroads from delivering ammunition and supplies...'

Korea was really the end of the story. Both the United States and the Soviet Union toyed with rail-mounted nuclear missiles, and in 1971 India made heavy use of railborne troops in its war with Pakistan. But the age when the railway was a decisive factor in war was over.

### Deadly fare dodger

One of the great feats of railway engineering was the Khyber Railway, completed in 1925. Starting at Peshawar in India, it ran for 58km (36 miles), zigzagging up the almost vertical sides of the towering Khyber Pass, and was used for British military expeditions into Afghanistan.

So daunting was the terrain that many experts doubted if even a narrow-gauge line could be built there. In the event, the Royal Engineers constructed a broad-gauge railway. At the summit, storage sidings were provided, and the crossing stations of the single-track line had loops to accommodate 305m (1,000ft) trains.

The local Pathans agreed not to attack the railway provided they were allowed to travel without tickets and to carry their firearms on the trains. An official who ignored the agreement and required one of the tribesmen to pay for his journey was shot.

# The armoured train

**Clad in armour plate and bristling with guns, the train took on the aspect of a formidable fighting machine. But appearances were deceptive, and although this new military monster would play an important role on battlefields from America to Africa, it was to prove highly vulnerable.**

The art of winning, according to an American Civil War general, consisted of 'getting there fastest with the mostest', so it is appropriate that this was the conflict that saw the first effective use of armoured trains. In an era of poor roads and horse traction, the rail-mounted gun was, indeed, the fastest way of getting heavy weaponry into position. The Confederates were the first to try this, mounting a 14.5kg (32lb) gun on a railway flatcar, encasing it in iron plates, and sending it off to fight in the Battle of Savage Station in 1862.

The Federals imitated the idea but, instead of single guns, placed an entire battery on rails. Before the end of the war they were operating what is regarded as the first authentic armoured train, which they used for reconnaissance and defence on the Baltimore & Ohio Railroad. This was not just an assembly of rail-mounted guns, but consisted of six vehicles with their own permanently attached locomotive, and with provision for infantry as well as artillery.

But the train came to an untimely end when its locomotive boiler was hit by a Confederate shell. In later wars, efforts were made to provide quite thick armour for the locomotive, but this was limited by the weight that the track could bear. Sometimes a fairly small locomotive had to be used simply to permit the use of heavy armour.

However, armoured trains were always vulnerable, for not only could they be immobilized by an unlucky shot, but a bold and mobile enemy could achieve the same effect by simply wrecking the track before and behind the train.

This meant that the armoured train could not usually be used in attack, where it could easily be cut off. But it could play a positive

▼ **In 1940, as invasion threatened, a number of armoured trains were assembled to help defend the British coast. Even the narrow-gauge Romney, Hythe & Dymchurch Railway in Kent acquired its own miniature Molloch. Made up of an armoured 4-8-2 coupled between two gun-wagons, the train was kept constantly at the ready, with steam-up 24 hours a day.**

role in defence, acting as a fast reinforcement for threatened sectors of the front.

Unfortunately, such considerations had little impact on military thinking in Britain. With the outbreak of the Boer War in 1899, the British fought a campaign over huge distances and made great use of rail transport. However, having failed to study the lessons of previous wars, the army command regarded the armoured train as a form of cavalry, to be sent out on offensive thrusts. So, although local foresight had ensured the building of ten armoured trains before hostilities began, one was destroyed on the very first day of the war.

Even this loss failed to change British tactics. In the months that followed, several trains were damaged while making narrow escapes and another was captured by the Boers. Among those on board was the young war correspondent, Winston Churchill.

In his book, *London to Ladysmith via Pretoria*, Churchill described the train as consisting of an engine and tender (situated, as usual, in the centre, which was the safest place for a train designed to run in either direction), ahead of which was a car with armoured, loopholed sides, and containing a platoon of infantry. At the front there was a car transporting a naval gun. Behind the engine came two more infantry vehicles, which also housed a breakdown crew and, finally, there was a vehicle carrying repair materials and tools.

▲ **Members of a British-based Polish unit man an armoured train at North Berwick in February 1941. The possibility of an armoured train had first been raised in 1859 by the English locomotive Engineer, William Bridges Adams. But it was the Americans, caught in the turmoil of civil war, who gave practical expression to the idea.**

As the train rounded a long curve, it ran into a Boer ambush based on the top of a nearby hill. 'The long brown rattling serpent with the rifles bristling from its spotted sides,' wrote Churchill, 'crawled closer to the rocky hillock on which the scattered black figures of the enemy showed clearly. Suddenly three wheeled things appeared on the crest, and within a second a bright flash of light... The Boers had opened fire on us... The train leapt forward, ran the gauntlet of the guns, which now filled the air with explosions, swung round the curve of the hill, ran down a steep gradient, and dashed into a huge stone which awaited it at a convenient spot.'

Although the vehicles in front of the locomotive were wrecked, the engine itself and the vehicles behind it were still intact. Under Churchill's direction, volunteers cleared the line of debris, and with the forceful young journalist by his side on the footplate, the driver reversed down the line.

But they had gone only a short distance when they noticed that the undamaged cars had been left behind. Somehow they had become uncoupled in the crash. Churchill and the driver then steamed back in the hope of rescuing their stranded comrades – only to fall into the hands of the enemy. Churchill later became a national hero by escaping from a Boer prison camp.

## Adopting new tactics

Eventually, the British commanders in South Africa adopted more sensible tactics. Armoured trains were to be used mainly for patrol and escort, and their offensive role was confined to cutting off enemy retreats when it was safe to do so.

### Aiding the enemy

In the early days of the Boer War, the British armoured trains were commanded by army officers rather than civilians – an arrangement that sometimes led to unfortunate consequences.

According to the head of the British Army's Department of Military Railways, Major Percy Girouard, 'Armoured trains were constantly rushing out against orders of the Traffic department, sometimes without a line clear message, and this caused serious delays to traffic.

'In fact, instead of assisting traffic by preventing the enemy from interrupting it, they caused more interruption than the enemy themselves.'

◀ During the chaos of the Russian Civil War, a Czech national army, formed in Russia to fight the Austrians, captured much of the Trans Siberian Railway and used armoured trains to patrol it. Here, under camouflage, Czech machine-gunners take up their positions.

▶ Unloading from trucks hauled by an armoured locomotive, British troops pile up earth for field works in northern France during the winter of 1916. Many locomotives were destroyed in the intensive artillery bombardments and both sides were forced to improvise, putting together strange looking hybrids such as the one seen here.

But there could still be complications. There was one celebrated occasion when the main line was blocked for hours after a local commander decided to allocate an armoured train to escort a herd of cattle making an on-the-hoof move parallel to the railway. For the most part, however, the armoured trains justified themselves, albeit fairly unspectacularly, in the later stages of the war.

With the start of World War I, armoured trains were used in the African campaigns and occasionally on the European fronts. But it was in Russia, in the civil war that followed the 1917 Revolution, that they came into their own again. The French and British troops based in Archangel and Murmansk, part of an international force that had been mobilized to crush the new Bolshevik regime, assembled several of these trains to patrol their own vital rail lines, while in the main campaigns between the Bolsheviks and their Russian opponents both sides used armoured trains. The war was fought with considerable savagery, with some prisoners being thrown alive, into the fireboxes of the locomotives.

It was again in Russia, with its vast expanses, scarce roads and severe weather, that armoured trains were most widely used in World War II. Although a great deal of improvisation was involved, a largely standard formation was developed. The Russian trains usually consisted of an armoured locomotive, flanked at each end by a

▼ The armoured train of Italian dictator Benito Mussolini, its anti-aircraft guns at the ready, halts by a bombed-out country station. In World War II, though still used for the rapid deployment of firepower, armoured trains began to lose their potency in the face of the new military factor of overwhelming air attack.

truck with anti-aircraft guns and then a roofed vehicle with two field guns and four heavy machine-guns. There were also four service cars – two at each end – which carried rails, sleepers, fire extinguishers, lifting jacks and other materials.

Such trains were used intensively against the German forces besieging Odessa and Sebastopol, destroying aircraft and tanks and breaking up infantry formations. Sometimes they operated in pairs, one covering the other. Many of them had a short life, but others moved from front to front and survived to take part in the great Russian counter offensives later in the war. One of these, named Klim Voroshilov and driven by a woman, took part in the defence of Rostov, Moscow and Stalingrad before being sent to support the attacking Red Army.

The Germans tried to obstruct the Russian trains by tearing up the track during retreat – a tactic which the Russians countered by fitting the trains with longer range guns. They also equipped some trains with rocket launchers.

## Trains of the invaders

Armoured trains were also used by the Germans in these campaigns, some built in Germany itself and some captured from the Russians. One vehicle that the invaders brought with them was their standard eight-wheeled armoured car, the Sd Kfz 231. This had been designed to run on road or rail.

The Germans also deployed armoured trains in France, where by 1944 the Maquis guerrillas were posing a serious threat. They had engineered many derailments, and the Germans used the trains to escort particularly important rail traffic.

In Britain during the early months of the war, armoured trains were regarded as a vital line of defence against an expected German invasion. Forty were built at Ashford works, with firepower provided by a Hotchkiss gun and a light machine-gun. The London & North Eastern Railway supplied for them small tank locomotives that were camouflaged and fitted with armoured cabs, and they were deployed on coastal lines in the south and east of the country.

Even the 15in (381mm) gauge Romney, Hythe & Dymchurch Railway, on the south coast, had an armoured train operated by an expatriate Polish brigade. One explanation for the railway's inclusion is that the War Office official who was in charge of deciding which coastal lines should have armoured trains put the Romney, Hythe & Dymchurch on his list, not realizing that it was merely a tourist attraction.

**▼ A German armoured train rests on a railway embankment near Helsinki, a reminder of Finland's involvement in the fighting between Nazi Germany and the Soviet Union. It was Russia, with its bad roads and vast distances, that became the main arena for armoured trains in World War II.**

# Women on the railway

**Few industries have a stronger tradition of male dominance than the railway. But twice in the twentieth century women have come to its rescue – in 1914 and 1939. And gradually over the years they have won the uphill struggle to receive a fair deal.**

Unlike some other enterprises which sprang up because of the Industrial Revolution, the railway was not a large employer of women. This was largely due to the type of work involved. Whereas women were generally well suited to dexterous, if repetitive, labour in textile mills, they lacked the physical strength required for driving and servicing steam trains.

Even the passage of more than 80 years did little to change the situation. By 1914, only 4,564 women were employed by the railway companies out of a total workforce of more than 640,000, and most of these were engaged in traditionally female tasks such as sewing, laundering and running refreshment rooms.

A notable exception was the Great Eastern Railway (GER), which had a female-operated section in its printing department as early as 1862. The September 1912 issue of the GER staff magazine included a piece about the section's Foreman, Mrs Attridge, who was retiring after service of half a century.

It was almost unheard of, however, for women to be involved in traffic operations. One of the first – perhaps, indeed, *the* first – was Mrs Hill of the Great Western Railway (GWR). In 1880, Mrs Hill's husband, a GWR employee at Chard station, suffered a serious accident and was given the less taxing job of crossing-keeper at Crowcombe, on what is now the West Somerset Railway. Mrs Hill,

**▼ Women porters employed by the Southern Railway load sacks of mail on to a train at an unnamed London terminus in April 1941. With the outbreak of World War II in 1939, thousands of women were drafted in by the Big Four to take over from male railway workers called away to the forces.**

who deputized for him while he was alive, was formally given the job after his death the following year.

In 1890, the GWR went even further by putting another woman, Mrs Town, in charge of Morebath Junction signalbox in Devon. It was not until World War I, however, that women began to make serious inroads into what had always been a male-dominated industry. As with other essential undertakings, the railway recruited them as replacements for men called to the forces, and by 1918, the mainline companies were employing some 55,000 women.

At first, most were engaged as clerks, but as the war dragged on and the demand for labour became more acute, an increasing number was brought in as porters, ticket collectors, dining car attendants, telegraphists, and carriage and locomotive cleaners. On the North Eastern Railway some women were also enrolled as police officers.

Much of the work done by the new recruits was arduous in the extreme. A gang of women was employed at the Midland Railway's sheds in Derby, for example, shovelling coal into the skips from which it could be loaded into the tenders of locomotives. It should not be forgotten, moreover, that the average railway employee at this time worked 54 hours a week, and no exception was made for women.

## Lack of discipline

Although most observers applauded the way they tackled their new roles, women railway workers were not without their critics. Writing in the *Great*

**Oh! Misses Porter**

One of the jobs taken on by women railway workers during World War I was that of porter. This could be hard, especially at goods stations, as an account by Lady Doughty, which appeared in *The Railway Magazine* in 1916, amply confirmed.

Lady Doughty, who was writing of Grimsby, noted: 'It is a strange sight in the goods shed and at the tracks outside. Women are trundling barrows, discharging cases, boxes, barrels, every kind of goods, and loading trucks with cheerful agility.

'There is no uniform. The women wear ordinary clothes. Some work in hats and jackets. Others without either, and arm themselves against damage to dress by a holland or print overall. At first sight there appears just a confusing and wild rush... in all directions. But a system prevails here just as implacably as in the office departments.'

**◀ Defiantly cheerful, in spite of the all-pervading grime and back-breaking labour, a group of women engine cleaners leave their depot in Sheffield in July 1941. 'All this heavy, dirty work...made our hands horrible,' recalled a female employee at the Kentish Town engine sheds in London, 'but we still managed to enjoy ourselves.'**

**◄The wife of a miner, Mrs Doris Sinclair pours molten metal into a mould for lining carriage bearings during World War II. She is pictured at a locomotive works of the London & North Eastern Railway, probably the one in Doncaster.**

**▼ Miss L. Smith, Deputy Stationmistress of Locheilside station on the London & North Eastern Railway's Mallaig to Fort William line in Scotland, hands over some letters to the guard of a train in 1936. Few women have been appointed to senior positions on the railway, and it was to take BR until 1981 to appoint its first female station manager.**

*Western Railway Magazine* in July 1917, one C. Smart deplored the lack of discipline shown by female railway clerks.

However, allowances had to be made, conceded Mr Smart, since 'They do not come to the business as a life's career. A few years and they leave to fulfil their proper destiny. Therefore, the same interest as actuates the young men, ambitious for promotion, can hardly be expected of them; but they do try to give satisfaction, and while they are with us they are entitled to encouragement.'

## Smart rebuff

Mr Smart's comments provoked a powerful rejoinder. Writing in the September 1917 issue of the Great Western magazine, Dorothy R. Dalton BA, observed that 'A woman is not a mentally inferior creature, or at least it is yet to be proved that she is. Woman is merely worse trained, or frequently not trained at all.

'She must be trained in the same school as the man, and I think one may safely say that the average girl can be made into as efficient and reliable a clerk as the average boy. At any rate the experiment might be worth the trying.'

One of the few companies that did try the experiment was the London, Brighton & South Coast Railway, which set up a training school for female telegraphists, booking clerks and office workers within its signalling school at East Croydon. The instructress, Miss Strevett, had herself been a clerk for many years at Hailsham in Sussex, where her father was the stationmaster.

## Trades union barriers

A problem encountered by these early women railway workers was the refusal of the railwaymen's trades unions to admit them to membership. It was not until 1915 that the ban was lifted, and even then women were at a disadvantage. Both unions

▲ **Miss Freda M. Jones, recently promoted from Warehouse Clerk to Stationmistress, tends the climbing roses at the village station of Pontdolgoch in mid-Wales in June 1941. Miss Jones had to run the station single-handedly, combining the tasks of booking clerk, porter and ticket collector with her administrative duties.**

and management regarded their employment as purely temporary – they were, after all, only filling in for men who had gone off to the forces – and this meant that their rates of pay were usually lower than those for permanent staff.

Faced with such bleak prospects, women saw little point in trying to pursue a career on the railway, and by the late 1930s only some 26,000 were working for the mainline companies.

The outbreak of World War II in 1939 saw another dramatic increase in the number of women working on the railway. By 1943, a sixth of its 660,000 workforce was female – roughly double the number which had been employed in World War I. In some places, women workers formed the majority of the employees, as at the Redbridge sleeper works near Southampton, where they outnumbered men two-to-one, in spite of the heavy work involved.

In his book *The Railway Workers 1840–1970*, Frank McKenna quotes Mrs Pat Foreman, who worked as a tube cleaner in the Kentish Town engine sheds during the war:

'Sometimes,' she recalled, 'we were taken off sweeping duties and put on "coaling", a job hitherto banned to the women. Some were sent to Cricklewood depot to "shovel up". I was detailed to a full wagon of coal on the shunting lines outside the sheds with three or four other women. On the adjoining line an empty wagon stood and more women stood in this. The purpose was for my crowd to throw the lumps of coal across to those in the empty wagon.

**Footplate advances**

Many of the controls on a large steam locomotive were not very accessible, even for the average man. To reach up to the brake lever on an express locomotive of the London & North Western Railway, for example, the driver had to be at full stretch. Other controls required considerable strength to operate, and it used to be said that there was only one man in Swindon works who was strong enough to operate the reversing lever of a Great Western 4-6-0 after overhaul.

Now, thanks to electronics, the 7,500hp Shuttle Locomotives for the Channel Tunnel have been designed so that they can be operated by the vast majority of adults in both England and France.

▼ **Women drill and tap a firebox for its stays at the Swindon works of the Great Western Railway in January 1946. More than 100,000 women were recruited by the railways during World War II, but with the return of men from the forces, their numbers soon dwindled.**

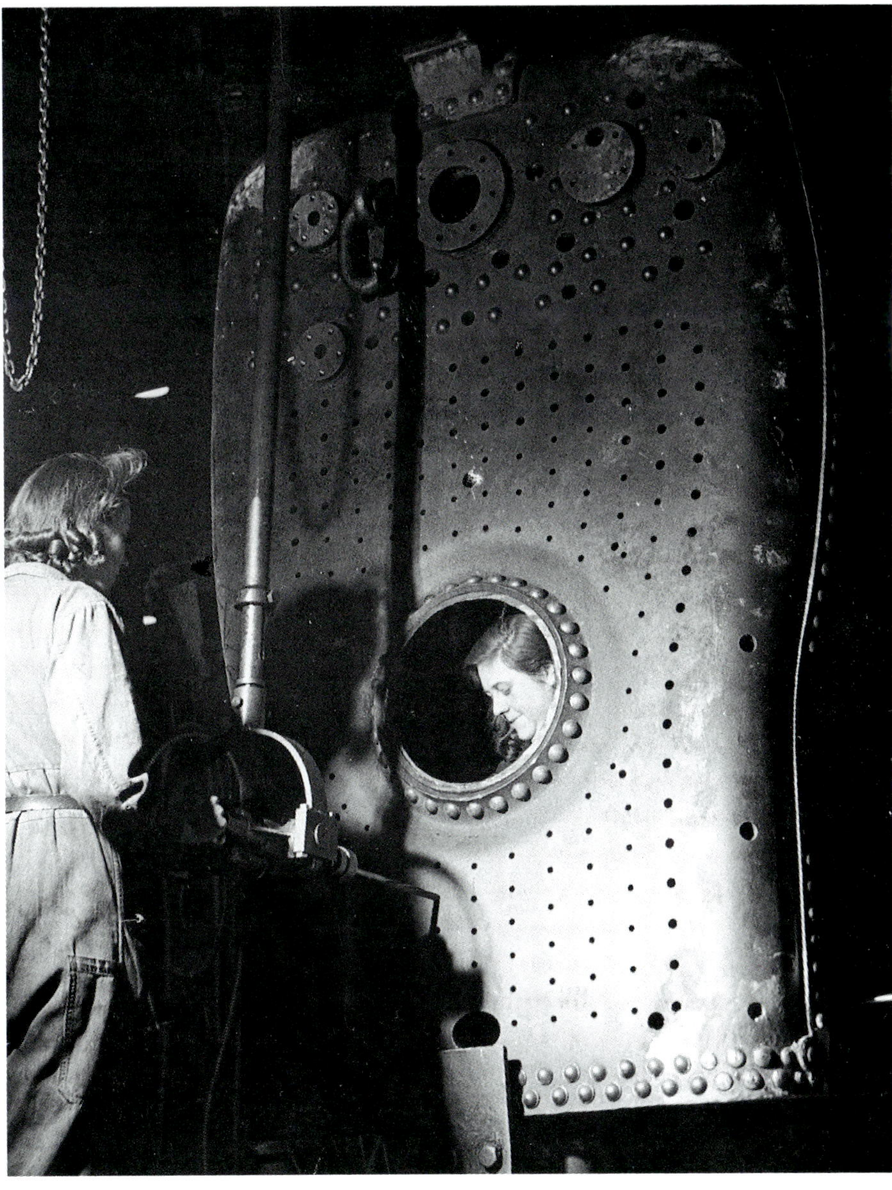

'It was very difficult work, as the coal we were standing on was shifty and sharp and cut our ankles as our shoes were not made for such treatment. The coal lumps were also very heavy and hard to heave the necessary distance.'

Mrs Foreman and her companions were not on that job for long as one of them was hit by a lump of coal, resulting in a broken pelvis.

Although the women workers were never put on 'coaling' again, they were expected to do one day a month on 'manual work' – which meant clearing piles of clinker with a large shovel. 'I refused to do this,' wrote Mrs Foreman, 'as I really felt it degrading on the grounds that I was taken on as a tube sweeper. (I had a "thing" about women with shovels.)...

'Why did we stick it? We could not get our release, but in any case, there is something about railway work that gets you. It is a way of life rather than a job. There was a lot of singing and laughing among the women on the railway; they worked hard, they shared the hazards of the men. They also shared their pastimes, a drink, a smoke, and game of darts in the pub across the way.'

## Improved opportunities

Extensive training courses were organized, which enabled some female railway employees to take on far more responsible jobs than had been possible during World War I. A number joined the operating grades on the Southern Railway, for example. By 1944, 60 women passenger guards had passed out from the company's training schools at London's Victoria station and Brighton. The youngest was Miss Edwards, who took her examination at the age of 19 and was then put in charge of electric trains between Charing Cross and Tattenham Corner.

A lower number – just 24 – was authorized to operate signalboxes. Among this élite was Miss Steel of Brighton. The daughter of a railwayman, she took over the box at Old Shoreham Bridge level crossing. This was a rather unusual posting, as her duties also included collecting the tolls from users of the road bridge alongside. In her spare time, Miss Steel was an air-raid warden.

As early as 1911, the Lancashire & Yorkshire Railway's telegraph office in Manchester's Victoria station was staffed by women. It was during World War II that women became associated with another type of information technology – making announcements through the public address systems at railway stations.

## On the air

Among the first stations to have women announcers was Paddington. This was on an experimental basis at first, but the *Great Western Railway Magazine* reported in 1941 that 'passengers have commented favourably on the clearness and audibility of their announcements'.

On one occasion, a female announcer at Liverpool Street station entertained passengers by reading out a string of unofficial items. On the arrival of a trainload of American troops on leave, she called out the names of those who had arranged for girlfriends to meet them, and told them which ticket barriers to go to. The railway authorities were less than delighted with this performance, however, and such announcements were never repeated.

As had happened at the end of World War I, the end of World War II saw a drastic fall in the number of women employed on the railway. Although for those who remained, career opportunities on the soon to be nationalized railway were much greater than ever before, they still suffered a major disadvantage.

It was not until October 1955 that the British Transport Commission announced that it 'was prepared to agree in principle' to the gradual introduction on British Railways 'of equal pay for equal work'.

**▼ It was during World War I that female station staff first became a familiar sight on British railways. Here a neatly dressed woman ticket collector clips a passenger's ticket in 1915.**

# Civilians on the move

**The trains and stations were barely lit, the carriages and corridors were filled to bursting, and slowness and delay were guaranteed. Yet, for all its danger and discomfort, wartime rail travel was not without its positive side.**

Railway journeys during World War II were often a nightmare. The trains were packed, they ran late and they often halted for no apparent reason – passengers could not be told why they were being delayed because that was 'information which could help the enemy'. Travelling during the night was extremely awkward and uncomfortable, with passengers having to avoid stumbling over one another in the dimly lit carriages and corridors.

On unfamiliar routes, the restricted window areas and removal of station nameboards meant that nervous passengers were always afraid of missing their stop or of recognizing it too late to struggle past standing passengers to the door. As the MP Harold Nicolson put it, 'St Pancras station on a wet midnight, and after three hours in a packed corridor, makes one realize that this is, in fact, a total war.'

In one notorious incident, the body of a woman who had become ill and died on a crowded train could not be removed until 95 of the other occupants had been ordered to leave the carriage.

And yet, the situation could have been worse. Common courtesies and consideration, far from being driven out by harsh circumstance, became much more prevalent. This, and a common external enemy who could be cursed for the discomforts and inconveniences, meant that passengers could feel good from the mere fact of coping, and delighted if they reached their destination in a seat.

▼ A helmeted policeman threads his way through the wreckage at Charing Cross station in 1940, following an air raid. By the end of the war, the railways had reported around 9,000 'incidents'. Almost 500 locomotives had been damaged and 4,000 goods wagons and carriages destroyed.

▲ The start of hostilities saw most commercial advertising on the railways being replaced by official announcements and exhortations. Typical was this poster urging people to avoid unnecessary travel.

The old and infirm were not trampled upon, there was always a cup of tea to be found somehow, and ticket inspectors tolerated unusual itineraries. It was possible, for example, to buy a Birmingham–London return ticket and use all of the Big Four railway companies on the trip.

The new mood was vividly described by the writer H.E. Bates. Writing in the *Spectator* in October 1940, he observed that 'The making of friends has never been so easy. In the whole history of British railways there has never been, I should think, so much conversation and friendliness per mile as now. The air of silent refrigeration, the arid cross-examination of stares, the snoozing behind the fat peace-time blankets of newspapers – all that has gone.'

## False start

The declaration of war in September 1939 was followed immediately by a well-planned evacuation of children from the inner cities, more than 800,000 alone being moved in three days. But with the railways' huge reserve of rolling stock this hardly affected ordinary passengers. Of more consequence was the decision to withdraw restaurant cars, some sleeping cars, seat reservations and cheap fares. However, in the following weeks, the war not having proved as demanding as first anticipated, these services were gradually restored.

The first major trial for rail passengers was the arctic winter of 1939–40, which caused more misery than the Germans. With points, water columns and coal stored in outside dumps frozen solid, dozens of trains were unable to run. Even the grease in their axleboxes froze up. Then, when the thaw finally arrived, it was accompanied by serious flooding and landslides.

In May 1940, the additional summer holiday services were cancelled, and there came the first of several fare increases. But in contrast to the hasty curtailments of the previous September, further restrictions came into force gradually, only as they were needed.

Overcrowding on London commuter services resulted in the abolition of first-class on those trains in 1941, and later the same year some restaurant and sleeping cars disappeared – a process that continued until, in 1944, all restaurant cars were withdrawn, enabling trains to carry more passengers.

A maximum running speed of 96.5km (60mph) was imposed at the start of the war, and for operational reasons there was a general slowdown of average speeds. The London–Brighton electrics,

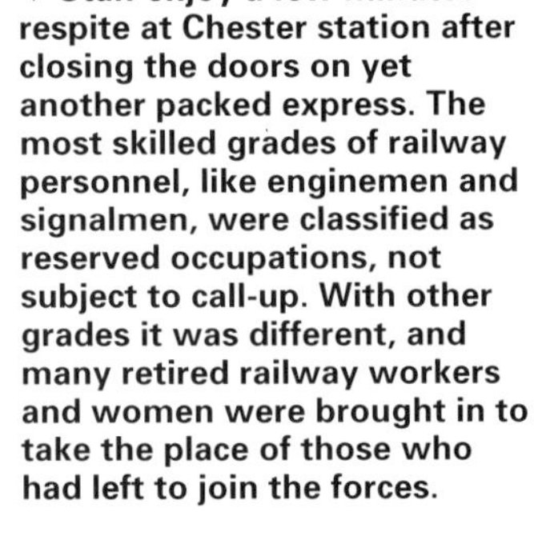

**▼ Staff enjoy a few minutes' respite at Chester station after closing the doors on yet another packed express. The most skilled grades of railway personnel, like enginemen and signalmen, were classified as reserved occupations, not subject to call-up. With other grades it was different, and many retired railway workers and women were brought in to take the place of those who had left to join the forces.**

▲ **A young servicewoman and her dog, both muffled against the cold, sit together on a cheerless platform. Passenger traffic rose by almost 75 per cent during the war, yet bomb damage meant there were ten per cent fewer coaches to cope with it.**

▼ **Waiting for friends or relatives, people keep an anxious eye on the arrival indicator at Euston station. Delay was an inescapable part of wartime rail travel, much of it caused by air-raid alerts and wrecked track or equipment.**

whose unexciting 83.75km/h (52mph) average speed was not considered worth reducing, became Britain's fastest service. Some passenger services were withdrawn during the war, but there were relatively few cancellations, and those were caused mainly by bombing.

There were also some cancellations in May 1940 to make way for trains evacuating the troops brought back from Dunkirk, but the discomforts of travel stemmed mainly from overcrowding, delays and slowness. The transportation of servicemen swelled the passenger flow, and track congestion was inevitable given the increased amount of freight being carried. Not only did rail traffic double, but it moved in new directions.

## The great escape

It was hoped that the withdrawal of holiday services in 1940 would persuade people to defer their holidays, but they flocked to the mainline stations anyway, determined to escape to the coast or the country for a few days.

Not even the discomfort deterred those wishing to travel on the railways. Rather than raise fares further or introduce travel permits, the government decided to use publicity, and 'Is Your Journey Really Necessary?' was the chosen refrain, appearing in countless advertisements and posters. The fact is that most people did believe their journey to be really necessary, and they continued to cram into the available carriages.

## Baggage ban

It was rare for a passenger to arrive at a station and find that it was impossible to enter a packed train. But the overcrowding was enough to bring a new regulation in 1942, forbidding civilians to take into the train more than 45.5kg (100lb) of baggage.

▲ **A morale-boosting poster proclaims the railways' ability to carry on despite the blackout. But the inconvenience to passengers was considerable, and those travelling on unfamiliar routes frequently went past their station. A spate of accidents also occurred, with many travellers tripping in the dark and breaking an ankle.**

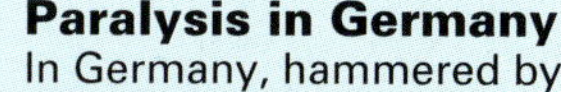

**Paralysis in Germany**

In Germany, hammered by three years of Allied bombing, the railways were virtually paralysed. One passenger recalled a journey from the Black Forest to Berlin that should have taken a few hours but instead took four days.

Merely getting on a train was a test of endurance. Travellers spent hours camping in the stations, and the carriages were so overcrowded that some people got on board only by climbing through the windows.

A woman who fought her way on to the Munich–Berlin express was appalled by the 'indescribable confusion: I had my dress half torn off me, my shoes spoiled. I was kissed by the soldier nearest to me and could not resist because I had my arms pinned to my sides.'

**▲ A young couple squat in a crowded corridor. 'After a night journey recently,' wrote one observer, 'the dawn broke cold and grim upon a packed corridor. People had taken it in turns to sit upon their luggage, but when morning broke other people emerged from the compartments and picked their difficult way towards the end of the car. Those who had to rise at their passing did so with a wan smile of forgiveness upon their sleepless, haggard faces...My admiration for these patient, patriotic, courteous people knows no bounds.'**

Although passenger trains were fewer, they became longer. This was one way to maximize the capacity of the overloaded main lines and, with the slower speeds, locomotives could handle heavier loads. Often, trains were longer than the platforms and, to avoid obstructing the tracks to other platforms, empty coaches were added to the ends of trains at the last minute.

The record was probably reached on 31 March 1940, when a Newcastle–London train was enlarged at Peterborough to 26 coaches totalling 850 tonnes (tons); the V2 mixed-traffic locomotive lost only nine minutes with this load.

Visually, the war brought great changes. Gone were the brightly painted trains and locomotives; there was a general layer of grime not only on and inside rolling stock, but also on stations. Because of the blackout, there was little or no station lighting. Although enamelled commercial advertisements remained in place, paper posters were largely confined to official pronouncements.

Most waiting rooms were closed, and the ones that remained open were unheated. New offices were set up at main stations, notably those of the Railway Transport Officers (RTOs), which were there to ensure that travelling servicemen actually turned up at their destinations.

## Tea on tap

Much in evidence were organizations such as the WVS and Church Army, whose activities included the dispensation of countless cups of tea. The red chocolate-bar machines of pre-war days remained in place, but were empty after the introduction of sweet rationing.

New types of train could be seen – ambulance trains, troop trains, fire-fighting trains and trains consisting of flatcars for military vehicles. The GWR put salvage vans into service, to encourage the pick-up of scrap metal from railway property.

## Into the blackout

For those travelling on the railways after dark, the most obvious sign of the war was the blackout. A wide black border was painted along the edges of carriage windows which, together with drawn blinds and very faint blue bulbs, was enough to keep down light emission, and more than enough to prevent passengers reading.

It was not until 1943, when the bombing threat had receded, that somewhat better lighting was allowed, with white bulbs in deep tubular shields. Colour light signals were fitted with long hoods, but covering the glow from locomotive fireboxes was never satisfactorily achieved, although tarpaulin sheets stretched between the cab roof and the tender helped to reduce it.

At stations, a few staff carried heavily shielded oil lanterns and, with the stations blacked out and nameboards removed, the shouting out of station names by platform staff was of vital importance. A white line painted on the platform edge showed passengers where to alight, but it did not always prevent them getting off at signal stops between stations, under the impression that they had arrived.

Quite a few broken ankles resulted, but the most spectacular mishap befell a passenger in a long train halted at Bath, with its rear standing not at the platform but on the bridge over the Avon. Mistaking the bridge parapet for the platform, the passenger found himself plunging into the river – an unorthodox arrival that he fortunately survived.

## Escaping derailment

In the early stage of the war, it was decreed that passenger trains should slow down to 24km/h (15mph) during air-raid alerts, and freights to 16km/h (10mph). This caused great delays, though in a few cases it enabled trains to escape derailment when the track ahead was damaged. By 1944, the passenger speed limit had been raised to

48km/h (30mph) for night movement during an alert, but this was no help when the unpredictable flying bombs arrived, and a Kent coast express came to lethal grief when a bridge it was approaching was blown up.

## Blitzed stations

Damage at stations could hold up traffic for days, due to the clearance work needed before actual repair could start. When Coventry was bombed, the London–Birmingham line was blocked for four days. York station was badly hit, and in May 1941 there was a period when seven London termini were out of action.

Occasionally, trains themselves were attacked by low-flying day raiders. The fireman of the Flying Scotsman received a bullet wound in this way, but one attacker was brought down when the locomotive blew up just as the aircraft was flying overhead. The pilot was killed, but the crew of the engine survived.

Air attacks on the railways caused about 900 deaths, of which some 500 were civilians. As H. E. Bates saw it, 'Death is a leveller; but death by bombing is, in more senses, than one, the greatest leveller of all. It has smashed the silence of the English railway carriage.'

▲ **A soldier chats with a young mother at a wayside station somewhere between London and Scotland. Ill-lit, unheated and grimy, and with their waiting rooms usually closed for the duration, wartime stations offered scant comfort. Even the chocolate machines remained empty.**

▼ **With the outbreak of war, many workers were moved out of London – including this typist in the passenger manager's department of the LNER. The whole department was installed in a four-coach train some kilometres (miles) from the capital.**

# Sabotage on the railways

**As soon as railways became a decisive factor in warfare, they also became prime targets. Cavalry raids, artillery assaults, air bombardment – all were used in an attempt to destroy them. But it was the stealth and guile of the saboteurs that posed the greatest threat.**

It was in the American Civil War (1861–5) that the strategic value of the railway was fully established. Each side sought to destroy the other's lines, engines and rolling stock, and attacks on such targets became a regular feature of the conflict.

What was to become known as the Great Locomotive Chase, in which a handful of Federal (Northern) soldiers hijacked a Confederate (Southern) train and proceeded northwards with the aim of destroying enemy bridges on the way, was the most spectacular railway raid of the war, but not the only one. Early in the conflict, the Confederate General 'Stonewall' Jackson managed to capture almost 60 locomotives and 350 freight cars of the Baltimore & Ohio Railroad, wrecking some and taking away others.

On the other side, General William Sherman, marching through Georgia, had as a principal objective the destruction of Confederate rail links. His men would tear up lengths of track, build bonfires with the sleepers, and heat the rails so that they could be bent out of shape.

In the Franco–Prussian War (1870–2), the Prussians became increasingly dependent on their railway supply lines as they advanced into France. The very speed and efficiency of their incursion spurred French civilians into acts of sabotage. The guerrillas, known as *francs-tireurs*, developed a derailment method in which a heavy charge of gunpowder was laid beneath the track, with an upright shell, its nose touching the underside of the rail, used as a detonator. An oncoming locomotive would depress the rail and thereby blow a hole in the track beneath it.

One of the most effective ventures of this kind was carried out in October 1870, when a 40-coach train carrying 400 Prussian troops was blown up.

**▼ The Northern Army of General Sherman uproots track and sets fire to railroad installations at Atlanta in Georgia in November 1864. Railroad wrecking was a favourite tactic of both sides in the American Civil War, but Sherman probably destroyed more miles of track than any other commander.**

▲ **Wreckage lies scattered on the Belfast–Dublin line in July 1921, following the derailment of a British troop train by Sinn Fein. Four men and 30 horses were killed in the incident – one of many in the Irish Troubles that erupted after World War I.**

**Multiple diversions**

The French Resistance scored a notable success in June 1944 when it disrupted a train carrying 1,500 German troops *en route* to oppose the Allied landings at Normandy. Held up by a sabotaged munitions train ahead of it, the troop train was diverted over a goods line. But the local Resistance group, forewarned of the train's arrival, jammed a point blade with a piece of rock, derailing it during the night. Having been set on to the track again, the train was then hauled back to the junction, where it was held for some days until the local mayor complained to the stationmaster that its hungry troops were robbing the district's precious reserves of food.

It set off again, but a local priest who headed the Resistance some way along its route arranged for it to be derailed a second time. It arrived at its final destination after 25 days, having averaged 2km (1¼ miles) per day over the final two weeks.

The train was thrown down an embankment, whereupon the 75 *francs-tireurs* waiting in ambush opened fire on the hapless Prussians.

The Prussians regarded this kind of activity as terrorism and countered with terrorism of their own. They arrested a number of leading French citizens and placed one on the front of each locomotive scheduled to pass over a vulnerable line. None of the hostages came to any harm, though whether this was because the saboteurs were unwilling to risk the lives of fellow countrymen or were simply less effective than they liked to believe is open to doubt.

## Derailments in the Desert

In World War I, the Middle East became the main arena for railway saboteurs. The railways here were vital to both Britain and Germany's ally, Turkey, and each side tried to bomb the other's lines, but with little success. It was Colonel T.E. Lawrence – Lawrence of Arabia – and his locally recruited irregulars who did the most damage, using explosive charges. They were responsible for many derailments, and the Hedjaz Railway, south of Ma'an, in what is now Jordan, was so badly damaged that it had to close for many years.

However, it was in occupied Europe in World War II that railway sabotage occurred on its grandest scale. Hitler's campaign in the Soviet Union depended very much on rail transport because of the poor roads. Railways were therefore a prime target of Soviet partisans, and there were periods when the interrupted flow of supplies had a critical effect on German operations. Delayed deliveries of anti-freeze for tanks were partly responsible, it was said, for the German failure to capture Moscow in 1941.

▼ **Russian partisans plant mines on a railway bridge in Belorussia during World War II. The destruction of such targets was a critical blow to the invading Germans, who were unable to move sufficient men and supplies by the country's inadequate road system.**

Lines passing through mountainous, sparsely populated terrain were the best targets, so Yugoslavia and Greece were the scenes of many spectacular attacks by the partisans. The sabotage of three mountain viaducts in Greece in September 1942 was perhaps the climax of this activity. However, for all their daring and meticulous planning, such exploits had relatively little effect on the progress of the war.

## French speciality

Strategy demanded not simply the destruction of particular railway facilities, but also their destruction at a time when they were most needed by the enemy. This policy was used to great effect in occupied France, where railway sabotage was carried to lengths unseen elsewhere, then or since. The key players were employees of the French railway system, SNCF. At first, their sabotage attempts were sporadic and un-coordinated, amounting to little more than an individual lashing out at the invader.

One elementary method, pursued throughout the occupation, was the exchange of wagon labels, so that goods would be sent off to the wrong destination. A variant of this was to place out-of-order labels on vehicles containing urgent German supplies – the vehicles would then be sent to the reception sidings of repair works, where they might wait undiscovered for weeks until inspected by an engineer.

As the Resistance, which contained a disproportionate number of railwaymen, became better organized, it transformed dislocation of the railways into a calculated, long-term campaign. Sabotage took two main forms – attacks in the open country, on major tunnels, bridges and tracks, and disruption and destruction inside railway installations such as locomotive depots and marshalling yards.

**▼ Colonel T. E. Lawrence, Lawrence of Arabia (left), leader of the Arab uprising against the Turks in World War I, poses with a colleague. So successful were Lawrence's sabotage operations that he was known among his followers as the 'destroyer of engines'.**

Attacks in the open country were usually conducted by the Maquis, who were guerrilla warfare specialists, rather than members of the conventional Resistance. Their particular hallmark was derailment. Resistance members of the SNCF – the rail workers were known simply as the *cheminots*, and their movement as Résistance-Fer – would tell the Maquis of important train movements. They would prepare accordingly, their usual method being to remove a rail or lay an explosive charge on the track. Either way, the effects could be catastrophic.

## Head-on collision

On one occasion, the track was blown from under a speeding troop train, with the result that more than 200 German soldiers were killed, 400 wounded and tonnes (tons) of arms destroyed. On another occasion, a Maquis group manipulated the switches on the Paris–Lille line, causing a head-on collision that killed almost 200 hated SS troops.

Moreover, if the location of an attack was carefully chosen, the line could be blocked for days. In 1943, for example, the vital Besançon–Belfort line was closed for 80 hours after a German supply train was derailed.

The *cheminots*, with their specialist knowledge, wreaked their own form of havoc at work. One outstandingly successful method was the running of locomotives into the turntable pit. Most French locomotive depots were of the roundhouse type, where engines exited over the central turntable. So an inoperable turntable meant the immobilization of all locomotives in the shed.

▲ **A photograph taken by Lawrence himself shows the aftermath of one of his train-wrecking sorties. His campaign, which centred on the Medina and Hedjaz railways, began in 1916 and remained a constant thorn in the side of the Turks until the end of the war two years later.**

**Peacetime disorders**
Railway sabotage occurs not only in wartime. During the 1926 General Strike the Flying Scotsman was derailed near Cramlington in Northumberland after strikers had loosened one of the rails, and the French labour unrest of the late 1940s was also accompanied by rail removals.

As late as the 1960s, America's Florida East Coast Railroad was liable to dynamiting as it fought striking members of the railroad workers' union.

The strikers carried on their campaign for 13 years, during which they blew up several trains, though all of them were fortunately empty at the time. After the strikers unwisely dynamited two trains during a visit to Florida by President Johnson, the FBI was called in, and the sabotage came to an end.

In June 1944, with the coming of D-Day and the Allied invasion at Normandy, the activities of the *cheminots* and Maquis moved into top gear. Subjected to a combination of Allied air bombardment and attacks by the Resistance, the French railway system virtually ceased to exist. On 7 June, only the day after D-Day, 180 trains were derailed and 500 railway lines cut.

In some places, the Resistance blew up locomotives in their depots, though placing the charges when the depots were under constant armed guard was a difficult job. At Amberieu, 52 locomotives were put out of action in this way on D-Day, the object being to hinder the transfer of German troops from Italy to Normandy. The Amberieu operation was the most successful of its kind, and involved assistance from the armed Maquis to overcome the German guards.

## Victims of the struggle

In all, the Resistance carried out some 6,000 effective incidents of railway sabotage and around 1,400 derailments. So successful was the campaign that it became known as the Bataille du Rail. The railways had, indeed, become a battlefield. But the price was high. Some 800 railwaymen were shot and more than 1,100 died in concentration camps. In addition, hundreds of French civilians unconnected with the railways were killed in reprisal.

The worst atrocity occurred at Ascq in northern France, just before the Allied invasion. One night, a train carrying part of an SS Panzer Division was derailed, whereupon the officer in charge shot the stationmaster. His troops then went to the village, kicked in the doors of the houses and hauled away all the males they could find. Eighty-six were killed before German military police put an end to the massacre.

In the post-war period, guerrilla-style wars have often involved the railways. In the uprising against the British in Malaya in the late 1940s, trains were frequently derailed by explosive charges. During the long struggle in Vietnam, lines were repeatedly sabotaged by the Communists. In Angola, the Benguela Railway has been put out of action by guerrillas. So the tradition of railway sabotage lives on. The IRA has occasionally placed explosives on railway lines in England and Ireland, although it is usually interested more in publicity than destruction.

In the Caucasus, where constituent parts of the former Soviet Union found themselves in conflict, the blockage of vital lines was quite common. A certain lack of expertise was evident here, with explosions often being engineered on the trains themselves rather than the track. This was perhaps an easier method of sabotage, but was unlikely to block the lines for more than an hour or two. Onboard explosions were also reported to have been caused by young men playing games with hand-grenades to while away the time on long journeys.

▼ **Splintered carriages straddle a railway track in wartime France in the wake of a sabotage attack by the Resistance. The large number of railwaymen in its ranks enabled it to paralyse the movement of German-controlled trains through French territory.**

# Crime on the railways

**The railways have long been a hunting ground for those in search of plunder or prey. The first railway police force was set up in 1830, since when an unremitting war has been waged against the railway criminals.**

The railways, with their loaded goods wagons and luggage-laden passengers, have always been a tempting target for criminals. As early as 1853 David Stevens, Goods Manager of the London & North Western Railway (LNWR), was complaining that 'Thieves are pilfering the goods from our wagons here to an impudent extent. We are at our wits' end to find out the blackguards. Not a night passes without wine hampers, silk parcels, drapers' boxes or provisions being robbed; and if the article is not valuable enough they leave them about the station.'

The protection of goods and passengers was the responsibility of the police forces raised by the railway companies themselves. Originally recruited to deal with the violence of the railway navvies, the railway police had powers and, eventually, uniforms similar to ordinary policemen, but could operate only on or near railway property.

By the 1860s the companies were establishing detective branches within their police forces. An investigative service was badly needed, and no doubt the companies were inspired by the example of the Scotsman Allan Pinkerton, who had gained wealth and fame by establishing

**▼ A witness testifies at the trial in 1864 of Franz Muller (left), the first man to be executed in Britain for murder on the railway. Muller's brutal killing of an elderly banker on the North London line provoked universal outrage, and more than 50,000 attended his public hanging outside London's Newgate prison.**

an American detective agency that attracted substantial railroad business.

In Britain, the railway detectives had an immediate effect in discouraging bogus damage and loss claims, which were costing their companies vast sums of money. Any minor accident to a passenger train was likely to bring claims for compensation, but the detectives soon became expert at weeding out the true from the false.

Traders, especially those whose businesses were doing badly, were tempted to make bogus claims. Some, for example, made a practice of claiming for eggs that had actually been broken by their own employees – a ploy which the detectives put an end to by marking eggs in transit with invisible ink.

There was little they could do, however, to reduce theft. Loaded goods wagons on isolated sidings were very much a sitting target at night, and the LNWR was not alone in bemoaning the loss of much valuable freight.

## Major gold robbery

Mail and bullion consignments were prime targets and attracted the most professional thieves. Often they would stalk the railways for weeks, watching how operations were conducted and looking for security weak spots. The first major gold robbery took place on a train travelling from London to Bristol in 1848. A box of 1,500 sovereigns was placed in a compartment next to the guard's van and the guard was able to keep it under observation through a hole in the partition. Nevertheless, the contents, though not the box, had disappeared by the time the train reached Bristol – a mystery that was never solved.

A few years later, thieves snatched a consignment of gold bullion from a South Eastern & Chatham (SE&C) train *en route* from London Bridge to Folkestone. Thanks to two SE&C accomplices, the Stationmaster at London Bridge, William Tester, and a guard on the bullion train, the thieves struck with faultless efficiency.

With a good deal of ingenuity they obtained duplicates of the keys used for the bullion safes, and somewhere between London and Folkestone the guard let them into the locked luggage van, where they opened the safes, substituted bags of lead for the bags of bullion and disappeared. The police remained baffled and it was only after one member of the gang fell out with another member and denounced him to the authorities that the conspirators were rounded up.

## Great Train Robbery

The main problem for train robbers has been to get off the train and make a clean escape with a bulky haul in tow. Even where a getaway has been meticulously planned, the thieves have sometimes come up against the unexpected. One gang operating in the early 1960s had planned to steal a cash consignment from a London–Bristol train, but was unable to leave the train at a prearranged point because the communication cord failed to work.

A few months later, the same gang tried to steal registered mail from a London–Holyhead train. Accomplices had changed the signals from green to red at a suitably lonely spot and it was here that the thieves had planned to unload the loot. But they were surprised by the train crew, one of whom pulled the communication cord. This time it worked and the gang was forced to make off empty handed.

In August 1963 some of those who had taken part in the previous two abortive raids were involved in a third attempt – and this time they hit the jackpot. The Great Train Robbery, as the newspapers called it, was of the London–Glasgow night mail. An inside informant had tipped off the gang that the second coach would be carrying a tempting consignment of used banknotes.

Again, the signals were changed to red at a lonely spot, then the locomotive and the first two coaches were uncoupled from the rest of the train and moved to a nearby bridge from where the mailbags could be conveniently dropped down into waiting vehicles.

**▲ This illustration of a notorious French railway murder of 1901 reinforced the fear of assault felt by many early rail travellers. In a letter to the *Derby Mercury*, a visiting American wrote: 'I am not a timid man but I never enter an English railway carriage without a loaded revolver. How am I to know that my travelling companion may be a madman escaped from confinement or a runaway criminal? And what protection have I against their assault, if it should please them to attack me, but the weapon I carry?'**

The robbers had taken great pains in their research – gathering vital information, finding the best location and learning to uncouple coaches. As a result, their activities went smoothly, though the locomotive driver was hit on the head with an iron bar and left bleeding and half stunned beside the track. However, having made a clean getaway, the thieves failed to solve the problem of disappearing without trace, and Scotland Yard was soon able to track them down.

Most railway crimes have been more mundane, but no less troublesome. Luggage thieves, pickpockets, prostitutes – all have been a constant headache for the railway police. So, indeed, has the railway vandal. The historian Frederick S. Williams in *Our Iron Roads*, published in 1883, noted that 'the amount of loss which railway companies sustain from wilful and wanton damage is as great as it is inexcusable. A railway carriage is often so mutilated that it has to be upholstered *de novo*; and brainless fops who wear diamond rings consider it a display at once of their elegance and wit to scrape the glass in such a manner as to interrupt the view, or even to outrage decency, so that the window has to be replaced before the carriage again becomes suitable for public use.'

A much greater source of concern to the Victorian rail traveller was the risk of being attacked. In fact, the risk was extremely small, but such violence as did occur underlined the vulnerability of passengers riding in the box-like compartments of carriages without corridors, and aroused a public alarm bordering on panic.

One case that attracted much attention in the 1850s concerned a young teacher who was

### Going for a snip

Railway theft reached an unrivalled peak of professionalism in British India. There was a tribe near Aligarh, just west of Calcutta, that cultivated rose plantations in the cool season, skilfully using a specialized long-nosed secateur.

In the hot season, its members would supplement their income by riding the night trains, snipping off the jewellery of sleeping passengers. When faced with travellers sleeping in an unhelpful position, they would tickle their feet with a feather until they turned over.

Another group, posing as pilgrims, concealed between the upper lip and the gum a sharp knife which they used to cut open passengers' baggage during the night.

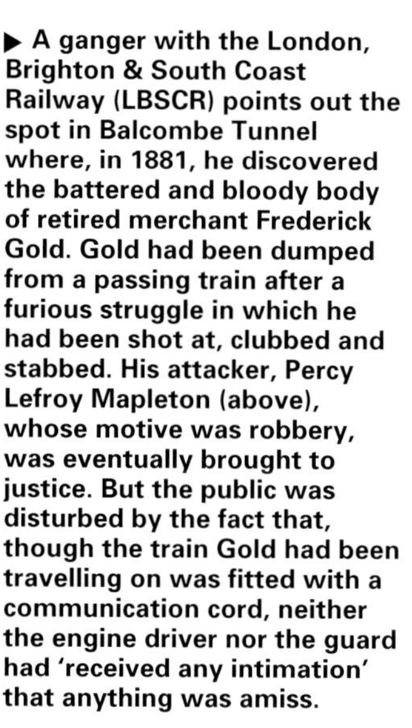

**▶ A ganger with the London, Brighton & South Coast Railway (LBSCR) points out the spot in Balcombe Tunnel where, in 1881, he discovered the battered and bloody body of retired merchant Frederick Gold. Gold had been dumped from a passing train after a furious struggle in which he had been shot at, clubbed and stabbed. His attacker, Percy Lefroy Mapleton (above), whose motive was robbery, was eventually brought to justice. But the public was disturbed by the fact that, though the train Gold had been travelling on was fitted with a communication cord, neither the engine driver nor the guard had 'received any intimation' that anything was amiss.**

knocked unconscious by a fellow passenger brandishing a revolver. As he started to recover, his assailant poured liquid chloroform into his mouth and stole his money and watch.

Captured and brought before the court, the culprit was sentenced to six years' hard labour. 'It would be frightful indeed,' said the judge, 'if men are to escape from the severest penalty of the law for cases of such a character as this. For, should they so escape, then no man will be safe when travelling in railway carriages.'

## Murder on the railway

The first railway murder in Britain appears to be that committed in 1864 by a young German, Franz Muller, who brutally attacked an elderly passenger in a first-class compartment on the 9.50 p.m. North London train from Fenchurch Street, this being the most promising way of obtaining the man's gold watch and chain. Muller then flung his victim out of the compartment on to the line, where he was later found dying of his injuries.

According to the trial evidence, Muller fancied his victim's hat, as well as his watch, so he took that and left his own in exchange, which was not a clever thing to do and led to his eventual capture and execution. Muller's counsel gave voice to the public concern the case had aroused: 'It is a crime which strikes at the lives of millions. It is a crime which affects the life of every man who travels upon the great iron ways of this country.'

To reassure the public, some railway companies installed small portholes – popularly known as 'Muller's Lights' – in the partitions between compartments. However, instead of welcoming the new measure, many travellers, especially women, condemned it as an invitation to peeping Toms.

In 1868, the railways introduced a more acceptable safety device – a rope which ran outside the carriages, with a bell connected to it at each end. But this proved hopelessly unreliable and travellers would have to wait another 25 years for an efficient communication cord to be developed.

**◀▲ Police confer at Cheddington station in Buckinghamshire in 1963 beside the looted coaches of the Glasgow–Euston mail train (above). The train was ambushed by a gang which uncoupled the engine and the two mail coaches and moved them to a nearby bridge. Having broken into the coaches (left), the Great Train Robbers then dropped the contents – worth £2.5 million – over the parapet and on to the road, where they made off in waiting vehicles.**

# Index

## ACKNOWLEDGEMENTS

Photographs: Roger Bastin 70(b); R A Bowen 30(t); Oliver Carter 150(bl); John A Coiley 82(t), 83(b); Sylvia Cordaiy Picture Library (Eddy Mayhew) 50(bl); Mary Evans Picture Library Ltd 19(b), 20(c,b), 25(t), 36(b), 96(tl), 120(b), 123(br), 138(t), 176(br), 186(b), 187(tr), (Alexander Meledin Collection) 183(b); Getty One/Hulton Collection 8-9, 10(l), 11(br), 13(tl,cr,br), 22(t), 23(tr), 27(tr), 28(b), 32(bl), 33(tr), 34(bl), 45(bl), 64(tr,bl), 67(t,br), 68(cl,sp), 69(cr), 75(b), 76(t), 78(bl), 85(t), 93(t), 94(b), 96(b), 97(tr), 101(t,br), 103(b), 104(tr,b), 106(tl), 108(t), 111(t), 112(b), 115(b), 117(b), 118(b), 121(br), 124(b), 125(tl), 127(tr), 140-141, 142(bl,t), 144(tl), 151(b), 152(tl), 153(b), 154(b), 159(b), 161(b), 162(tr,bl), 163(bl), 166(tl), 172(b), 173(bl), 174(tl,br), 175(tl,br), 177(b), 181(b), 184(t,b), 186(cl), 188(cl); Glasgow Herald & Evening Times 39(t); John Hunt 31(b); The Illustrated London News Picture Library 11(tl), 12(b), 17(c), 33(bl), 37(t,cr), 38(b), 62(bl,tc), 63(tr), 87(t), 116(t), 118(t), 126(bc), 128(sp,b), 131(b), 165(tl), 183(t), 188(br); Imperial War Museum 107(tr), 160(t,br), 161(tr), 164(b), 165(br), 167(b), 168(b), 169(tr), 170(tl,b), 171(tl), 177(tr), 178(b), 179(tl,tr,b), 180(l), 181(tr); Richard Joby (Pontypridd Library) 145(tr); Chris Kapolka 46(t); G & P Kichenside Ltd 59(b), 121(tl), 122(t); Anthony Lambert 26(tl,bl), 41(bl,br), 146(b), 147(cr), 149(tr); London Borough of Camden 40(b), 41(tr), 42(tl), 43(t); London Transport Museum 111(b), 113(t); Millbrook House Picture Library 4, 7, 21(t), 23(b), 26(bc), 35(br), 42(bc), 49(br), 50(tc,tc), 53(b), 57(b), 58(b), 59(t), 65(c), 66(sp), 72(br), 76(bc), 78(tc), 79(br), 86(b), 91(bl), 92(t), 99(tr,b), 100(b), 102(t), 105(r), 109(br), 110(b), 125(br), 134(t,b), 136(b), 148(sp), 152(tr), 163(t), 171(b), (PM Alexander) 98(br), 158(b), (Hugh Ballantyne) 68(bl), (CRL Coles) 95(b), (HGW Household) 49(t), (RG Jarvis) 84(b), 91(tr), 112(t), (GD King) 29(b), (Eric Treacy) 44(b), 47(tr), 80(bl), 106(b), 119(t), 122(b), 139(b), (PB Whitehouse) 154(t), (John S Whiteley/AC Cawston) 24(b), (JS Whiteley) 156(b); Mirror Syndication International Ltd 71(tr), 126(tl), 143(br); Brian Morrison 48(b), 132(b), 133(b); Peter Newark's American Pictures 98(tl), 182(b); Dr L A Nixon 135(t); Popperfoto 67(bl); Press Association Ltd 61(b), 189(tr,bl); Rank Organisation 155(b), 156(t), 157(t), 158(t); RAS Publishing (FR Hebron) 94(tl), (TG Hepburn) 90(b), (W Rogerson) 137(tl); Rex Features ltd 137(b); RC Riley 29(t), 31(t), 60(b); Geoff Rixon 51(br), 52(b); Science & Society Picture Library (National Railway Museum) 3, 14(bc), 15(tl,bc), 16(t,cr), 17(b), 18(t), 38(t), 45(tc), 77(tr), 88-89, 103(tr), 105(br), 108(bl), 129(b), 130(sp,b), 132(t), 138(bl), 144(b), 147(t), (Science Museum) 53(t), 54(t), 55(t), 56(b), 86(t), 114(t); Topham Picturepoint 80(t), 81(br); Ullstein Bilderdienst 85(b); Viollet Collection 185(b); Jim Winkley 34(t), 72(t,bl).